WAR WIVES

COLIN AND EILEEN
TOWNSEND

WAR WIVES

A Second World War
Anthology

GRAFTON BOOKS

A Division of the Collins Publishing Group

LONDON GLASGOW
TORONTO SYDNEY AUCKLAND

Grafton Books
A Division of the Collins Publishing Group
8 Grafton Street, London W1X 3LA

Published by Grafton Books 1989
Reprinted 1989

Copyright © Colin and Eileen Townsend 1989

British Library Cataloguing in Publication Data

War wives: a second world war anthology.
   1. World War 2. Role of women. Biographies.
   Collections
   I. Townsend, Colin   II. Townsend, Eileen
   940.53'15'0420922

ISBN 0-246-13388-0

Printed in Great Britain by
Mackays of Chatham plc, Kent

Contents

Preface

When the Second World War was at its height, and the civilian death-rate ran at tens of thousands per day, Heinrich Himmler announced, 'In three or five hundred years who will care anyway whether the Mrs Smiths of this world were unhappy?' This callous prophecy has not yet had time to run its course, but the mere fallibility of human memory could have, in itself, fulfilled the cold cynicism of those words, had those 'Mrs Smiths' he so summarily dismissed not been given the chance to speak out for themselves. In this book, we have allowed them to do just that. No one could read the following pages without believing that what they have to say is well worth recording.

Between 1939 and 1945, for the first time in human history, with the advent of the bombing of civilian targets, war was brought right into the family home, and death became an ever-present companion for those left behind to 'keep the home fires burning'. That last cosy sentiment from the First World War was to take on a whole new, chilling meaning in the Second, when husbandless families cowered helplessly beneath the bombs, with their homes burning about them.

If mankind is to progress, then we, the succeeding generations, must not forget the Mrs Smiths of those years. And 50 years later, we remember them not as Himmler's faceless mass, but as young mothers, struggling to create and protect life when the war machine appeared bent on its destruction. We remember their love, and their anger, their resourcefulness as well as their anguish. Above all, we remember them as individuals who struggled to cope with a situation they neither wanted nor understood, and who displayed more reserves of humanity and resilience than Himmler and his like ever dreamt of. The pages of this book are the abiding proof that there is nothing 'ordinary' about the Mrs Smiths of this world.

The conviction that the women of that generation had their own stories to tell – stories that merited telling just as much as those of ex-servicemen – came about during a conversation with Marjorie Townsend, the mother and mother-in-law of the editors of this book. On being asked one day what it was really like to live through those years, she spoke freely and vividly of her own experiences. Then, when asked why she had never spoken of such things before, she replied, 'I was never asked.' We, her listeners, knew then that there must be many other women with just such tales to tell, who, quite simply, had 'never been asked'. From that moment on, we knew it must be our task to put this omission right. Since then, we have been in contact with hundreds of women, both in Great Britain and in Germany, all of whom merit inclusion in this book. Unfortunately, space has dictated that we can offer only a cross-section.

What follows, however, is more than an anthology of the experiences of wives and mothers during the Second World War. It is also a tribute to that generation of women, in Great Britain and Germany, who waited for husbands, sons, and loved ones, and fearfully watched the skies as the conflict between their two countries carried havoc and destruction into their own homes. Their war was the same war as the tank generals', the fighter pilots', and the political leaders', whose exploits, both fair and foul, have been amply chronicled; yet their war was a distinctly different war, too. It was not fought in the skies, or on the field of battle, it was fought within the home itself, where, as sole protector, they endeavoured to bring up their children in circumstances that were often little short of desperate.

But for them, when the hostilities were over, there was to be no limelight and acclaim. Their only reward was the survival of the family, and the hope that their children would grow up in peace to inherit a better world than they had known. They asked for and received no recognition, so it has fallen to us, the editors, as children of that generation of remarkable women, to pay this tribute and ensure that, in the words of at least a few of their generation, their stories will not go unrecorded in the annals of history of those fateful years we now know as the Second World War.

On 8 May 1985, Richard von Weizsäcker, President of the Federal Republic of Germany, used the occasion of the 40th anniversary of the German surrender to speak of the role of women in war:

> . . . of all the burdens that mankind had to carry, the heaviest was surely born by the women of the various nations. Their suffering, their self-sacrifice, and their silent strength is all too easily forgotten by world history. They worked and they worried, they carried human life in their hands, and they protected it. They grieved for lost fathers and sons, husbands, brothers, and friends. In the darkest years they kept alight the flame of humanity . . . When their menfolk returned after the war, the women often stepped aside again. But, because of the war, many women found themselves alone, destined to live the rest of their lives in loneliness. If the devastation and destruction, the barbarism and inhumanity did not inwardly shatter the people involved, if, slowly but surely, they came to themselves again after the war, then they owed it first and foremost to their womenfolk.

Richard von Weizsäcker's words were addressed not only to the women of West Germany, but to women everywhere. The mother who cradles her badly-injured son in her arms in the ruins of her home in Sunderland, or the one who sees her small son blown up by a shell while sheltering from the bombs in a cave in the White Cliffs of Dover, shares the same emotions as the mother who buries her frozen child in a roadside ditch in Pomerania, or the mother who walks for miles pleading for a single egg to fulfil the wish of a desperately ill child, in Bad Wildungen. The young woman who stood on the station platform watching the diminishing figure of her husband returning to the Front could be found in any country. All over Europe, women stood on the streets confronting the ruins of what was once a home. The anguish was universal.

In compiling this collection of memories from the Second World War, what we offer the reader is the personal voice of history; the voice of a generation of women – the wives and mothers of Great Britain and Germany – to whom this book bears tribute and is dedicated.

Acknowledgements

To list all who have shown interest and encouragement in compiling this book would be an almost impossible task. The names that follow represent those who were kind enough to take the time and trouble to help over the past two years that it has taken to compile this anthology. Our special thanks go to our dear friends Jan Brinkmann and his wife Olaug, of Wedel, near Hamburg; and to Jan's mother Elisabeth Brinkmann, formerly of Lüdenschied, Westphalia, who all gave generously in both time and effort. Also to Rosemarie Gratz, of East Berlin, who gave such invaluable help in contacting and interviewing 'war wives' across the German border. We are indebted to Alex Robertson, of the Extra-mural Department of the University of Dundee, for using his good offices with the Liga für Völkerfreundschaft to enable us to make contacts in East Germany. Our thanks go also to Elise Arnecke, of Bremerhaven; Audrey Aveyard, of Ludlow, Shropshire; Irene Ballard, of Balham, London; Eileen Benifer, of Thornton Heath, Surrey; Waltraud Beyer, of Rees, North Rhine-Westphalia; Mary Bloomfield, of Garmston, Shrewsbury; Mile Braach, of Frankfurt; Eva Breithaupt, of Düsseldorf; Christel Bröcker, of Spaden, North Rhine-Westphalia; James M. Brown, of Rugeley, Staffordshire; Johanna Buder, of East Berlin; Gerda Butz, of Düsseldorf; Wilma Christel, of Frankfurt; Ange Christoph, of Oberursel, Hessen; Gladys Cleaver, of Charlemont, West Midlands; Emmi Costa, of Nürnberg, Bavaria; Helga Collatz, of Düsseldorf; Irmgard Dallmann, of Solingen, North Rhine-Westphalia; Hans-Jürgen Dörr, of Bad Camberg, Hessen; Christel Ebisch, of Frankfurt; Mrs E. M. I. Escott, of St Austell, Cornwall; Ray Fear, of Hilderstone, Staffordshire; Mrs M. Fordham, of Norwich, Norfolk; Rose Gardener, of Bradmore, West Midlands; Johanna

Gerhold, of Mönchengladbach, North Rhine-Westphalia; Vera Gettins, of Trefonen, Shropshire; Mrs V. Gibson, of Fulwell, Sunderland, Tyne and Wear; Miss M. H. Giles, of Middlesbrough, Cleveland; Else Giste, of Hamburg; Else Gossmann, of Simonsberg, North Rhine-Westphalia; Jessie B. Gould, of Dairsie, Fife; Nellie Green of Albrighton, West Midlands; Gertrud Haake, of Sievern, North Rhine-Westphalia; Heidi Hagen, of the *Neue Westfälische*, Bielefeld, North Rhine-Westphalia; Gertrud Hannes, of Cologne; Gabriele Hasenberg, of Dormagen, North Rhine-Westphalia; Elsie Hay, of Strachan, Aberdeenshire; Lina-Luise Heepmann, of Bielefeld, North Rhine-Westphalia; Maria Held, of Essen, North Rhine-Westphalia; Gudrun Hermann, of Bad Rothenfelde, North Rhine-Westphalia; Margaret Heywood, of Wolverhampton; Hertha Hoffman-Lang, of Mannheim; Mary Hollins, of Saltaire, West Yorkshire; Edeltraud Hönsch, of Gladbeck, North Rhine-Westphalia; Dorothy Horton, of Kingswinford, West Midlands; Walter Johé, of Wesel, North Rhine-Westphalia; Dorothy Jones, of Waterloo, Liverpool; Mrs I. V. Jones, of Brinnington, Stockport; Mrs P. M. Jones, of Aldershot, Hants; Mavis K. Jubb, of Oakengates, Shropshire; Marianne Kammerer, of Voerde, North Rhine-Westphalia; Hedwig Keil, of Frankfurt; Vera Kersten, of Hamburg; Geoffrey Kirkland, of Manchester; Ernst Kohleick of Wuppertal, North Rhine-Westphalia; Sabine Komoss, of Düsseldorf; Hannelore Kronen, of Neuss, North Rhine-Westphalia; Marlene Kruse, of Mönchengladbach, North Rhine-Westphalia, Olivia Kunz, of Bremerhaven; Mrs D. Lamb, of Spennymoor, Co. Durham; Mrs E. Lee, of Walsall, West Midlands; Lilian Lewis, of Walsall, West Midlands; Mrs D. McIntosh, of Woolton, Liverpool; Marianne McKinnon, of Glasgow; Margaret McWilliam, of Ballindalloch, Banffshire; Ursula Maeghs, of Kevelaer, North Rhine-Westphalia; Hilda Mason, of Keighley, West Yorkshire; Maria Mehren, of Düsseldorf; Ruth Meissner, of Bad Homburg, Hessen; Barbara Memsell, of Shrewsbury, Shropshire; Eileen Midgley, of Bradford, West Yorkshire; Gertrude Miller, of Ashford, Kent; Nellie Mirow, of Meerbusch-Büderich, North Rhine-Westphalia; Wanda Muecke, of Neuss, North Rhine-Westphalia; Muriel E. Munro, of Ringwood, Hants; Ilse Natschinski, of Hilden, North Rhine-Westphalia; Irene Neuber, of Düsseldorf; Gerhart Niemeyer, of Leverkusen, North Rhine-Westphalia; Cyril Nixon, of Stafford; June Noble, of Sutton, Surrey; Ingeborg Nolte, of Mannheim; Gwendoline Nye, of Ashford, Kent; Johanna Ohlig, of Mönchengladbach, North Rhine-Westphalia; Maria Otto, of Krefeld, North Rhine-Westphalia; Phyllis Overton, of Bromley, Kent; Christine Parkin, of Ashford, Kent; Mrs P. Parrett, of Christchurch, Dorset; Margarete Pauls, of Weeze, North Rhine-Westphalia; Shirley Peckham, of New Milton, Hants; Dieter Peil, of Düsseldorf; Ilse Portmann, of Hamburg; Margaret Price, of Penn, West Midlands; W. Reibel, of the *Frankfurter Neue Presse*; Cläre Richter, of Bielefeld, North Rhine-Westphalia; Helga Roeber, of Viersen, North Rhine-Westphalia; Elisabeth Rogge, of Bremerhaven; Rosa Rotermund, of Bocholt, North Rhine-Westphalia; Anneliese Roth, of Hilden, North Rhine-Westphalia; Irma Rupert, of Hamburg; Udo Semrau, of Düsseldorf; Rhea Scheddon, of Kennoway, Fife; Inge Schild, of Hamminkeln, North Rhine-Westphalia; Helmut Schönert, of Kaarst, North Rhine-Westphalia; Thomas Schmutz, of Mannheim; Gerd Schuster, of Munich; Olive Smallwood, of Keighley, West Yorkshire; Molly Smith, of Farnborough, Hants; Mrs M. Smith, of Wednesfield, West Midlands; Nellie Smith, of Hellesdon, Norwich, Norfolk; Eileen Stapleton, of Haywards Heath, Sussex; Elsa Stelling, of Hamburg; Hilda Sumpner, of Crosby, Liverpool; Käthe Theilmann, of Mannheim; Betty Thomas, of Barlaston, Staffordshire; Mrs V. M. Townsend, of Caldmore, West Midlands; Betty Upham, of Speke, Liverpool; Anneliese Vogt, of Frankfurt; Brunhilde Vollmerk, of Kriftel, Hessen; Paul Weingart, of Mönchengladbach, North Rhine-Westphalia; Elfriede Weiss, of Kiel; Mrs Western, of Pringe Ville, West Yorkshire; Elisabeth Wiesenhöfer, of Ratingen, North Rhine-Westphalia; Violet Williams, of Orpington, Kent; Martha Willing, of Düsseldorf; Erna Willms, of Garbsen, Lower Saxony; Agnes Wilpert, of Würzburg, Bavaria; Frances Whitehead, of Stockport, Cheshire; Louisa Williamson, of Onchan, Isle of Man; Sophie Wörmann, of Bielefeld, North Rhine-Westphalia; Mrs A. Worrall, of Wye, Kent; Marjorie Wright, of Purley, Surrey; Klaus Zöller, of the *Kölner Stadt Anzeiger*, Cologne; Renate Zollinger, of Oerlinghausen, North Rhine-Westphalia.

To the above listed we express our special thanks. Their contributions may not be visible in the pages of this book, but without their assistance, either by way of establishing contacts, or providing information, documents, pictures, newspaper-cuttings, and tape recordings, the compilation of a book of this sort would not have been possible.

Finally, and most of all, our very special thanks go to those contributors whose memoirs, letters and diaries fill the pages of this book. It has been our privilege to be allowed to share your experiences and your often very private thoughts and feelings during those terrible years. We, of your children's generation, have been enriched and at times humbled by your resourcefulness, courage, and care during those years when bombs fell and fathers did not return. It was a world we could not understand at the time, but which we understand the better now you have spoken. We pass on willingly to the next generation the message which so very many of you expressed so earnestly at the end of your letters to us: No more war, *nie wieder Krieg*.

WAR WIVES

ELIZABETH SMITH, from Sunderland, Tyne and Wear. Elizabeth suf-
fered as much as any woman in the war – experiencing her home bombed to
the ground around her, her husband and sister-in-law killed in the inci-
dent, and her only son so badly mutilated that he had to undergo years of
plastic surgery operations:

'God makes the back to carry the burden'

We lived very near the coast and our first heavy air-raid was on a
Thursday lunchtime when all along the coast bombs were dropped.
One completely destroyed some semi-detached houses in
Sunderland and so many shop windows were shattered we were
almost ankle-deep in glass. The reason Sunderland was so heavily
bombed was because the whole length of the River Wear were ship-
yards, engineering works, Wearmouth Colliery, and a large goods
station etc. . . . . Well, let's just say, it was an industrial area.

Every day I used to meet my sisters in town and we would join the
queues when a few oranges, fish – in fact, when anything that was
unrationed was on sale. Oh, the laughs we used to have listening to
the conversations of the people! The things some of them would
have loved to do to Hitler and his gang was nobody's business! In
spite of our fears, we could always have a good laugh.

The first time I bought frozen fish I thought one just prepared and
fried it like ordinary fish. Those were 'pre-fridge' days. De-frosting
never entered my head. I had a pan of revolting stuff, as tough as
leather.

It was a hectic life getting up early to get my housework done before shopping, dashing home to prepare a meal for Jim, my son, coming home from school at lunchtime, after being in the Anderson shelter in the garden half the night.

Well, time went on with daylight raids as well as at night. Hundreds of people were killed in Sunderland and countless buildings devastated. On 10 May 1943 a landmine landed on our house killing my husband and his sister who was staying with us. Jim, our son, received terrible injuries. Mine were not quite so bad.

When I was able to visit Jim in Newcastle General Hospital I could have died at the sight. I can just picture him now and hear him saying, 'It's lovely to see you, Mum, but why did you come? You're not fit to be out. How is Dad?' I'd been advised not to say anything about the fact that his Dad and Auntie had been killed. You can imagine how I felt when he managed to write a little letter for me to give to his Dad. I still have it.

When Mr Robotham discharged Jim from Newcastle General he had to go straight into the Eye Infirmary for an operation. He'd lost the sight of his left eye in the bombing. He was then transferred to Hexham Hospital to have bones set. After that he was transferred to Shotley Bridge Hospital for plastic surgery repairs to his face. He returned there every few months until 1946. The nurses and staff of every hospital told me what a wonderful patient he was; although terribly injured he never complained. He had his 16th birthday in Hexham Hospital.

After almost a year of visiting him in hospitals, which were never local, I got him home . . . or rather, we had no home after the bombing, but lived with my niece Kathleen and her husband Bill and family until we managed to get a flat. They are a really wonderful couple who were our mainstay in those awful days.

Towards the end of the year Jim was discharged from hospital and to keep him occupied, the doctor suggested he should start college and begin his studies again. I saw the billeting officer and asked if it was possible to get a house as we couldn't stay with Kathleen and her family indefinitely as Jim would need a place to study and somewhere to put his books and drawing-board. We were soon provided with a nice flat in a house that was being requisitioned. It was in a private park. The rooms were huge. It was a three-storey house with cellars. We had three rooms and no furniture. Sunderland Corporation allowed us a large trestle table and four chairs, no beds, and horrible grey blankets. I could have cried when I looked at them. But Jim had a terrific sense of humour and used to make me laugh at the things he would say about our 'wonderful home'.

Then something that was really wonderful happened. We had a visit from one of the men who had helped to get us out of the rubble that was our home. He and his family were moving to London to stay with his parents and instead of storing his furniture he said we could use it until they returned. So we now had a dining suite, bedroom suite, and a three-piece lounge suite. It was a miracle.

I received £2 10s per week for ten weeks after the bombing, and after that 17s 6d per week widow's pension and a £12 death grant for my husband being a war casualty. I received £1 4s 6d injury allowance and Jim got £1 17s 6d. This was all we had. We had no furniture, no household possessions, no clothes, nothing. And never at any time was I given a travel pass to visit Jim, although he was never in a local hospital.

A Board of Trade official visited me to assess damages. I had to tell him the price of all our furniture that we had lost, in fact, the full contents of our five-bedroomed, semi-detached house. Then he would reduce the price for what he called 'wear and tear'. No allowance was to be paid for such things as a piano, camera, etc., only for furniture. In the end he awarded me £300, but can you imagine anyone in my condition, in those early days, thinking in terms of money? I couldn't have cared less, in spite of being penniless. The only thoughts in my mind were of Jim.

We were only in our night attire when the bomb fell and all our clothing was destroyed, along with all our other possessions. When I had to ask for clothing coupons and cash to buy something to wear it was deducted from the £300.

Being severely crushed from the waist down to the feet in the bombing, I was unable to walk properly for some time. The pain in my back was awful. I've had to receive regular hospital treatment since that awful night of 16 May 1943. Arthritis set in and I've had prolonged injections and treatment, including a particular course which made me look like a roll of navy pebble-dashed wallpaper. But gradually I was able to get about, although the doctors told me they were unable to cure my injuries; they could only try to ease the pain. But, with a struggle, I coped. My Mum used to say, 'God makes the back to carry the burden.' I've been thankful for the back He gave me.

When Jim could go back to work he also went to night school and studied. I still have his evening class exam papers: Maths; Drawing; Science; English – First Class, with distinction.

With Jim back at work we gradually saved a bit of money with his wage and our pensions. He had to go into hospital for a few weeks for plastic surgery in 1944. He got over that and, after a holiday, started work once more. I'd saved enough to buy him a piano and he was delighted. His friends used to bring their girlfriends and we had some happy times. Then the time came when the house was to be de-requisitioned. I received a postcard from the Housing Department to view another house. It turned out to be a tiny flat in an awful district. One very small room containing a gas cooker, zinc wash-boiler and just enough room for a small table and two chairs. The bedroom was just big enough to hold a bed and either a dressing-table or a wardrobe, not both. The second bedroom was only big enough to take a single bed and it was an upstairs flat. I had enough difficulty walking without having to walk upstairs. I took the key to the office and was told they would try to get me something more suitable later.

The following week I received another postcard, so, hopefully, I went for the key thinking maybe this would be something nice. When I saw the address it was the same flat I'd seen the previous week. I explained to the elderly clerkess that the type of furniture I'd bought for the large rooms which we were then living in wouldn't fit into such a tiny place, only to be told it was people and not furniture they catered for. I told her not to bother me again unless the premises were more suitable. I was feeling pretty desperate by this time.

The result was I wrote to the owner of Belle Vue Park House, where we were living, and asked if I could rent the house from her. She replied saying she was returning to Sunderland to see about de-requisitioning and would visit me, but, in any case, she intended selling the house as she was much too old to be bothered with the property and was quite settled in Wales.

Well, she kept her promise and came to see me and said she would sell me the house for £650. But the fact remained, I didn't possess £650. I'd only managed to save about £200. My late husband's aunt offered me £250, but I was still £200 short. I told Mrs Sadler, the owner, I only had £450 and she suggested arranging a little mortgage, as she termed it. I refused saying a widow's pension of 17s 6d a week couldn't cope with debt and I would have to see if I could afford another house which was for sale lower down the Park.

She visited me every day for a week making various proposals as to how I could buy the house. Then, one night I was just going to inspect the other house; in fact, I was just placing the key in the lock when I heard a voice saying, 'Mrs Craig, I've decided to let you have the house for £450. You can also have whatever compensation the Corporation consider is due to me. I'll see my solicitor tomorrow, then I'm returning to Wales. Thank you for taking such good care of the house. I wish you good luck, health and happiness in the house I lived in for so many years. Goodbye, my dear.' Before I even had time to thank her, she was out of sight. So a few weeks later I was a property owner.

During these years dockets were issued to war victims to buy utility furniture and I began to buy furniture of my own, so when the time came to return those pieces which had been loaned to me they wouldn't be missed. I used to attend good-class house auction sales hoping I could obtain the type of furniture suitable for these large rooms. Unfortunately the prices were usually much too high for my meagre amount of cash. But with what pleasure and pride everything I did buy was washed with vinegar and water, then polished until it looked as good as new.

An advertisement in the *Echo* sent me off to a nice house where they had an HMV gramophone for sale. I waited on tenterhooks for Jim's return from work and off we went full of hope. We were overjoyed at our luck in being the first customers. When the lady asked if we had transport and we said, No, I remarked that if we were still living in Atkinson Road we could have carried it. She asked where we were living and I told her about the bombing. Well, the result was she gave me a lovely pair of heavy lace-panel curtains, cream with a heavy fringe on the bottom; two water-colour pictures with narrow black frames; four fine china teacups, saucers, plates, a preserve jar with a silver lid; a cut-glass vase and a lovely white table-cloth. And they had everything delivered to us. How lovely that room looked. Later I bought a large gilt-framed mirror at a saleroom for it.

Binn's advertised blankets and eiderdowns for docket holders, so off I went and managed to buy cream woollen blankets – two pairs. The assistant must have liked the look of me because he let me have two eiderdowns and one pair of white sheets into the bargain. I didn't mind switching on the light when I went to bed now that I could see a white sheet and cream blankets and pink eiderdown. When you have had to put up with detestable things, it's only then that you appreciate the nice things you once took for granted. How much I appreciated what we were gradually building up between us no one will understand.

Jim always gave me his pay packet unopened (as his Dad had always done). It was such a joy to me to give him extra pocket money to buy records. It always astonished people the knowledge he had of composers and music, both classical and jazz. I remember him booking two seats at the Empire to see Oscar Petersen. This was a special appearance and I gladly went with him, but, although to me it was agony, to him it was sheer delight. He would sit for hours playing the piano or listening to records. How close we were, sharing so much trouble and caring for each other. He was so thoughtful, understanding, with not a selfish thought in his head. As a 16-year-old, with his Dad dead, he seemed to take on a man's responsibility. What he and I crammed into those years no one could understand.

Then, in 1945, Jim became ill with a particularly virulent type of meningitis and was taken to the Isolation Hospital. We were told there was no cure for it. Dr Cram, a tropical disease specialist, Dr Thorpe, the hospital doctor, and our own doctor tried every possible place for something to counteract it but without success. Every day I used to visit the hospital but was only able to see Jim through a small window. I was told he was critically ill and they couldn't give me any hope. The only thing they could do was draw the fluid from his brain, and from his spine through lumbar punctures.

That period was one of the worst I ever endured. I cannot describe the agony at the thought that I might lose him. Especially the day Dr Madan, our own doctor, called saying that he had to pass our road and he would give me a lift to the hospital. We were talking about Jim when the doctor said that they had tried so hard to get something to cure him. Then he said, 'You wouldn't want him to recover if this virus was going to leave him affected in any way, would you, my dear?' I immediately thought that Jim had died or was insane. I turned completely numb.

Everyone agreed that Jim's eventual recovery was a miracle. He was discharged a few weeks later and afterwards started work with an engineering firm as a draughtsman. Everything went fine for 15 months until he was again admitted to hospital with cerebro-spinal meningitis. You can imagine how I felt. Dr Thorpe, the hospital doctor, was told of Jim's war injuries and what he'd already been through by our own doctor and said, 'God knows what's going on in that boy's head after that lot!' Few boys suffered more so uncomplainingly. Never at any time did he refer to either his injuries or his illnesses, although he had to go back to hospital constantly for plastic surgery repairs to his face. He simply referred to these operations as a necessary nuisance.

I was delighted when, in 1949, he married Jean and later on had two daughters, Jean and Helen; two lovely girls, now married, with the same caring ways as the Daddy they both adored. After suffering so much during the war, Jim died tragically in September 1975. He passed away, in the Hexham Spinal Unit, five weeks after a bus drove into the back of his car and severed his spinal cord. He had had his 16th birthday there and was to have his last one there too – his 49th.

I often ask myself why we didn't both go along with his dear Dad when he died under the bombs that awful night. Why we, especially Jim, had to suffer so much and then go the way he did. God must have the answer. I have not.

Elizabeth Smith (formerly Craig) remarried after the war and, now in her eighties, still lives in Sunderland.

SIGRID WENDT, from Brunswick, Lower Saxony, remembers how they coped with the shortages in ways they would never have imagined in peacetime. Her hometown of Brunswick suffered badly from the bombing raids. It lay right in the path of the north-western approach run to Berlin, and its industries and railway network attracted frequent air attacks. She also knew the nightmare of living beneath the bombs with small children:

'Our own house is ablaze around us'

The six years of war certainly depleted stocks of clothing, but replacements had to be found. You could hardly get anything worth having for your clothing coupons. So we had to find our own solutions. Make eyes at the shopkeeper on the corner and you could get an empty flour- or sugar-sack. Sugar-bags were the best for unravelling. You got piles of shiny, silky strands which could be knitted or crocheted into lovely pullovers and jackets. The flour-sacks you undid and then, in the hours when the bombs left you in peace, you could either hand-sew or – if you still had one – machine them into underwear for the children. Often you couldn't get off the lettering and it just gave a nice individual touch to see them going around with the firm's name stamped on their backsides.

If a mum wanted to look her best, she could fix up an old hat with a new ribbon or sew on a feather she had found. For everyday wear, you wound a piece of material artistically round your head or put on an old ski-hat to keep out the wind and cold.

The children kept on growing, and that led to problems with shoes. Once again the local shopkeeper came to the rescue. His packets were done up with plaited straw string. You could use this to make the most wonderful soles for shoes. You just added a couple of stiff cloth straps for the uppers. They were only any good for dry weather, though. You just had to bribe the shoemaker with a few cigarettes to take on another shoe-repair job, if you wanted to keep your children dry-shod and healthy. If you didn't have enough coupons for a pair of stockings, there were articles in the paper on how to use the sewing-machine to make one new pair out of three old pairs. The war made you use your imagination. Situations were always changing, and there were even things to laugh about.

The dire clothing shortage affected the soldiers, too. On the Russian Front the army issue was completely inadequate. So we women unravelled tea-cosies and unpicked bolsters for knee-warmers and balaclavas.

If the children were at school, or out playing in the street or garden, that gave mum a chance to go round trying to get in something to eat. That was a time-consuming business. It meant going along to the butchers with your empty jug in your hand to see if you could get a few blood and meal sausages or a drop of offal soup. There were always queues and often the person in front got the last bit and you went away empty-handed. If that happened there was no good meat broth on the table the next day, just an extra bit of bread topped with a spread we made from dried egg and skimmed milk. We made it by scrambling the egg powder in an almost dry pan with the milk, or occasionally with mustard.

One of the best times of year for us was autumn when we gathered beechnuts in the nearby parks and woods. We took them to a mill where they made a lovely-tasting oil out of them. We heated it up with salt and onions and poured it over our potatoes. A real feast!

Shortages taught you to think ahead. If in summer there was a birthday or special occasion in the offing, you would suddenly remember where there was a poppy field in the surrounding countryside, and, armed with bags and scissors, off you would go to fill up your containers with fat ripe heads from the edges of the field. But you were thrifty, too, and never took more than was needed. The poppy seeds were cooked together with powdered milk, sugar, and semolina, and that gave you a thick, tasty filling to put in an almost fat-free flan-case. What a treat that was!

We bartered pieces of silverware and good quality underwear for food from the local farms. If you were lucky, the farmer might even get out his horse and cart and drive you back to the tram stop at the edge of town. Rides like that were an extra-special treat for the children. You always had to try and get home before nightfall. The blackout made it impossible to find your way around in the dark and the children used to get frightened. They gave you luminous patches to wear on your clothes, but they were not a bit of good. Neither were the feeble little torches you could get.

There were so many bombed out that special billeting offices had to be set up to find accommodation for the affected families. It was a question of all squeezing in together, which didn't make it very easy for the women when it came to preparing meals in the kitchen. The gas and electricity were turned off at certain times of day to save energy. That was when cooking boxes and stoves from granny's day came in handy – as long as you hadn't thrown them away. All you needed was something to burn in them, but allocations of fuel were pretty mean. It was in such short supply that coalmen stopped making deliveries. You had to go to them to get your ration. Mothers used to rent out prams, but they had to be strong ones to stand the weight of briquettes or beech logs without collapsing. Often the children's help was needed to push it along.

Although winters were very cold, we only ever managed to provide a bit of heat after work, when we all used to gather round the stove. In our garage there was an old car-seat. We had taken it out when they came to requisition the car. After we were bombed out in 1944, this was put next to the stove and it became our most luxurious and most prized seat.

If anyone in the family fell ill, they hadn't a hope of recovering in the cold, so that you just had no choice but to turn to criminal ways. We all knew about the night coal trains that came from the opencast mines near Helmstedt-Offleben. They used to pass through Brunswick East Station. There was always quite a gang of people with the same idea. Because of the blackout you needed torches to find the pieces of coal lying between the rails. But we used to 'help' them fall off the goods wagons, too. Often you got home in a lather of fear and sweat with a couple of bulging bags, only to find half of what you had brought home was bits of ballast off the track.

Added to the problems of missing husbands and the ever-increasing air-raids came the worries about evacuating children. They were sent from the blitzed towns to special evacuation centres in the country. Here they were looked after by NSV [National Socialist

10

Welfare] nurses and RAD girls [girls of 17–18 on compulsory war-time service]. It was too much for these young girls to cope with, and they often felt completely useless when faced by howling homesick children, bed-wetters, moody teenagers and cheeky, boy-mad girls from the towns. The evacuees were just as worried as the mothers they had left behind to face the bombs. But 'Germany's future lies in Germany's youth' (Nazi slogan), and they had to be rescued at any price.

10 February 1944: morning
The early warning siren sounds, followed shortly after by the full alert. The block we are in stands right next to a boys' grammar school, which they have been using for a reserve hospital and is now full of casualties. There aren't many people at home in our block, but the few that are left are just making their way to the cellars when the bombs start whistling down and exploding. Rubble starts trickling down from above and the smell of burning gets into our noses. Our next door neighbours have been trapped in their house and are shouting for help. Our own house is ablaze around us, and we have to get out quickly. With us is an expectant mother with three children, whose husband died of leukemia not so long ago. So here we stand looking at the ruins of our home. Soon we shall have to write on the walls that are still standing, 'Still alive. Gone to . . .' She went to her parents in Lüneburg. We went back to the family home and were taken in by my mother.

Day in, day out, there are great queues of homeless people waiting for a hot meal at the emergency kitchens set up by the army. A few days later we are searching for our belongings in the rubble of our home. Our children are with us, in case there is another air-raid warning, and we see people searching for dead bodies in the total ruins of a hospital. (It was bombed out despite the fact that it had a red cross painted on the roof!) There are human legs dangling out of the crane bucket. The sight gives the children nightmares. 'Mummy, where were the other bits of the soldiers?'
Towards the end of the fifth year of the war the bombing got so bad that we had to start using the proper communal air-raid shelters,

rather than our own cellars. We always had our air-raid luggage standing ready to hand. The children each had their little rucksack with their favourite toys in it. When they were down in the shelter they would snuggle up to each other beneath a woollen blanket in the naïve hope that it might give them extra protection. We sometimes spent hours in the foul air of the shelter and were always very relieved to come out again after the all-clear and find that the house was still standing. We never undressed at night. We slept on our beds with all our clothes on.

15 October 1944: midnight
Strong contingents of British and American troops have made Brunswick their target and tonight have destroyed almost the whole of the town centre with its medieval, half-timbered houses. It was a sea of fire, burning for days. We weren't much better off out in the suburbs and had to stay in the dark shelter until daylight dawned. The asphalt on the streets is glowing red-hot. The fire brigade had to hose down a pathway so that we could get out. Then we set off through the smoke-laden half-light into the unknown. You could still see the old slogans on the walls that were still standing: 'Take Care! The Enemy is listening in.' 'You are Nothing, the Volk is Everything.' 'Give all for the Führer, the People, and the Fatherland.' 'Wheels must turn for Victory.' A macabre spectacle.

The only time you dared to talk about political issues was with people you knew and trusted, and then only in whispers in places where it was safe to do so. The Nazi Party had its spies: block wardens and air-raid wardens especially. So walls had ears. People did listen-in to foreign radio stations, but it was a risky business. You could be denounced by someone and then it was the death penalty. Sometimes people told each other political jokes. It was a way of letting off steam.

Before the Russian campaign began, which brought the great turning point with the catastrophe of Stalingrad, the loyal Nazi Party members were all keen and willing. They had supreme confidence in Hitler's 'Final Victory'. So everyone was encouraged to do their bit for arms production by donating garden and graveyard railings. Those in two minds were 'encouraged' by articles in the newspaper: 'It would undoubtedly have been the dearest wish of the deceased to give up his graveside railings for the sake of his own beloved German People.'

Hitler's attack on Russia in June 1941 alarmed and worried everyone. Could we succeed where even Napoleon had failed? Newspaper headlines proclaimed: 'Final Victory in East Assured', and, in the autumn of 1941, Hitler stated that 'The enemy is broken.' Winter taught us otherwise, though right up to the very end the radio and press tried to keep flagging hopes alive. The end of the war was going to be a full-scale apocalypse. It was no longer 'Guns Not Butter', but 'Total War'. Thinking people, who had always been hated by the Party, began to doubt whether the war was going to bring victory. Amongst themselves they were talking about Germany's defeat. The slogan they had invented so long ago turned out in the end to be right:

> Everything vanishes, everything passes,
> Even Hitler and his Party asses.

LOIS ROE, of Stourbridge, West Midlands, remembers the humour that occasionally shone through the horror:

'There shot into the room an apparition'

The sirens had sounded their nightly warning. My friend and neighbour came into my home. We decided that we would not get my two children out of bed unless we heard planes overhead.

The arrangement was that she would get my son David, who had just turned three, from the back bedroom, and I would get my daughter Jane, aged five months, from her cot in the front room.

We were knitting as usual when we heard the planes. We pulled the settee away from the wall so that we could get down behind it. This was to save being hit by broken glass. Our knitting needles were still clicking away when we heard the whine of a bomb. We ran as quick as lightning, dived into the bedrooms, grabbed a child each, then ran back down again – even quicker this time. We threw ourselves, with our precious bundles, behind the settee and tried to regain our breath.

Suddenly the door burst open and there shot into the room an apparition. Yes, it really was an apparition – another friend from four doors away dressed in a long white nightie (you know the type – frills around the neck and wrists and long enough to wrap your feet in). She was holding under her arm a large black bag, and panted, 'I didn't wait to get out of bed properly. I jumped out over the bottom and grabbed my bag.'

'Whatever is in the bag?' we asked.

'Oh,' came the reply. 'It's the Bright Hour money from the Chapel.'

The bomb fell into a marl hole half a mile away and shattered scores of windows in the surrounding area. But the Chapel money was saved.

LUISE MEIER, who died in Gütersloh, North Rhine-Westphalia, in 1984, at the age of 81, was a wartime mother with four brothers in the German armed services. Her daughter, Helga, here describes a scene from a day in 1944, when Aunt Marie brought her mother news from the Front:

'She covered her eyes with her arm'

I shall never forget that damp, cold autumn day. Mother was helping our neighbours with the potato lifting. It wasn't done by machine in those days. The women were kneeling next to each other and gathering the potatoes with their hands into wire baskets. When they were full, they were tipped out into a big horse-drawn cart. It was hard work, kneeling in the cold earth with bent backs for hours on end. Mother was always so happy when evening came and the work was over.

Aunt Marie arrived on her bike. She had such a serious look on her face that my stomach immediately started to churn. I saw her go across the field to Mother and speak to her. Mother stood up, the moist earth falling in lumps from her apron. She covered her eyes with her arm, and I could see that her shoulders were shaking. She was weeping so much. Aunt Marie had brought the news that two of Mother's brothers were dead, the youngest killed in France, the other in Norway.

RENE SMITH, of Wolverhampton, West Midlands. When war was declared, Rene had been married for only three months. Her husband worked for the Central Electricity Generating Board and, as they lived in a three-bedroomed house, like others in the small town of Coalbrookdale, they were told to prepare to take in evacuated children from the bomb-stricken city of Liverpool:

'Two girls – fair hair and blue eyes, please'

My husband was on the committee for placing the children with local people. He had asked if I would like girls or boys, dark or fair, blue eyes or brown. I (smilingly) replied, 'Two girls – fair hair and blue eyes, please.'

They were two of the poorest little scraps of humanity you could imagine. They were dressed in what had once been blue velvet dresses, much washed and faded, several sizes too big, that reached down to their ankles – and the extra width was taken up with two large safety pins, centre waist! They wore a pair of navy knickers each – minus elastic – plimsolls, and grey socks, which at some stage had once been white. To top this, there were two little, thin, drawn, tear-stained faces – tired, bewildered and very insecure. All they had was what they stood up in.

After a warm bath, milk and biscuits, and each one attired in one of my nighties, they were soon soundly asleep. *We* sat up until the early hours of the morning deciding what we could do – and how. I nearly despaired; none of the clothes they had arrived in could be used again. They were even past being washed. They had no vests, no knickers – in fact, no clothes at all. Margaret, the elder one, was eight, although so under-nourished she looked six. Winnie, the little one, was six and looked about four. At this age, of course, they needed school clothes as well – footwear, underwear – the lot!

There was an accommodation allowance made but it didn't even cover their food, let alone clothes. However, the next morning (Saturday) we got a friend to come and stay with them while we went into Wellington, the nearest market town. We had to buy them everything – complete sets of underwear, dresses, coats, macs, socks and shoes. Most people in Coalbrookdale and Iron Bridge who had taken in evacuees found themselves in the same predicament. They also had to rush out and get clothes for the majority of these children. The tradespeople in Wellington were wonderful and knocked quite a percentage off the total expenditure for us. They decided that was a way in which *they* could help.

We got our little girls a beautiful coat and hat set each – lovely quality. Later I would have loved to have been able to afford coats like those for my own children, but rationing made it impossible. They were thrilled to try on everything when we returned. They really did look better after a good night's sleep and dressed in clothes that fitted.

We decided that they should call us Auntie and Uncle and to this they readily agreed. In the next day or two we had a visit from the clinic people to help advise with any problems that may have arisen, and to point out those that *would*. The inherent problem that most of us found out to our cost was bed-wetting – on a problem scale! And verminous heads which had to be tackled daily, night and morning, combing with a fine-tooth comb over a large piece of paper, applying a special pomade and washing regularly with clinical soap. It really was quite a chore, but to them it became almost a game. They would regularly vie with each other to see who had the most lice and would become quite excited over the grand total. They would greet my husband when he returned in the evening with, 'Uncle, I had 138 today and Winnie only had 120!'

It ceased to be funny when my husband, at a conference with his Chief and several other GECB executives, in response to a tickle on his cheek, brushed off one of the aforesaid offenders on to his notes – much to his chagrin! So he too had to line up with them night and morning to have the 'livestock' removed with the fine-tooth comb.

The bed-wetting proved a *much* greater problem in many homes – very difficult to eradicate and the endless washing incurred was heartbreaking. There were no machines in those days – it all had to be done the hard way, by hand. To say nothing of the endless ironing and drying. The clinic advised there should be punishment when the bed was wet and praise when it was dry. They suggested keeping something that they really enjoyed from them when they had fallen from grace and restoring it on 'good' days.

They had never used cutlery before for eating, only a spoon when necessary. With us they had their own knife, fork and spoon with which they were thrilled. On days when there was not a good report, just a spoon was set out for the guilty one, while the other had the full set of cutlery. This they soon learned to accept without a word – and it worked wonders. Gradually it became perhaps twice a week and then they would be dry for a week or two, and eventually scarcely a lapse – and finally DRY!

My life had become very different from what I had imagined as a new housewife. I had acquired a ready-made family of four, so our life together as husband and wife was severely curtailed. Our social life was practically non-existent. On the other hand, it was quite amazing to see how those children blossomed physically. It was most heartening and gratifying to see them develop into two plump, healthy, well-behaved, really very nice little girls. We both found it very rewarding.

On several occasions we took them with us to visit my home in the heart of the country. They were thrilled to stay there and see all the sights, and hear all the sounds they had never heard or seen before. Domestic animals were completely new to them and to be able to see them at such close quarters was indeed a novel thrill to them both. They had new dresses to go in and were made a great fuss of by all branches of the family. They were thrilled with everything that was happening to them and lapped it all up. Life was really wonderful for them and so different from what they had known. They had seven brothers and sisters back in Liverpool, who they maintained all slept on the floor in the 'garret'. And they would boast that they all wet the bed!

They were all staunch Catholics and it would take half-an-hour extra to get them to bed at night fitting in all their prayers, and after each one a 'Hail Mary' had to be chanted. These were never missed. Church was a MUST each Sunday. We could go with them to *their* church but we must not take *them* to our church.

They had settled down very happily with us and had adapted

to their changed lives very well. We had become very fond of them and they of us, so it was a sad day for all of us when my husband first learned that he was to be transferred to Wolverhampton. We knew of course that this would mean parting with them because Wolverhampton was definitely a 'non-reception area'. In fact, it was one of 'high risk' in the Black Country, in the heart of heavy industry – steel and manufacturing of munitions of all kinds.

My husband had a friend in the RAF (a bomber navigator) who was shot down without a trace in the first year of the war. His mother was a widow and my husband talked her into taking on our children. She lived in Iron Bridge and readily agreed to have them. We were glad to have them fixed up in a good home but were still apprehensive as to what would become of them eventually. They were very excited at the prospect and didn't seem to mind too much when we took our farewell, amidst many promises to keep in touch. They would never forget us, nor we them.

We moved into a bungalow on the outskirts of Wolverhampton and, from the start, life became much more involved in every way. My husband was in a reserved occupation and was turned down medically (C3) for the military, but served in civil defence and part-time in the auxiliary fire service.

Quite soon the bloodcurdling sound of the air-raid siren was to be heard more and more – 'Wailing Winnie' as we called it. Just as you were sitting down to your evening meal this wail would penetrate the quiet. As my husband was on duty about three nights a week, he would have to report straight away he heard it. Two nights a week I had to go to the Red Cross.

If we weren't on duty, we would wait until the drone of the *Luftwaffe* planes could be heard before we made for the shelter. Sometimes they would be droning over us at a great height. This would probably mean they were making the north their target – Hull, Sheffield, Manchester or Merseyside. When they approached at lower levels our local gun-site would open up at them. Flak would be flying, searchlights would pierce the darkness to try to pick up the enemy planes for the guns. The barrage balloons were an eerie sight lit up by the searchlights. Falling incendiary bombs and flares added to the spectacle. Once the fires were flaring, the planes would often unload the heavy stuff before reaching their intended target.

Our neighbours were builders and had constructed a brick-built shelter in their garden. It held about 20 people. Knowing I was usually alone, they insisted that I made use of it with them. This I was glad to do – often emerging in the early hours of the morning, when my husband came off duty and called for me. My neighbour on the other side was the wife of a policeman. Her husband was nearly always on duty at night. She was what was termed a 'mature mother', meaning she was in her forties, with a very young baby. She was reduced to the state of a nervous breakdown – night after night having to collect the baby and all his paraphernalia (hot water, dried milk, bottle, nappies, etc.) and go next door to the shelter belonging to the builder. Often there would be more than a dozen people – noisy, some smoking – so you can imagine what it was like trying to feed a small baby and get it to sleep in there. Finally she became so distressed that they had to pay for their own brick shelter to be built underground in their garden. I think this finally saved her sanity.

Food coupons were issued in books that lasted a month. We were allowed 4oz of bacon, 4oz of butter, 2oz of cheese and 12oz of sugar per week. Milk and dried eggs were available which did help out when you could get them. Meat was rationed to 1s 10d worth per week for all over six years of age. Later it became 1s 1d per person, but ½lb was available for farmers and miners, and all who did heavy work.

My husband and I managed to snatch a week away from it all in the summer of 1940. We chose our nearest seaside resort – Aberystwyth, in mid-Wales, about 80 miles away. It was June and extremely hot and that particular weekend all the British Expeditionary Forces were evacuated from Dunkirk. They were so desperately exhausted and worn out, they just lay on the beach, where they had been brought by army coaches. They were so tired that *nobody* heard the bugle call for meals. They just continued to lie there, in the heat of the sun, getting terribly burned. Many of them had been rescued from the sea by tiny rowing and sailing boats. Everyone with anything that was seaworthy helped in their rescue.

We had, like everyone else, been instructed to make a 'safe room' in our house. We decided that the bathroom would be our safe room. So out of the window came the glass and it was duly boarded up. One afternoon I was intending to visit a friend on the other side of town. It was about five minutes' walk to the bus terminus and I was about halfway there when, all of a sudden, 'Wailing Winnie' set up her dreaded wail. Now should I proceed or would it be more sensible to retrace my steps? I decided to return home and await the all-clear. I sat down to write a letter whilst waiting when I heard a plane droning overhead. I knew by the sound that it must be fairly low. Then suddenly there was the unmistakable scream of a BOMB!

I threw down my writing things and made a dash for our safe room. I had my hand on the door knob and made to rush inside when, with one almighty roar, every window in the house was sucked out. All the doors were blasted open and every ceiling in the bungalow, in every room, crashed to the floor. I was still standing at the door of the SAFE room – but could not get in as the ceiling lay behind it! By a miracle nothing had even touched me. I really had been lucky – particularly as, by then, I was pregnant.

The bomb, all 500lb of it, had buried itself almost opposite my house in the soft earth of the playing field of a school for backward children. The children, thank goodness, had just been marshalled off the field into the shelter and no one was hurt.

Strangely enough, it had been a perfectly fine, warm afternoon, but almost immediately it started to pour with rain. But, with no ceilings or roof left, it fell as a thin mud. Soon everything – beds, carpets, and all our furniture was having mud rained on it. But within a very short time, the rescue squads had completely sheeted over the entire roof and had secured temporary doors and windows. We had to stay with friends for a month till proper repairs were carried out.

My daughter Joy was finally born during the longest alert of the war. It was quite an eventful night all round. The police came twice to report that the arc-lights in the operating theatre were much too bright and could be seen through the blackout.

By this time air-raid shelters, known as Anderson shelters, were being distributed to every home according to levels of income. They were built underground in your garden, but not so close that your house could fall on top of it. The next grade were Morrison shelters. These were constructed of steel. You could either have them in your dining room and use them for a table, or in a bedroom and have your bed on top of it. The latter choice seemed better in our case. We put ours in the bedroom. It was a huge flat piece of steel on four posts. The sides were of steel mesh. We put our mattress on top of it, then, when the alert sounded, we lifted the baby in the carrycot inside and then we would get into it, and lie down on another bed and (hopefully) carry on with our sleep.

By 1943 I had had our second baby – a boy. Even infants were issued with gas masks. For Joy there was a Micky Mouse gas mask and for David, the baby, we had what was termed a 'cradle'. We had instructions to let the children wear the masks for a time each day, to get them used to wearing them. It was quite easy to call it a game with the Micky Mouse respirator, but the baby didn't much like being lifted into his 'cradle'. It was a little alarming for them both, although there was a large perspex window through which we could see them – and they could see you. They thought it was quite funny when I wore mine. I thank God that we never did have to actually use them.

I will never forget that dreadful night when the city of Coventry was devastated – the terrible noise as wave after wave of bombers came across, and the roar of the anti-aircraft guns. There was a blood-red sky all over the West Midlands from the fiercely burning fires, as the city blazed beneath the bombs. Although we were many miles from Coventry, it was a night we shall never forget.

By the end of 1942 we got news from Iron Bridge that all evacuees had now returned to Merseyside, despite the dangers. We both wondered how our two little girls were faring. In 1945 we got a chance to find out. My husband had to go on a business trip to Liverpool. He arranged to stay overnight so that he could go down to the dock area and try to find out what had become of them. But first he had to discover where Railway View was – their home address. To his horror he discovered that the railway bridge there had received a direct hit and all the surrounding houses had been reduced to rubble. He never managed to find out what happened to all the families affected. I should love to know what became of our little girls and their family. If they survived, they would now be middle-aged women.

When the war finally came to an end, every street held a party for the children. Trestle tables, laden with cakes, jellies, sausage rolls and sandwiches, were laid out in the middle of the road and a huge bonfire was lit. The menfolk rigged up floodlighting in all our gardens and put fairy lights in all the trees and at night we carried on the festivities in the local school canteen. We had games for the children and dancing for the adults. It was a night to remember for us all. And to add to the joy, one of our road, who had been a prisoner of war, was released. He walked into his home just in time to join the party. His family was thrilled, as indeed we all were.

Almost 50 years on, I still live in our bungalow in Holly Grove. Sadly alone. I have been a widow for over 10 years. My children are now happily married and living not too far away, so I see quite a lot of them and my grandson. I *still* consider myself to be one of the lucky ones.

HEDWIG G., of Blankensee, East Prussia, and her husband owned a farm in the Ermland of East Prussia. Christmas 1944 was a cosy and peaceful family affair, celebrated with her husband and three small children. Three weeks later, however, they could hear the rumbling of the guns on the border. By the end of January the Front was only three kilometres away. With her husband gone, Hedwig G., her three young children, her aunt and her two sisters found themselves caught by the rapid advance of the Russian winter offensive of January 1945. With the Russian guns just over the horizon, they left their farm and fled north in an attempt to reach the coast. They journeyed on foot, carrying few possessions, and as the fighting closed in around them, they were often forced to leave the roads and take to the open fields. They slept in abandoned farmhouses and cottages and scavenged whatever food they could find. By the beginning of February they were within reach of the coast, where they counted on finding a boat to take them back to the German heartland. That journey was to prove one of great heartbreak and suffering for the small family:

'God took her for one of His angels in Heaven'

After some days we moved on again over ploughed fields and reached a village from where all the inhabitants had already fled. We found shelter in a cold, empty room. The next day we were told that the soldiers could not take us any further. Little Russian Panje carts arrived with civilian Russian drivers. What followed was a nightmare journey. We were hemmed in between army trucks and columns of troops. Whenever the road ahead cleared, the Russians drove like madmen. A wheel came off on one of the bends and we nearly tipped over. After that it kept coming off. After 16 hours, in constant fear for our safety, we finally reached Rosenberg. We had made it to the coast. But we couldn't find anyone to take us in and eventually ended up in a school, where there were so many people they were sleeping on top of each other. During this whole time we had had nothing to eat. Then there was an announcement: 'Boarding cards for the ships are being issued. All refugees to leave and assemble at the saw-mill.' There were 6,000 of us there. The wind came howling in through the gaps in the boards. Everyone was frozen stiff and sick. Anyone who was able to walk had to cross the tidal basin on foot to get to the harbour. We then waited for four days before a little ship carrying wounded soldiers sailed with us to Pillau. There we were able to wash again for the first time. In Pillau the search for quarters started all over again. The big halls that were used for refugees were already full, but we managed to squeeze in.

The next day it was announced that ships were leaving for Germany. Thousands of people pressed forward. Everyone wanted to save themselves. We managed to get on a transport ship that had been used previously for carrying horses. Old people and children were lowered the 20 metres into the hold on a rope. Others had to use a ladder. If the height made you dizzy it was just too bad. You got left behind. No one cared. Everyone was shouting and scrambling to get a place to sit. We tried to make ourselves comfortable on top of our bundles. For two days the ship waited to sail, whilst mine-sweepers attempted to clear a passage out. We came under artillery fire on one occasion, and the ship was hit. Finally we sailed for Gotenhafen, near Danzig. There were 3,000 refugees on board.

My children were half-dead with the cold down in the hold of the ship, so I managed to fight my way up to the deck, where I got them a place in a cabin. The other women were very hostile. They were all just thinking of themselves. After a passage of about eight hours the ship docked at Gotenhafen. Then it was a question of picking up our bundles and setting off again in search of lodgings. We were taken in at the army barracks. But we had only just arrived when the announcement came that convoys were leaving. With no chance to recover from the previous journey, we got the children together, picked up our few possessions and set off to walk the three kilometres to the railway goods-depot.

We arrived at about three o'clock in the afternoon of 15 February 1945. An icy wind was whipping through the streets. We were to travel on an open goods train. We crouched down in the corner of a wagon, shivering and miserable. The storms, freezing cold and snow made the situation unbearable. I could hear a rasping in the throat of my little daughter, Gabriele. It was the death-rattle. The suffering had been too much for her. God took her for one of His angels in Heaven. Lord, Thy will be done . . .

The train stopped. Lauenburg, the sign read, in Pomerania. There were just a few people around, some of them SA men, and they helped us down, loaded our bundles on to a truck and drove us to a school. There, for the first time in nearly three weeks on the road, we were given warm tea and jam sandwiches. It was three days before we were able to bury our little Gabriele in the cemetery there.

We still had a long way ahead of us. We set out for the station again. A goods train once more. It took us 12 hours to reach Bublitz. It was a rainy day. Everyone had to get off the train and wait. I took the chance to go and look for a doctor for my little Arnold. He was so bad they admitted him to the hospital, where the nurses were kind to us and gave us soup and pudding. We just had to leave him there, whilst we were taken off by truck to a village called Gust about five kilometres away. The people there gave us rooms. Old beds were set up and straw was laid on the floors. Three days later we even got a little peat to burn.

One night while we were staying on a farm there we heard the rumble of gunfire. The farmer's wife said it was just the Volks Sturm [Home Guard] on exercises. But that same night she harnessed up her horses, loaded up and departed. We were on our own again in a strange land. We decided that we would leave, too. We found a little hand-cart and loaded up our things and put little Gregor on board as well. We set off that night heading for Köslin.

We were still on the road the next morning when, at about nine o'clock, we saw dark shapes approaching. The monsters kept on advancing, and then guns started firing. Russian tanks. Frightened out of our lives, we threw our belongings into the ditch and took cover behind a fence. Irmgard, my sister, tore all her legs and stockings on the barbed-wire. Shots went whistling over our heads, but we weren't hit. My little son, Gregor, was yelling his head off. I think it was this shock that finally did for his health.

Our only thought was to find a house to take cover in. We did, but it was all locked up. The owners had fled. Finally we managed to open a door and went inside. Ten minutes later the Russians arrived. They were Mongols. They demanded watches, but did us no harm. The next day whole columns of troops and trucks passed along the road. Reinforcements were being brought up. A couple of hours went by before there was a banging on the door and shouts for us to open up. The Russians came swarming in. They robbed us of all our jewellery and ransacked everything. They dragged my sister outside and set on her like hungry wolves. They were devils in human form. There must have been over 100 Russians came through the house that day. They kept demanding watches and searched me from top to bottom, stealing my wedding ring and my signet ring in the process. That afternoon we were given five minutes to get out of the house. We left all our things lying where they were and were driven into an old dilapidated house. In the end there were 20 of us penned up in there. They put guards on the door. From the sound of activity outside we were convinced they were going to blow the whole place up.

After a sleepless night, the next day finally came. Once again it was a question of moving on. The Russians forced us to walk another eight kilometres to the next village. Anyone not capable of walking was promptly shot. We took it in turns to carry Gregor on our backs. Once they got us all to stand in a line and trained a machine-gun on us from the other side of the road. We thought our last hour had come. But then we moved on again and were finally driven into a pig-sty whilst the Russians fired shots over our heads. At least there was straw down on the floor.

The next day we were moved on again another 12 kilometres to the farm estate of Zeblien. There we were kept in a shed that had previously been used to house the prisoners who worked on the estate. All the domestic buildings were empty. The cows – there must have been about 90 of them – were just roaming around wild, and Aunt Maria managed to catch one and milk it. There were 20 people in one room; women, children, and a few old men. By this time Gregor was very seriously ill and running a high temperature. He looked desperate. He lay beneath the wagon cover, on a bed of old straw. Every night the Russians came in. My two sisters, Irmgard and Cäcilia, were raped time after time by the devils. Cäcilia was only 19. The experience left her a mental wreck. They had kicked

27

her in the face and she looked in a terrible state. There was an old Pomeranian among us. He spent the whole of one night in prayer, then went up to the attic and hanged himself.

Gregor was worse. He was obviously dying. When it was all over we thought we should give him a proper burial. We wheeled him out in an old pram and buried him in the garden. Arnold, my last son, had been left behind in the hospital at Bublitz to get over the journey. I had given the nurses some money to take care of him. I never saw him again. I suppose he must have died when the German staff took flight and just left the children lying there. A few days after Gregor's death, my two sisters were taken away by the Russians. They both ended up in Siberia. Cäcilia died there, and I didn't see Irmgard for another five years, when she eventually returned from forced labour.

Hedwig G.'s sufferings were far from over. Some weeks after the events narrated she was interned in a camp at Gaudenz, together with over 2,000 other German refugees. The camp was broken up in May 1945, and Hedwig G. then trekked back towards her native Ermland. She crossed the Weichsel into East Prussia in early May. She had now lost over five stones in weight, and her whole family was dead or missing. She walked for 10 days and found herself back on what had once been her husband's farm. There was little left. The house had been ransacked and the contents destroyed. Machinery and animals had been scattered to the four winds. She was put to work on the farm, first by the Russians, and subsequently by incoming Polish settlers, after the Russians departed in the summer of 1945. On top of all her other hardships, she became suspected of being a partisan, was imprisoned and then received a sentence of 120 blows of the rubber truncheon, as a result of which she nearly died. The diary she kept of her experiences broke off shortly after that.

In 1947 Hedwig G. came to the West and found refuge in Hildesheim, Lower Saxony. Shortly before her death, some 10 years ago, she entrusted her diary, written in an old exercise book, to her close friend Erna Arntz, who thought that her friend's hardships should not go unrecorded, and so contacted us.

MRS E. EMBERTON, of Salford, Lancashire, remembers her brother John, and also a friend who came home from church one Sunday to receive a terrible shock:

'Her whole family had been wiped out'

My brother John was in the navy and his ship was ordered into Portsmouth for refitting, so he got three days unexpected leave. During that time he visited me and said that he had a strange feeling about going back. I asked why and he said they had a new captain and no one seemed to trust him. But he returned to duty and the next thing we knew, we had a telegram to say he was missing, presumed dead. His ship had been torpedoed in the English Channel. As far as I know there was only one survivor, who visited my very upset mother and told her that the last time he saw John he was on watch in the crow's-nest. We got word that his body had been washed up on the coast of Brittany, where he was laid to rest in a war graves cemetery.

After the blitz on Manchester (which includes Salford) there were so many bodies they had to be put in a local cinema. No one would go into that cinema after that and it was eventually demolished. I remember a friend of mine going to church one Sunday in December and when she got home her whole family had been wiped out. Salford Royal Hospital was bombed, with the loss of some doctors and about 25 nurses. A great pity. The local cemetery was also bombed and consequently closed down. One can imagine why.

AFIENA ALBERS, of Einhausen, was a Dutch girl married to a German, a Rhine bargeman. But even life on that great river was changed drastically when war broke out:

'The war had taken away everything'

I was born on a little sailing ship in Holland and as a child was always aboard a ship. In 1938 I married a German Rhine bargeman who had a motor-ship of 500 tons. Together we travelled the Rhine, the Weser, the Elbe, and all the other navigable rivers and canals in Germany. We called at many ports and harbours: Antwerp, Rotterdam, Amsterdam, Bremen, Hamburg and even Berlin.

The day war broke out, we were loading in Basle, Switzerland, and then set off for Bremen, collecting our ration cards in Mainz. That was the beginning of a bad period in our lives. Things were not so bad at the start, but it wasn't long before we were having to ask the farmers for food, because the rations were just not enough. With the war on, there was often a shortage of sailors, so that in those days I often found myself working on deck or at the tiller. Things got bad after the occupation of Holland. Mines came drifting down the Rhine and I remember seeing them exploding. Whenever we were berthed in the large towns like Hamburg, Bremen or Cologne, we could never make it to the bunkers, because we were alongside for loading or fire fighting with our hoses. We had to survive the air raids as best we could. That's the way things went on right through till March 1943.

On 15 March 1943, just six weeks after my daughter was born, my husband got his call-up papers. He went off with the army to the Eastern Front, and I was taken in by my in-laws in Cologne. Then the war really got started. Every night spent in the air-raid shelters and all day standing in queues for food. It was like that the whole summer of '43. One night my in-laws' house got a direct hit and was flattened. We survived because we were in the shelter.

At the end of September I was offered the chance of evacuation to

Limburg in Holland. I went instead to my parents in Rotterdam. Three months later I was told by the German authorities there to go back to Cologne to join the Labour Force. But I stayed on with my parents. The only thing was I got no more rations or money. The food shortages in Holland were terrible, too. You were just happy if, after queueing for three or four hours, you got your 100 or 200 grammes of food to take home. There were also fleas and lice. Just imagine! In Holland which had always been so clean! Although I was not getting rations any more, my German pass enabled me to travel to the country areas which were prohibited to the Dutch. Here I swapped all my possessions for food – my last clothes and my last shoes.

So it went on until the war finally came to an end. I had still heard nothing from my husband for a whole year. But at last came a sign of life from him. He was alive and well and living with his parents in Cologne. He had returned there after being in the east since March 1943. But another year would pass until we were together again. It would have taken even longer if I hadn't stowed away on a barge in Rotterdam and escaped to Cologne that way. We were together again but standing in front of a total void. The war had taken away everything. We now had absolutely *nothing*! But we had our health, were together again, and had made it through the war.

My husband has been a pensioner since 1971 and today life is good to us. We live with our daughter and two grandchildren in a beautiful house in Einhausen. Our only wish: NO MORE WARS!

ALICE HAY, of Forres, Morayshire, was the wife of a 'key' worker on a farm in the north of Scotland, when war was declared, so he was not called up. A nearby mansion house was turned into a battle training school and, consequently, the local people got to know the soldiers who passed through the course there:

'They were all somebody's sons'

We were pretty poor then as farm wages were only £5 per month. To make ends meet I cleaned bothies. For cleaning one farm bothy, and cooking and baking for two men, I received 15s a month. For cleaning and making the beds in the gardeners' bothy, which housed four men, I received 8s per month. I also took in men's laundry at 2s per month. When I think of all those shirts and starched collars! And I only had a cold tap in my house, no electricity, only paraffin lamps and candles, and an open fire to heat the water. I had a big pot outside which I lit a fire underneath to boil all the white sheets and towels. The ironing was all done with a box iron and heaters.

My husband had to join the Home Guard and, despite all his long hours and hard work on the farm, if the alarm went, he was often out all night. It was so tiring during harvest time. I would be left alone with the baby. I remember one night a new squad of soldiers arrived at the 'battle school' and were down by the old castle firing live ammunition. They had no idea our house was at the top of the brae. The bullets were pinging off the slates of our roof. I was terrified.

Another time, there was a big exercise on. Trucks started to arrive and before long the fields all around were filled with tents. There were 400 or more men from different companies. There were pipe bands amongst them. One night 100 pipers, and as many drummers, played on the lawn of the mansion house and we were all invited down. I danced an eightsome reel with General Ritchie, who was there inspecting the troops. It was a lovely summer's night and a beautiful setting, with Highland cattle by the river in the background.

One night we were sitting by the fire having a cup of tea, with the baby asleep in his cot beside us, when a knock came to the door. It was two soldiers asking for hot water. We took them in and gave them a cup of tea. One was English, the other from Lanark; the Scottish soldier said his name was Harry Noble. When he had had his tea, he took the badge from his cap (Argyll and Sutherland Highlanders) and laid it on the cot beside the baby and said, 'Some day he may wear that.' It was a kind gesture. My son still has that badge. I never heard from them again.

As time went on, prisoners of war began to arrive at the camp and came to work on the farm as replacements for the men who had left to fight. We had Italians first, then Germans, and Polish men. We found if treated with respect, they would work and, in turn, respect us. They were all somebody's sons.

HERMINE JUNDT, of Mannheim, Baden-Württemberg, and her husband Ignaz had their own radio shop in the centre of Mannheim. When the heavy bombing raids began in 1944, the Jundts faced a difficult decision: should they join the thousands who were being evacuated to the country areas, and thus abandon their livelihood, or should they remain where they were and risk the bombs, in order to save what they could from the destruction and looting that inevitably followed an air-raid? They decided to remain, and, during the anxious nights that followed, Hermine wrote regularly to her relative and friend Anna, who had left Mannheim for the safety of the countryside in the late summer of 1944. Here are a few of those letters:

'You won't see many of your old neighbours again'

Mannheim, 22 October 1944

Dear Anna,

Today you're going to get a lovely long letter. I got yours yesterday and what a big one it was. It really cheered me up to get it, so many thanks for writing. We were very happy to hear that you like it where you are. You certainly seem to be having lots of variety in your old homeland of Thuringia. Well, you can imagine that boredom is no problem here either. Life is no picnic here and we don't seem to get a minute's peace. I'm writing to you sitting in the kitchen and I've to keep my ears open for the sirens going. Since the last bad raid lots of the sirens have been put out of action. The one near us isn't working any more. The radio stations aren't transmitting either, so we're really in the dark as to what's happening.

Things are awful here now, Anna. Thirteen big bombs have dropped round about us – the craters are the biggest I've ever seen, and the dirt and rubble in the house and yard is worse than ever. The only clean place was the cellar. When we got back home I just wanted to howl. I didn't know where to begin. No lights, no water, no gas. I tried to light a fire and what a smoke came into the room!

When I looked outside there was a piece of a mattress landed on top of the chimney! Everything had just been whirled up into the air and the whole place is littered with bricks and bits of wood. We've managed to clear up most of it. The presbytery got a direct hit and our lovely church was also badly damaged. But the priest is still keeping cheerful.

There were 180,000 incendiary bombs dropped on the town, so you can imagine that the fires were burning for days on end. Anna, I'm afraid you won't see many of your old neighbours again. In the H1 district a bomb dropped down an air-shaft into an air-raid shelter and exploded. There were over 300 people down there and the only ones to get out alive were those at the entrance. The blast simply blew them outside. They've brought out well over 100 bodies already and they're still digging. I don't know all the names. You'll find out next time you come. Our butcher, Herr Knapp, is among the dead. He always used to go to that bunker. His wife, and the other women who served in the shop, are badly injured in hospital. They were all naked. The blast had just ripped all their clothes off.

Trucks have been carrying out the bodies for days. Oh, I can't tell you how gruesome and eerie it is at night, with all the fires burning. There are three pumps running all night long in the market square. There isn't a single window left in the rooms at the front of the house. With no electricity, we are having our evening meal by torchlight. And can you just imagine me, lying for three whole nights on the chaise-longue in the kitchen listening for the sirens going once again, and wearing my full air-raid rig-out the whole time. I didn't dare go to bed. Ignaz did, of course, and, thank God, we managed to get through three whole nights, from midnight to eight o'clock in the morning, without a single air-raid warning. We still have them in daytime though.

Ignaz and Herr Walter have been busy for two days doing repairs and putting in windows. Gradually we're getting back to normal. The two lovely plants in the courtyard were damaged by heavy cobble-stones flying in from the square. One is completely done for and the other badly damaged. In the N3 district there were 56 people killed in a cellar.

On top of everything else, we had to go to Unterflockenbach on

Friday afternoon. The siren started up just as we were setting out and by the time we arrived I was positively squint-eyed with watching out for low-flyers. Things were in just the same state there, too. Six bombs had fallen near the Voosens' house. All the windows and doors had been blown out and the rooms were open to the elements. All the blackout material and curtains were lying in a corner covered with splinters of glass and clods of earth. Ignaz started work on the doors and windows, and I got busy with cleaning up. By evening our joint efforts had got the place shipshape once more and we got back to Mannheim just in time for another alarm.

I must tell you, the window sausage-dogs [to keep out the draughts] were like pincushions, with all the broken glass stuck in them. The big one had a splinter right through the heart! In Drösel six barns and four houses have been burnt out. Flockenbach was only hit by normal-sized bombs, but other places had big thousand-pounders dropped on them.

Frau Winkler sends her regards. She had a bad time when the train she was on was badly shot up, so she's off to her daughter's and says she doesn't know whether she'll ever be back.

I'll get the material for you. If we see Herr Dehus, we'll ask about underclothing. We're sending you the usual little present and something for little Franz as well. Frau Käferle asks me to remind you about the left-over wool you promised. Thank God the stove chimney is now fixed and the fire is burning well. We're picking up the art of stoking very well.

Today was Sunday and we managed to get a proper rest for a change. At five o'clock I went to church while 'his lordship' stayed here and fixed a puncture on his bike. There was a splinter of glass in it again! At half past seven I was just taking my basket of things down to the cellar when the siren went. Full Alert. We rushed off to the bunker in Parade Square. We never would have made it to Q6, what with all the streets blocked off.

Anna, we're both in good health and are managing fine. Ignaz is busy writing to Arthur. You'll have had letters from him already.

And now to you, dear Anna, and your relatives, our very best wishes.

Extra special greetings from Ignaz,
Your Hermine

Dear Anna,

Many thanks for your nice letter of 14 January, which arrived safe and sound. For some reason the men's letters seem to take less time than the women's. Your letter took four weeks to get here! I do hope the food coupons arrive safely. I sent them off to you as soon as the post in Mannheim got going again. Anna, you'll see from the newspaper cutting that we had to de-register you here because you're not here in person. If you think you can manage the journey back, then don't forget to bring the form with you.

Frau Besseling has arrived back after a journey of eight days. From her home in Breslau she had to walk 40 kilometres in 26° of frost. Her luggage still hasn't got here. I'm afraid, Anna, you're just going to have to do without your lovely wool and I'm going to miss getting my silk thread. The fat boatman's wife is dead. She went down with the boat. Our neighbour, Kurt Unger, has also been killed in action. And who else do you think has been killed? Frau Simons! Her whole shop was destroyed. The Keibels also got a direct hit – but perhaps I told you that already. He's still keeping the shop going, though, and has got half his house stored in the shop. Herr Link is dead. He lost both his legs.

What an awful shock we had last night. The alarm was too late. I can't bear thinking about it. There were 14 people killed on the stairs leading down to the bunker at the station. There were two killed at the Q bunker and two at the one in Parade Square. There are 3,000 slates missing off our roof and we can't get a carrier to bring new ones from Wiesloch. We've had to brick up the shop windows. We were told we had to make room for another shopkeeper, so Ignaz has taken in Herr Weick, the tobacconist, and cleared a little space for him. Better him than Herr Joos, with all his pans and cooking stoves. Three Frenchmen have just spent the last 10 days clearing rubble out of the house. Ignaz has bought himself an iron wheelbarrow. We've got enough firewood to last us for years. But the heating isn't working because the frost has burst some of the radiators. The windows still haven't been repaired. On Sundays Ignaz now has to go off to shooting practice with the Volks

Sturm [Home Guard]. Everyone is being conscripted, even the sick. On Wednesday he has to go to Wiesloch for an army inspection. I must close, it's getting late! Goodnight!

For now to you, dear Anna, and all your relatives, very best wishes from,

Your Hermine

Ignaz sends his love. He managed to get 760 kilos of torch batteries in Heidelberg and we're distributing them around. We'd send you some, but the post office isn't accepting parcels.

Mannheim, 6 p.m. Sunday

Dear Anna,

We have just said goodbye to Hertha after a simply dreadful Sunday. It's only now that I've got a moment to write and thank you for your lovely letter. Today was the seventh massive terror raid since you left us. The Neckar and the eastern part of Mannheim were the main target for the bombs. I can't begin to describe the terrible hours we spent in the cellar today. It was too awful for words. Hertha and I were just clinging on to each other in the corner. We didn't have a chance of making it to the bunker. Since the Front moved closer to Mannheim, the Luxemburg radio station has stopped broadcasting, and our splendid Mannheim officials are nearly always too late sounding the alarm. That's what happened today. You just can't imagine how we had to dash for the cellar and how the bombs made us sweat. By the way, your old bunker friends all send their best wishes. There isn't one who doesn't envy you where you are. We don't get a moment's rest. Hertha was with us last weekend, too, and we had to take to the shelters four times in all! You should have heard how the people were all screaming in the street here today. Everyone was outside and on the move when the bombs started falling. Well, you know well enough what it's like.

Can you imagine the mood here now, Anna? The Front is getting nearer and nearer. Just between ourselves, everyone is saying that the Americans will be here in a few weeks' time. Many are in complete despair. Where are we supposed to go? Germans are flocking

38

in from Alsace. The entire youth of Mannheim has been called in to work on the defences. All drivers have to report to Metz with their vehicles. They've got to bring back supplies into Germany. Never a day passes without some new development! Oh, and another thing. From last week we have to keep the shop open till eight on Tuesdays and Thursdays. And we're not allowed to close on Wednesday mornings any more. So, as you can see, we're kept busy. But please don't worry about us. We're managing fine.

Did you get the things we sent? We got them packed one night between air-raid warnings. Heinz had to wait for hours at the station because there were so many people sending off bags and cases. Hertha wanted to go to Weinheim this evening, but the Neckar station is just one great pile of rubble. The trams have stopped running, and there are no trains out of Mannheim at all. So Hertha has gone back home to get her bike so she can ride to Weinheim. I hope she gets there safely, because I've just heard a warning that there are enemy fighter aircraft approaching. Herr Walther's going to be out of his mind with worry. I can just hear him: 'God, oh God, what if they come!'

I'll not be sorry when these few weeks are over, I can tell you. Last week there was an awful shock for our family. Poor Arnim has been killed in action on the Narwa Front. Just imagine! My brother's only boy. I nearly fainted when the telegram arrived.

Shortly after this letter was written, Hermine Jundt's radio shop, and their home above it, received a direct hit. The building was completely destroyed. Hermine and her husband survived, however, having made it in time to the air-raid shelter. They rebuilt the shop after the war and continued trading for many years. Now in her nineties, and as cheerful and active as ever, Hermine Jundt still lives in her native Mannheim.

VERA MANTELL, of Wimborne, Dorset, recalls the difficulty of getting children to respond quickly to an air-raid alert:

'I knocked out two of his front teeth'

During the war I lived in Poole in Dorset. We lived quite near the sea and the Sunderland Flying Boats used to come in the bay to land on the water, and, of course, the German planes used to follow them in. The first bombs that were dropped in Poole fell in the afternoon and had the children been at school many would have been killed. Luckily they were not at school that afternoon as they only went so many times a week. We had quite a number of bombs dropped on Poole. There is an island in the bay, not very far from the shore. It is called Brownsea Island and there were soldiers billeted on it. One night they set it alight. That was a very bad night, but we always felt that in setting the island alight and attracting the bombers to it, they saved the town that night.

It was a harrowing experience, but we had some laughs as well. I had two boys at that time and, when the sirens sounded, I used to get the elder one up first, then get the younger one up and, while I was doing that, the elder one would get back into bed again. In those days we had oil lamps and some nights, when the siren went, I used to put my hand out to pick up the box of matches, but instead I would knock them on to the floor. I used to get so worked up when I couldn't find them in the darkness. Another night, I got my elder son up and, in my haste to get him dressed, I knocked out two of his front teeth.

I had a friend who had a young daughter and they had a cellar with a fireplace. My friend's husband put mattresses in the cellar and she would light the fire so it was really warm and cosy. While all the noise was going on, my little boy used to shout out, 'I want some bread and butty', and my friend used to laugh and laugh. In the end she had us all at it.

But, as time went on, things began to get worse. My friend's husband thought we had better go to the big cellar just down the road. In years gone by it used to be a brewery and they kept all the barrels in the cellar. It was very large, so there were lots of people down there. As time passed, it was very well equipped and they had wardens there. But, when the sirens went, by the time I got the boys in the pushchair and ran down the road, I couldn't get down the steps to the cellar because my legs shook so much with fright. But then a warden would come along and help me down. In due course we would stay down there all the time and only go out for shopping. Even when my husband came home on leave from the army we still stayed in the cellar.

LILLIAN THOMPSON, of Croydon, London, found that what came after a bombing raid could be a harrowing experience in itself:

'A mug of tea and some dry bread'

I was 18 years old when war broke out in September 1939. I got married in June 1940, and had my first baby in July 1943. I was in the first London air-raid, which took place at Croydon Airport, on a Thursday evening, on 15 August 1940 at 6.45 p.m. We had no warning. As the German planes followed our planes in, they dropped screaming bombs all over the place. Many were killed and injured. Our house was badly damaged. Those bombs really did scream. It was a terrible noise, coming from out of the blue like that, and is an experience one cannot describe, or ever forget.

The air-raid wardens bundled us into ARP ambulances and took us to Queen's Road Homes – a workhouse then. The staff there stripped and bathed us, inspected our heads, then made us put on stiff white linen gowns, with a split right down the back. They then put us in cell-like rooms until morning. All we got was a mug of tea and some dry bread. We cried to think we had come to that. (Although we had a good many laughs about it afterwards.)

Next day they took us to a Colonel Garwood's mansion at Combe Cliff. We stayed there for 10 days then went back home. The top of the house was still off, but we had to manage as best we could with the rest of the house, and the air-raid shelter. We had many near misses in the remaining six years of the war.

In mid-June 1944, I was on my way to Elmwood Road School to be evacuated with my cousin's wife. We had our babies in our arms. My uncle was pushing a pram with our cases on top. No one else was in sight as there was an air-raid on. The school was at the top of the road. We always walked in the middle of the road in case of unexploded bombs or falling masonry. We were almost there when, suddenly, this plane dives on us, spraying machine-gun bullets all around us. We left the pram and ran to hide behind a fence. He must have been hovering up there waiting as we never saw or heard a plane until then. He meant those bullets for us.

We did get away that day – to Yorkshire – but we came back three months later, to the flying bombs (doodle-bugs), which we had been trying to leave behind.

Lillian Thompson still lives in Croydon, just around the corner from the house she grew up in. She calls it, 'my house of memories'. She is now both a mother and a grandmother, and still very active.

ERICA HILDEBRANDT, of München-Solln, Bavaria. During the war Erica was called upon to help out on her cousin's estates at Zeitlow in the Prussian Neumark, some 95 miles east of Berlin. She undertook administrative duties on the estate and remained there for several years. Her memories cover the Russian occupation and the expulsion of Germans from those areas in July 1945. These extracts are from a much longer journal she kept of her experiences throughout 1945:

'Save yourselves! You're on your own now'

End of January 1945. The latest army report speaks of battles at Posen and Thorn. The great Russian winter offensive has hardly been going three weeks and already Warsaw has fallen, Gnesen has been taken, and the battle for Breslau is on. For the past two weeks endless columns of refugees have been passing through, making their way from the east back to the German heartland: German settler-farmers, Germans from the Black Sea and Bessarabia. Horses slip and stumble as they pull the chains of covered carts along the icy roads that lead west. Most of the carts have women leading them. Small children, frozen blue with the cold, lie among bundles and sacks. Even the furs that they are wrapped in offer little protection against the freezing winds. They neither speak nor cry; they die mutely, and mutely they are buried in the roadside ditches. No milk for days. The bread frozen like a stone. The gunfire is getting nearer. The whips crack harder on the backs of harness-sore, exhausted horses. Day and night they move on. Who knows what suffering and misery still awaits them.

We got orders to pack a few days ago. Our bags are all ready and waiting. The blacksmith and the wheelwright have been working feverishly to put covers on all the available carts. Männe has been working out which family goes on which wagon, and how much luggage everyone can take. Four hundredweight isn't much, and the estate women look sadly at the pickling tubs we have only just filled.

Männe and I go every day to Friedeberg, our nearest town, to make final arrangements. All the offices are in a panic, but I make use of the general confusion to get the biggest possible allocations of clothing for our Polish farm-workers. Every evening we have a share out: wool, darning materials, coats, shoes, all the things that have been so scarce these last few years.

On the estate the daily work goes on as normal. A team of six is harnessed up to pull the mash-wagon over the icy roads to the distillery at Hohenkarzig. The Polish and Russian reapers are loading dung in the farmyard. Foals are chasing after each other in the midday sunshine. The rumble of the guns gets louder and tells us that the Front is rapidly getting closer. Some claim they have seen the first Russian tanks – the advance guard of the Red Army – in Kreuz. There are reports that Himmler has gone in an armoured convoy to Schneidemühl and that there is a U-boat lying ready for Hitler in Danzig.

Every evening we listen to all the radio stations to see if we can get information about the general situation. But the British aren't very forthcoming, and the only positive piece of news is that the Russians are drawing in the nets. Mechtild and I are kept busy sewing wadding into all our underclothing. There is a bitter northeaster whistling outside. We make a point of enjoying our last evenings before the blazing fire and try to avoid leaving the Russians too many good things in our wine-cellar.

I have been almost five years at Zeitlow now. It was in August 1939 that my cousin Mechtild asked me to come and help out. I had been taking part in the horse tournament in Halle at the time. Männe, and all the other men who worked with horses, had been called up almost overnight because of the impending Polish campaign. We sensed war was coming, even though nothing was known for certain. More recently, as the war took a more threatening turn, Mechtild and I had finally succeeded in persuading Männe to take me on permanently as estate secretary.

Every day at Zeitlow has been somehow special. New Year was the best time of all to arrive at Zeitlow. As the horses trotted up the dark, snow-covered drive you could see the lighted candles on the Christmas tree shining through the trees. Mechtild lit them specially to greet visitors. The household, which Mechtild ran so smoothly and comfortably, used to fill up with guests. The New Year could begin. How different things are now.

Recently a phone-call from Papa – a clear line for once – to say he's sending special horseshoes and nails to cope with the winter conditions. Two days later Mechtild comes up to my room at five o'clock in the morning. The air-raid siren has been sounding from Friedeberg. It was the signal. We knew what it meant: save your-selves, you're on your own now!

Up till now they had refused to allow us to evacuate. There were notices hanging over the streets warning you not to disobey orders. The people from one of the neighbouring estates had taken to the road, despite the warnings, and had been forced to turn back. At Zeitlow Mechtild has been the one to insist that we stay. She thought rightly that it was the only way of securing the property for their sons. And Männe agreed with her. But now the time for debating the pros and cons is over. We dress mechanically. Männe goes down to see to the harnessing of the horses. Even now he's still telling every-one, 'Now just keep calm!' Downstairs the breakfast table is laid as normal. The only unusual thing on the table is Ziry's cognac flask.

By eight o'clock the yard is full of covered wagons. The coupé for Männe's 82-year-old father is standing at the door, together with Männe's jaunty little hunting trap pulled by one of the trickier horses. He's going to travel in that so as to be able to supervise the convoy.

As we come out of the front door we are astonished to see the Polish farm-workers standing in a long row. Sobbing, they run up and kiss our hands in farewell, begging us to return soon. They don't want to join us on the trek. They had been forced on to the roads in Poland in 1939 and know only too well where that got them. Only the Polish horse-team leaders are having to go with us, since there are just not enough German men available. So they are ready and waiting with their wives. They could easily have gone into hiding until we had left. The Russian workers want to come with us at all costs, and we let them. The send-off we get makes us smile a little. According to Nazi propaganda this should now be the moment when the Poles murder us all. If the Red Army is no worse . . .

The horses start to pull. For the very last time the carts creak and cut deep ruts across the snow-covered yard. After a few hundred metres the old chestnut trees lining the yard fall away and we have a view over the infinite white wastes, with a blood-red sun just rising in the east. The snow turns mauve and pink. The whole sky blazes with silent flames.

I have tied our two Scotch terriers, Benjamin and Fat-Madam, together on a long lead. They keep up well considering how small they are. Then one gets tangled round my left leg and one round my right. I think to myself, they're going to have to learn fast. We've got another 300 kilometres ahead of us yet, if we're going to escape the Russians!

The roads are pretty clear as yet. We pass through Friedeberg without stopping. New snow has fallen and it gives good, safe going for the horses. The whole convoy is going at a cracking rate and it's not too long before we hear Männe bellowing 'Whoa there!', which brings us to a halt and lets man and beast take a breather.

At the Wildenow crossroads we are held up for the first time. Army trucks are coming in our direction, and there are French prisoners-of-war crossing in front of us. A little further down the road a cart has slewed side on. Then we get going again and keep moving till we get near Büssow, where we are halted yet again. We're stuck here for ages at the edge of a wood which is being lashed with snow pellets born on an icy north-east wind. In front of us is the convoy from Hohensalza. Behind us are dense columns of people fleeing from Friedeberg. In the distance we hear the rattle of machine-guns. Männe decides to go on into Büssow to see what's going on.

We wait. There is more firing. It seems to be coming from every side now. From the north and south, the east and west. Machine-gun and artillery fire. We get tired of standing about and creep up on to the carts. There we pass the time eating. The eggs have all frozen solid, but the bread is still all right and we help it down with a gulp of cognac from Ziry's flask. Fat-Madam and Benjamin were put in one of the wagons the first time we stopped. The poor creatures were dreadfully frozen. So the time passes. At least we are well fed. We walk up and down beside the wagons for a while. The snow is falling thickly. It's the coldest day of the winter.

The fat man who runs the distillery is having problems with his horses. They allocated him one of the two-year-olds which Männe didn't want to leave behind. It is getting bored with all the standing around. It has started prancing, jumping and leaping around, and finally somersaults clean over the other two horses and ends up lying helplessly on its back. Cursing, the man leads it away and hitches it to the back of the wagon.

People who had been ahead of us on the trail are now returning. They tell us that the Russians are in Büssow. One of the men is excitedly showing everyone a bullet-hole in his scarf; they'd shot at him! They report that the vet, Dr Arndt, is dead. The Russians had completely demolished his car. Herr Wedemeyer-Schönrade and Herr von Langenn from Wildow have also been shot. More people are returning from Büssow. But Männe is not among them. Mechtild and I go along the road to meet him. We pass policemen burying their weapons in the snow beside the road. Soldiers in full flight run past us but they can't tell us which way we should go. A horrifying thought suddenly strikes me: I have left my pistol hidden under the seat of Männe's hunting trap. He knows nothing about it. If they search him . . .

Suddenly we see a small vehicle coming along the road towards us. It looks like a little tank in outline. We make a dive for the cover of the wood, and from its safety we see the first Russian armoured reconnaissance car pass us.

Finally, a long time later, Männe returns. In Büssow he had tried to get a tank to stop to get information. It wasn't till it opened fire at him that he realized it wasn't a German tank. We offload all our pistols and sporting guns into the ditch. The trek turns back. Männe decides to head for Braunsfeld to see if there is any chance of escaping the net that the Russians seem to have drawn around us.

At Braunsfeld Frau von Schröder and her daughters are busy loading up. It is very hard to convince them that there is no point in setting out. They are even continuing to slaughter pigs.

At last we can warm ourselves up. I have already had enough of being on the road and the whole idea of carrying on for hundreds of kilometres holds very little appeal. The Braunsfeld household is full of refugees. We have our midday meal and finish off with coffee. A Baroness Schilling from the Baltic tells us a lot about the Soviets and maintains that they have not changed their attitudes since 1917. Männe's father paces up and down. The circulation in his feet is failing with old age and he has a bad cough. He is just not up to strains of this sort.

Eventually Männe manages to get through on the phone to Friedeberg. There is still a German army command post set up in the Savings Bank. According to them there is little hope of getting out of the Russian encirclement except with fast horses via Landsberg. So we decide to stay the night in the sheep-shed at Braunsfeld together with the other people from the estate. We think it best to stay together, just in case a chance should present itself during the night. Only Ziry and the old gentleman stay on in the house.

In the darkness, we load up with furs and blankets and move into the sheep-shed. There's plenty of room for us and it's quite warm, too. It's just the noise that is so unbearable. It is lambing time and hundreds of high-pitched, strident lambs' voices mingle with the deeper bleatings of the mother sheep. It doesn't seem to disturb the fat man from the distillery; he just snores away, and the ewes put their heads on one side and look at him in astonishment.

Two of Männe's hunting guns are still in the main house, and Mechtild urges him not to leave them there. Inside the house everyone is still up and about. The last of the wine bottles are being opened. We don't stay, but soon come out again into the cold snowy night. In the moonlight the village street is bright as day. There are people moving about. Soldiers in flight. They look completely demoralized and tell us that their unit was wiped out at Altkarbe. In the distance we hear the rattle of machine-guns. At the end of the village a German tank waits menacing and massive in the shadow of a farmhouse. Fires light up the sky in the east.

Männe disappears with the guns into a clearing at the end of the estate. He is gone a long time. I wait on the street for what seems an eternity. Finally he finds a good place to hide them. We go through the sheep-farm to see if we can find a place where we can look out over the open fields. There are fires to the north, too. About 200 metres away we see a group of soldiers feeling their way down a snow-covered bank. 'Russian infantry,' whispers Männe. 'They'll pass us by.'

Back in the sheep-shed we lie down and try to get some sleep. Very soon the sound of the machine-guns gets nearer and louder. The bleating of the sheep really wears our nerves down. Amidst the other sounds comes the harsh bark of tank guns. Suddenly the door bursts open and in crowd about 40 German soldiers. They stand between us and the sheep, smoking cigarettes. Our menfolk begin to protest. We don't want the whole shed burnt down about our ears. The presence of soldiers is endangering the lives of women and children, if the Russians come. Reluctantly they leave again, no longer soldiers, just men in need of refuge.

Through the high windows we see bright tracer bullets spraying through the night sky. Outside the noise is deafening. We cower in the straw, petrified with fear. Männe says drily we should be glad we're not under artillery fire. His words bring little comfort. Any moment the whole shed could catch fire, and what would happen to us, wandering around outside in the hail of bullets?

The door opens again, and two German soldiers come in. They stand in the doorway, their rifles beside them. The last thing we want at this moment is a pair of sentries, so I get up and persuade them at least to hide their weapons. That's the first thing the Russians would see when they came in.

A long time passes, or so at least it seems to us. The fighting is now in the village. Wild cries are heard above the racket of the tanks and the machine-guns. The noise gets nearer. They are obviously now in the sheep-farm. Only thin walls and the barn doors separate us now from the leading Russians. Männe, who seems to be taking it all very calmly, gets up and cautiously goes over to the door, to see where they are. Just at the same moment a slant-eyed Mongol pokes his head round.

'Come on in, chum,' says Männe in a friendly tone. 'We're all civilians here.'

The door swings open, and someone shouts for a light. The light goes on. With deafening yells, a terrifying horde of Mongols bursts in, brandishing machine-pistols, and with knives clenched in their teeth.

If Männe's polite 'Come on in' had brought us a moment of relief, we are now filled with horror at the sight of these bellowing brutes in shaggy furs. 'Don't worry, their bark is worse than their bite,' says Männe, standing there quite casually.

When the Mongols saw that we really were all civilians, they put their squat machine-pistols aside and came towards us, knives in their hands. I was sure the one who approached me was going to cut my fingers off with his kitchen-knife but I soon noticed to my relief that all his shouting was because he wanted my watch. I didn't have mine on, but to keep him quiet offered him a gold arm-band I happened to have in my pocket. He took it, looked at it briefly, then pushed it back into my hand.

Meanwhile other Russians had discovered the two German soldiers and there was more roaring and shouting. Waving their guns, they drove the men to one side of the barn and the women to the other. The space they allowed us women was so small that we could scarcely stand upright. Then they set up two machine-guns in front of us. We all knew what to expect now, and I pushed my way forward, so that it would at least be over quickly. But the soldiers all round us were friendly and laughed, and made gestures that we should not be alarmed. They raised their machine-pistols and sent wild bursts of fire through the ceiling above us. Were they trying to set fire to the place? We stood in the clouds of dust whilst silence returned. Even the sheep had stopped bleating in fright. The Russians obviously just wanted to see whether there was anyone hiding in the hay-loft over our heads.

When the dust settles, we see the fat distillery man sitting at the other end of the shed, his 84-year-old mother beside him. Close by, Männe is sitting. They had just stayed where they were when the other men were driven outside. Probably it's just as well. We crouch down again in exhaustion. It's too crowded to sit down. The Russians look quite friendly. Fine looking lads, a lot of them. Obviously they are not so bad after all.

But it's not long before the first comes over to drag off one of the girls. Irmchen, a fifteen-year-old farmhand. The lights have been switched off. Now the soldiers come in one after another. They take their torches to light up the faces of the women and all you hear is their hoarse, 'Frau, come.' It goes on till morning. I pull my brother's hat well down over my face and keep my head down on my knees all night. Outside they are queueing up for their turn at each woman. Then they bring her back, only to fetch her out again shortly afterwards. It's always the same girls.

They are getting more and more drunk. They're certainly making the most of the fact that there is a distillery on the farm. They reel around, fetching water for their horses. Then stagger in to get a new woman. Then one of them sways in Männe's direction. We have no idea what he could be after. Männe's boots have long since gone. I see Männe standing there, trying to establish some sort of communication with the drunken brute, whilst the blood runs down his nose from the blows that have landed on his face. 'Do you want a cigarette . . . ? Have you a cigarette for me . . . ?' Männe is fighting the psychological battle of his life with a drunk who stands there swaying, with a pistol in his hand. Suddenly the soldier turns and goes out.

It is daylight now. Outside are the 15 covered carts we started out with. The Russians are standing by directing the Poles who are looting them. They have already driven off the horses and oxen. We go over to the plundered carts and see piles of our belongings scattered in the snow. But what's the use of picking them up, we can't take them with us? All we can manage is our rucksacks. I see the picture of my brother Siegfried's grave lying there. But I don't dare to pick it up. I had stuck the picture on a map of the area where he was buried, right down in the south of the Soviet Union. It might be misinterpreted. There's my pretty yellow suitcase lying there, with all the cheerful luggage labels from hotels in Rome, Florence, Budapest and Vienna. It's been slit open.

We feel as though the floor in the shed is burning under our feet. The two rifles that the soldiers left there last night are still lying under the barrow where we spent the night. We want to get out before the Russians find them. After much toing and froing, the Russians finally allow us to get on our way. Männe's father and Ziry appear in the farmyard. The estate house was overrun in the night by Russian soldier-women, all with guns in their hands. Afterwards things took very much the same turn as with us.

We pick up our rucksacks and I call the dogs. What sort of state will poor Fat-Madam be in? She always used to head straight for home whenever Männe took a pot-shot at a crow. But she comes trotting along, when I call. She springs up at me and tries to hold me in her two front paws, as if begging for help. I promise to do my very best to look after her and she trots along happily enough by my side. Not so Benjamin. He is licking out a jar of black sausage lying under one of the carts. He would much prefer to stay. One of the Russians stole the dog-lead off me, so we just have to leave without him.

We leave the sheep-farm and skirt the village, heading towards the north. Eventually the gentle hills lead us down, and when we raise our eyes we find ourselves right in the heart of the war: burnt-out houses, toppled telegraph-poles, wrecked vehicles. Dead horse-men lie beside their dead mounts, clinically clean in the white snow, except for the bright red blood on their mask-like faces. And silently, their footsteps muffled by the snow, trek endless columns of men heading west: hulking Kirghizinians, Mongols, Tartars and Ruthenians, with fur-caps and fur-gloves, in thickly padded uni-forms. They are laughing and singing as they ride along, with wiry little horses pulling little carts no bigger than a table-top. How dif-ferent they look from the emaciated, downcast figures in field-grey, who, with sunken eyes, darting glances and whistling lungs, strive to find a way out of a trap that is inescapable.

Erica Hildebrandt and her family had unwittingly been caught by the surging advance of Zhukov and Konev's First Belorussian Front, which began on 12 January 1945 and by 2 February had swept through Poland and Prussia as far as the River Oder. There was no escape.

The family returned to their home at Zeitlow, which was burnt down a few days after their return. Living in farm buildings, they survived the Russian occupation, and saw the Poles take over the land and towns. Throughout winter and spring they worked for their new masters. Erica Hildebrand was appointed spokeswoman for the German people in the Zeitlow area, doing her best to shield them from the reprisals that inevitably followed the German defeat. At one stage, she herself suffered imprisonment and the threat of a Russian prison camp. The whole of Prus-sia as far as the Oder was to be cleared of German inhabitants. On 28 June the eviction order reached Zeitlow and the long, painful trek west began.

Erica, Männe, Mechtild, and Ziry all survived the war. Männe, the original owner of Zeitlow, settled in East Germany and died in Braunschweig in his eighties. Erica Hildebrandt, herself, made it back to her native Bavaria and now lives in Munich.

EVE POORE, of Bristol, Avon, was in the thick of the air-raids, even when giving birth to her son David. She also suffered the agony of having a husband still fighting the war against Japan whilst the rest of the country celebrated the victory in Europe:

'Silvery suits in the brilliant sunshine'

Bristol's first air-raid warning siren was sounded at 0.15 a.m. on 25 June 1940. Between then and 25 September that same year there were 150 warning sirens; the 151st siren heralded the daylight attacks on Bristol aeroplane works at Filton. I was in the Bristol Maternity Hospital, following the birth of my son on 15 September, and had to endure many terrifying raids whilst there. The hospital was on high ground overlooking the city and most of our nights were disturbed by the bombers.

When a raid began, the patients would be taken on stretchers down in the lifts to the basements until the all-clear sounded. At 11.30 a.m. on 25 September there was a horrific raid on Bristol and the nurses were rushing around and climbing up into the window recesses with binoculars, giving us a running commentary on the enemy planes crossing from Knowle, across the centre of the city, to Filton on the outskirts. During the early evening a patient was brought into our ward in a very distressed state as her husband was one of the workers reported missing during the bombing. (In 45 terrifying seconds that day, 168 bombs were dropped on the Bristol aeroplane works, causing a high death toll and much havoc.) The staff were wonderful to this lady and the six of us in the ward spent the night alternately sympathizing and crying with her.

Then in the early hours the matron herself, Miss Nora Deane, came into the ward with the news that the patient's husband had been traced to another hospital, and was not too seriously hurt. She had a taxi waiting, with a nurse escort, to take her to see him to put her mind at rest. This was a wonderful moment for us all to share. She returned in about an hour and her baby was born later that day. We were all as thrilled as she was.

The following year saw most of our city destroyed by bombs and, apart from the total destruction of all our city centre, I can still vividly recall seeing familiar and much-loved landmarks ablaze, such as our local church of St Francis in Ashton Gate.

I well remember several nights when we couldn't get out of the house quickly enough and huddled together over the baby's cot in the kitchen, with the ceiling falling down on our shoulders. Then we would make a dash, one by one, to the shelter my father had constructed for us in the garden. We had a lot of rockings in it, but were very glad of the protection it gave.

My husband was called up into the army in August 1941, and I was given the opportunity, along with my mother and father and baby son David, to stay on a farm about 10 miles out of Bristol. From the farm we could see the air-raids over Bath. We were only a mile from the airport and one Saturday afternoon I was walking with my son in his pram and we saw several aircraft approaching very, very low, and obviously in trouble. Then we saw several of the crews eject and parachutes floating down. They were a wonderful sight, in their silvery suits, in the brilliant sunshine, but, as we had been warned to look out for enemy parachutists landing, we could not hang about to appreciate the effect. My first thought was whether I could reach the farm with the baby before the airman, as one was only 50 yards away in the adjoining field. Most of them had baled out much too low and had been killed on impact. They were Americans returning from a raid. My father helped the nearest one into the farm. He had a broken leg.

David was 14 months old when that happened and he was five years old, and had started school, by the time my husband returned from the war. I remember the day after VE Day: I was in a local shop and everyone was in high spirits and when someone mentioned that the war against Japan was still going on, they laughingly said that that didn't concern them, it was too far away. Naturally, I was very upset. When the shopkeeper explained that my husband was still out there, they didn't know what to say.

JULIA KRAUT, of Düsseldorf, North-Rhine Westphalia, was born in Hildesheim, Lower Saxony. She moved to Düsseldorf on her marriage in 1938. A year later her husband was called up. She moved back to Hildesheim during the war and had three children. In 1945 the house was destroyed by bombs and her mother killed. She was now homeless, without news of her husband, who was on the Russian Front, and already seven months pregnant with her fourth child:

'I gave birth to my baby on the bare earth'

The first time we were bombed out was in February 1945. The place we were given to live in had neither doors nor windows. Everything was wrecked, and there was no cardboard or nails, let alone better materials, to make the place habitable for young children, and to keep out the winter storms and rain. So we were taken in by relatives, where it was pretty overcrowded. Whilst we were there a huge bomb fell right in the garden. It felt like an earthquake hitting us, and it was a miracle we weren't all killed. We had to be evacuated once again.

We were taken in by a small farmer, but only very unwillingly. My baby and I were put in a storeroom, and the two boys – three and four years old – had to sleep in the passageway of the pig-sty. I complained to the National Socialist Welfare Organization about the disgraceful and unhygienic conditions, because I was in the advanced stages of pregnancy. It is easy to wonder nowadays why we let ourselves get into that state when times were so bad. But there was no pill in those days and a young wife couldn't deny her husband, when he perhaps only got home to see his family once in the year. The fact that my children all have their birthday in the same month tells its own story.

They allowed me to move out of these unhygienic conditions. But then, pregnant as I was and in the middle of winter, with a babe in arms and two others hanging on to my coat, I had to walk eight weary kilometres to the next village. Soaking wet and shivering with cold I reported to the village mayor, who was helpful and understanding and took me in.

On a temporary basis, we were given two rooms in a bomb-damaged barn. At least it was a roof over our heads, but the windows were draughty, and the door led straight out on to the farmyard. I had a little tin stove to heat the place and do my cooking on. When February came, thick crusts of ice covered all the inside windows and walls. It was condensation from the cooking, I suppose. Our only hope was that spring would bring release.

Because I was expecting the baby any day now, I had to be moved out. There just weren't any doctors or midwives in the area. The farmer's family, though complete strangers, took in my three young children – the youngest, Gerda, was barely a year old – and I was sent by the Welfare Organization to the Harz Mountains.

I arrived at a very well run maternity home. But the war was still raging and the Allies were getting closer and closer. I was so tense and anxious that the birth was delayed. I wanted to go back to my children, but they wouldn't let me because the low-flying enemy aircraft attacked anything that moved on the roads. You just couldn't take the risk of ending up dead in a ditch. From where I was in the mountains I could see a glow in the sky. It was my home-town of Hildesheim, 60 kilometres away, ablaze after a big bombing raid.

My fears for my little family became impossible to bear. The day the baby was due had long passed. Finally they moved me out. I was the last of the expectant mothers, the enemy was closing in, and the place was needed to billet troops on the move. I was put in a rattling old cart and taken to a rat-hole of a house. That night the British started shelling the place and the tanks moved up. The only people left to defend it were youngsters from the Hitler Youth who had been issued with bazookas and were stupidly trying to block all the roads by felling trees. My labour pains started. No doctors, no trained help at hand. I gave birth to my baby on the bare earth down in the cellar. There in the candlelight a woman – who she was and where she came from I don't know – saw to the delivery and then disappeared again.

Troops were entering the village. The cellar started to burn; the house above was already ablaze. Barely an hour after giving birth, with my newborn baby wrapped in paper I ran out into the freezing snowstorm and made it the hundred metres to the nearest bunker. A while later the English fetched me out again on a stretcher. I was put in an empty house. Every day I went to the command post and begged milk for my baby, who was barely alive. No success. So I said to myself, it's either help yourself or die. I lived off potato peelings and potatoes that had been half-eaten by rats. I made tea for the baby by boiling nettle leaves.

When finally, eight weeks later, I got my pass, the baby was even lighter than it had been at birth. I travelled on the Allies' supply trucks. We moved from place to place, always changing from one vehicle to another. We were always stopping and being held up by obstacles. Often I was set down out on the open road, as were other refugees, and had to continue on foot. So, after all sorts of detours and delays, I finally got back, completely exhausted and worried to death about what had become of my three children. How happy I was to find them there. They had been well looked after, and went absolutely wild when they saw me, crying and hanging on to me. But no one had heard anything about my husband in Russia.

But I was back again! All together again in our little kitchen and communal bedroom. Back with the farmer. Even they weren't having things easy. The mayor had been carted off by the Poles, and cattle had been slaughtered in their stalls. We just had enough to keep us alive. Once when I asked for milk for the baby I was told that every last drop had been requisitioned. When I dared to ask for some skimmed milk instead, I got the prompt answer, 'That's needed for the pigs.' It was the same with potatoes. We had to go out with rucksacks to gather them where we could find them, when all the time the barns were stacked to the roof.

They were just the same with vegetables from the garden and windfall apples. The children were given the freedom of the garden to play in but were not allowed to touch the windfall apples. Only if they were entirely honest, and gathered them all up properly, without eating any, were they occasionally given one. Sometimes sticks and wood were available. But the rule was always the same: first the farmer, then us, the evacuees!

There was just nothing to be had anywhere: no thread, no needles, no paper, no household utensils. With no toilet paper, the children's bottoms had to be wiped with rhubarb leaves. We adults could count ourselves lucky if we got a scrap of newspaper.

Once that winter I noticed my baby was turning blue. I thought it was heart trouble and managed – for the first time – to get hold of a doctor. It wasn't her heart, though. It was frostbite in her cheeks and limbs. We had to bring the bed in from the ice-cold room and set it in the kitchen, where the stove was. We packed warmed-up bricks carefully around her. A girl helper who had been allocated to me slept in the same room. Under the couch she slept on, we stored our wood to dry. It just wouldn't burn otherwise. We were able to wash the babies' nappies every third day in the farmer's wife's wash-tub. On the days in between we used to boil down scrubbed and sliced beet from the fields.

Although it was supposed to be temporary, we spent five years there. In winter there was the cold and ice; in summer there were the flies – swarming over the windows and all the furniture.

Julia Kraut's husband was captured in Czechoslovakia by the Americans and made a prisoner of war. He was lucky. Instead of delivering him up to the Russians, as they were supposed to, the Americans released him and he returned to Germany on foot. One day he knocked on the farmhouse door in Lauental, where his wife and family were living. After the war they returned to Düsseldorf, where they lived until his death, aged 86, in 1983. Now a grandmother in her eighties, Julia Kraut lives not far from Düsseldorf.

CICELY BOWER, from Langton Matravers, Dorset, moved in 1936 from a farm to a house in the centre of a little village in the Isle of Purbeck, near Swanage, on the south coast of England. When war came, along with other women in the village, she joined the Women's Voluntary Service. Her three brothers were in the Royal Air Force. Always ready to lend a hand, she became affectionately known to all Service personnel in the neighbourhood as 'Mrs B.' and her house, which many regarded as a second home, as 'The Bowery'. Their village was chosen to house evacuees from the East End of London and she, as always, was willing to do her bit:

'I can't stand chrysanthemums now'

I took four children – a brother and sister and two girls. I already had four of my own and would have another before the war was finished. One of the girls stayed with us right through the war, attending the local grammar school, and to this day comes to see us several times a year and is still part of the family. Her mother had been evacuated to the Midlands. There they received 'Bundles for Britain' from America which she shared with us. My girls became the best dressed in the district. They could change their clothes twice a day and did too! They loved to wear the lovely Shirley Temple frocks that were sent.

The father of two of my evacuees came to see them and really played up. Apparently his children were used to pineapples and melons! We, of course, never even saw such things. We had only apples and pears here. His children went back home after a few weeks.

Evacuated families were put up in the sanatorium of a nearby preparatory school, which wasn't very satisfactory; there was no privacy, and they were very short of basics. We did what we could to make things easier for them, but some soon returned to their own homes. They must have found it such a contrast, coming from the East End of London to a quiet little village like Purbeck.

We had a radar station in the next village right through the war and it became very much a target of the bombers later on. One of the prep schools in the village was taken over by the RAF. At first they had no NAAFI canteen so we took pity on them and invited them home for a taste of family life. I obtained a food permit from the local office for tea, sugar, etc. and made apple pies, pancakes, etc. – good old dried egg! I also made lots and lots of tea – buckets of it. Sometimes there were so many in the house they had to sit on the stairs!

At last they got an RAF canteen of their own, run by the WVS. I helped out some evenings. Our leader, a Miss Dymond, OBE, affectionately known as 'Auntie Di', always did her fair share of the hard work and would never ask anyone to do anything she wouldn't do herself. A saying of hers, still used to this day when buttering bread is, 'Right into the corners, dear!' She worked every day, including Sundays. She would come up to the church in her green overall and soft shoes, park her pots, etc. in the church porch, and take 8 a.m. Communion. That's what I call a real Christian. How that dear old lady worked.

In 1940, or 1941, I organized a fête in aid of the Red Cross in the garden of a local house. All was going very well, there were lots of people there, when suddenly a Spitfire came in over the cliffs and crashed in a nearby field. End of fête.

During the so-called Phoney War, the ARP wardens would go round on bicycles blowing whistles as a warning, then they would ring a large handbell for the all-clear. During an alert a party of WVS would sit in a hut in case we were wanted. One night we were sat there playing cards from 9 p.m. to 6 a.m. They forgot to tell us that the all-clear had been sounded!

I sometimes put up the wives of some of the RAF boys in our home. One weekend it was a case of changing the sheets for night – and day – use! A boy in the RAF and a girl in the WAAF were married from this house. How we conjured up the dresses, the cake, and the eats, I'll never know. It's a lovely memory. I still have the photographs.

There was a long consultation on how we should go about organizing the wedding. 'We must have a cake,' said the men. And it was after that that things began to appear from the camp up the road, such as dried fruit and butter, and two airmen came back from leave with some eggs! So, with a bit of this and a bit of that, we conjured up a large wedding cake. I ground down some precious sugar and, with dried milk, I iced it. We decorated some of the mixture with the blue bag from the washing to colour it. With the dried egg we already had, it turned out to be a darned good cake.

The wedding was to be by special licence, so this was put, along with all the bills and things, behind the kitchen clock on the mantelpiece. It was always the first place one looked for anything. As we had a big family, and very little money, we had plenty of clothes coupons, so we bought some lovely spring-green material and a friend made up dresses for my three eldest little girls. We had to make all three the same for the sake of peace and quiet. We made headbands out of bits and pieces of ribbons. My husband's cousin ran the only florist shop in town, so it was no problem to borrow flower baskets. The girls went down to the woods, just across the field, and picked their primroses. It gave them something to do and kept them from getting under my feet.

Their really lovely fair hair was washed with yellow soap – no fancy shampoos in those days. My Mum and Dad lived with us and they went in to Gran to have it done up in rags. Gran was a dab hand at it.

I had spent the evening before the wedding making anything I could out of what we could find. We had dried apples that I had saved from the year before, and some blackberries I had bottled, so we made piles of little tarts and some small cakes.

There were no clean sheets that weekend – we had to use them for tablecloths! We made everything look as pretty as possible with lots of flowers and pussy willow. It was a real April showers day and the front passage of the house was a real mess with muddy feet, with all the coming and going of the RAF preparing the flowers for the church and so on.

Come dinnertime, we had sausage and mash – lots of mash. When dishing up time came, there were no plates. They were all up at the hall for the reception. So we used saucepan lids – wiping them clean with a piece of bread, then using them to hold a piece of jam tart. It might have looked a bit queer, but hunger is a good sauce!

By then, of course, the sun was shining and that made that house look worse than ever, but there was no time to do anything about it.

I had borrowed a wedding dress and veil for Margaret, the bride, and Rose, the bridesmaid, was in uniform. Our cousins, the florists, had obliged with a lovely bouquet, so at last all was set.

The WAAFS were billeted in the town, but, as the church there had been bombed, the wedding was held at another church nearby. Eventually, we all got there. My oldest three little daughters were so excited, and I carried the youngest, who was not yet a year old, in my arms. I then had four daughters – Rosemary, Heather, Jasmine, and Veronica, and one son, John.

Looking back, I think I must have had thirty hours to my day, but I never seemed to be tired. I certainly never needed sleeping tablets! I just did what had to be done and left the rest to 'The One Above'.

Well, there we all were at the church. There were RAF personnel everywhere. The flight sergeant was to give the bride away. Out came the parson and asked, 'Can I have the licence?' To which all replied, 'It's behind the kitchen clock!' There was a mad drive of one and a half miles up the road, by RAF transport, to get it.

At last we were all back in the church. The organ played and in came the bride. I was opposite the door. Veronica shouts, 'Oh, lubby Marget!' I clamped my hand over her mouth and she promptly bit my finger and made it bleed. In the meantime, Jasmine, the youngest bridesmaid, was rocking about with her legs tightly crossed. Trust her! But she held out – she had to!

The car was outside ready to take the bride and groom to the reception. The boys had been busy and it had large bully beef tins strung out at the back. As it swept round the corner, to turn into the main road, the tins lifted and those watching, and in the way, had to jump aside. It did look funny.

The reception went very well. Many joined in from the camp just up the road. Suddenly the cry was heard, 'Here's the CO!' Out the back door and over the wall went those who shouldn't have been there. The CO said he thought he might as well come and join in with all the rest! We breathed again.

At the end of the evening, wearily we packed up, cleaned up, and left the hall. At home, I lit the old copper and washed out the sheets.

All the guests, along with the bride and groom, had left. Life had gone back to normal, but there was no time to mope after all the excitement.

My brothers, themselves in the RAF, would occasionally come home on leave. One was a senior test pilot throughout the war, the other a bomber pilot who took part in the Normandy landings, the other (the eldest) was a sergeant observer. One dreadful evening, in October 1940, we got a much dreaded telegram. My eldest brother had been shot down over Stratishall. My God! The whole crew were lost. He was given a military funeral in the local churchyard, next to the house. I can't stand chrysanthemums now.

The RAF boys were constantly going and being replaced by others. At one time we had the RAF Regiment here. One day they went on exercise and came back to my house. They all sat round the kitchen table drinking tea and going over things with their leader. With the constant changing as the war went on, we lost a number of good friends.

The American 1st Army arrived and were soon introduced to our house. I did a lot of washing for some of the officers. There were no washing machines or spin-driers in those days – just an old copper and good old elbow-grease. I'd get it all done, nicely ironed and folded and they'd come and grab everything and ram it into their kit bags! They were very grateful, though. They loved my children and the kids got plenty of chocolate and chewing gum! Tragically, they were killed at the Battle of the Ardennes. I heard from their commanding officer. They had left my small son a gift of £10. We missed them so much. I wrote to their families for some time.

Looking back over the years, I like to think that we helped a bit – made up in some small way for what those young men were having to face some time in the future, or even the next week.

I remember one of our young visitors was Jock, a Scots boy. When he went back home on leave he brought back a haggis. I hadn't a clue what to do with the darned thing. But we ate it. I just listened to what was said – and I got quite a few hints about it! Anyhow it was food and not to be wasted.

We were always being told to 'Dig for Victory'. We had lots of vegetables from the garden and also used dandelion leaves and fresh cow parsley for salads. Those of us in the WVS got extra sugar from 'above' (a food official) and made hedgerow jam from sloes, blackberries, rosehips, elderberries, etc. We saved every bit of fat and rendered it down and salted down sliced beans.

Every full moon for some months the authorities cleared out some house in the village and fixed up anti-aircraft guns. The road was closed for some nights and this meant that men living on the far side of town had to take a very wide detour to get home from the pub opposite here. We thought it was a good laugh, but I doubt if the men thought so!

By now, of course, we had proper sirens and as we were on the coast, we got a lot of hit-and-run air-raids. The enemy aircraft would also get rid of their bombs by dropping them on us when turning back for home. All the corners were knocked off our local town and there were even bomb holes in our air-raid shelter. Looking back over the years, it was a good job we didn't realize at the time what a dangerous spot we were in!

There was much talk of where and when the invasion of Europe would take place. There had been much coming and going of troops of all nationalities. The rumours were widespread and the feeling in the air that it would be soon grew daily. I had a WAAF girl, Joyce, and her husband billeted here. She was on Radar – that much we knew.

My husband and I walked to the top of the hill one evening and looked down over the sea towards the Isle of Wight. We could see what we took to be boats tucked in beneath the cliffs by the Needles. We knew that boats were also moored by our own cliffs, in and by the old cliffside quarries. In my mind's eye, I can see the scene now. The island looked so near – and all those black shapes . . . We held our breath and our tongues!

Joyce went on duty that night, as usual, but she did not return for two days! Apparently they were locked in and even escorted out and back if they needed to go to the toilet! All night there was the roar of aircraft and the roads were blocked with lorries coming south. Next day the boats had all gone! We heard the news and prayed. This part of the Dorset coast was the nearest point to Normandy. Afterwards a sailor remarked that the army could have walked across to France – there were so many boats in the Channel!

My Mum and I sat in our back garden for days and watched the transport planes go over – each with its shining cord tied to a glider, and we closed our eyes and prayed. They were all somebody's sons.

Then, for days, they came back with the wounded and the dying. It went on and on and we felt so helpless . . . The noise of the planes never ceased and I knew so many who were closely involved.

Some came back to renew old memories and even now, after all these years, I can visualize them and thank God that we were able to invite them into our humble cottage and let them share, for a moment or so in that terrible war, the ordinary world of home and children once again.

I can remember one Sunday in late December. I can't remember what year it was, but it was two years before Nye Bevan introduced National Insurance. My little son John, then 18 months old, was asleep in his pram in the garden, underneath a tree, complete with a hot-water bottle. He was still asleep as we started our meal and I remember saying, 'Let's eat in peace and then bring John in and feed him.' I brought him in after we had eaten but he wouldn't eat and was crying and miserable, so I just sat by the fire and cuddled him. All night he grizzled. After breakfast I brought him out of our downstairs bedroom and sat him in an armchair. He slid out of it and his legs folded under him. Immediately I said, 'Infantile paralysis!'

He was running a fever too, so I rang the doctor, but he said, 'Oh, it's probably just his teeth.' When I told him about his legs he altered his tune. Three doctors arrived and held a parley. There had been an outbreak of polio at a nearby school and another child, a girl, in the village was ill. But John had hardly ever been out of the garden. With six children to look after I had little time for walks. Ten days later I took him by ambulance to an orthopaedic hospital in Bath and left him there – screaming, 'Mummy! Mummy!'

Before John went into hospital I had grumbled for weeks about him standing at the foot of the stairs just screaming at the others, but I'd have given my soul on my return home to have heard him scream once more.

In all, he had to have 11 major operations. He holds the Scouts' VC for bravery. Now in his forties, he has his own business. He is a watch repairer. A wonderful ending to a grim beginning. But faith, prayers, hard work, and many friends won through in the end.

One of our RAF boys was John's godfather. They all loved him. Young men came and went away – some never to come back. But there is a saying in Purbeck, 'You see we are an island, and once you have crossed the Wareham river you will always come back during your life.' Thank God, so many of them have done so. Even today, many of them still call and say, 'Do you remember . . .?'

LISABETH HELMERKING, of Cologne, North Rhine-Westphalia, was born of a farming family, from Hasselberg, East Prussia. She married a farmer from her own area. Her husband was called up at the outbreak of war, served in Poland and France, then volunteered for service on the Eastern Front, so as to have the chance of spending his leave at home. In January 1945, Lisabeth, now with a son and daughter and expecting her third child, became a refugee and fled from East Prussia to escape the advancing Red Army. She embarked from Pillau, on the Baltic, in an over-crowded ship and took a full six days to reach Stettin. The remainder of the journey to Berlin, only 68 miles, took a further three days, without food or water, on unheated trains, with standing room only. But, subject to heavy air-raids, Berlin was no refuge. She therefore moved on to relatives at Lüneburg:

'You're just a lot of thieving scoundrels'

We had relatives in Lüneburg who were prepared to take us in. So my sister and I – she with three children and me with two and another one five months underway – packed together our few meagre belongings and set off for Lüneburg. Our relatives gave us rooms to live in and looked after us well. But things weren't to last long here either. The bombers caught up with us. Then there were the low flyers on their evening raids shooting in at the windows. It

66

wasn't much fun at all, lying in bed and being shot at. Almost every night we had to drag the children out of their beds and run to the air-raid shelter in the wood. At first that only happened at night, but later the planes came in the daytime, too. We spent hours sitting in that shelter. The children would get restless and hungry. Once, when things were very quiet, I ventured out of the bunker, even though the all-clear hadn't sounded. We lived up on the third floor and I had just put the potatoes on when I heard a whistling sound. I knew immediately that it was bombs dropping, so I rushed out into the lobby. There I was, standing between the two walls when all the windows and doors were blown out. The whole house was shaking, so I dashed downstairs, as quickly as I could, in the direction of the cellar.

My uncle lived underneath us and he never went down to the cellar or to the shelter. He was standing on the stairs when the house next door got a direct hit. The blast threw us down the stairs into the cellar. As soon as we could think straight, we realized that we were all right, apart from a few cuts and bruises. We thought our last hour had come. The neighbour's house was completely destroyed, all except for a pile of rubble and a few bits of clothing hanging from the trees. It had just gone completely.

My sister decided it would be best to head for the country to look for somewhere quiet to live. She managed to get an empty room for us in one of the big farmhouses. We only had straw and blankets, but at least we could sleep in peace, until one night, without any warning, there was a raid and several bombs dropped on the nearby railway line. They hit some of the tanker wagons standing on the line and the next morning the oil was running in rivers down the embankment. A little further down the line there were other goods wagons with spools of silk and yarn, obviously intended for some spinning mill. The Poles had broken into these hoping to find cigarettes. The spools of silk and yarn were simply thrown down the embankment, so some of us decided to go and help ourselves. They just might come in handy for bartering, which we were all involved in from time to time. Other wagons were carrying food-parcels and the Poles had ripped them open to look for cigarettes. When the farmers saw what was going on, they started arriving with horses and carts. We managed to get a wheelbarrow and loaded as much as we could. Then we cleared off as quickly as possible.

We weren't far from the big barn when the English arrived. 'Hands up! Everyone back over here!' We were right by the barn, so we dashed into it and pushed all our packages into a gap between the straw-bales and the wall. Then the English came in to see what was going on. They came into our room, where the children were playing, and they asked us whether we had been taking things. We said we hadn't. They just looked at the children, took pity on us, and left again.

Now the problem was how to get the things out of the barn without being noticed. We couldn't try it in daylight because the farmyard was full of Polish workers and they would have made trouble for us if they had seen us. We weren't allowed out at all at night because of the curfew. So we had a good think. The Poles celebrated almost every night and were often drunk. One night, when things were quiet, we crept along the passage and across the farmyard into the barn, and then through the cow-shed. We kept bumping into cows and treading in something soft. It wasn't that easy even getting to the packages, but we managed it somehow. We only brought the small ones into the house, then unpacked them and ripped the cardboard and paper up small and hid the shreds in a nettle patch.

A few days later two Polish women dragged me and my sister off to the English and told them we had pinched things off the train. But the English didn't believe them.

The packets we had hidden away were a great help to us. They meant we didn't have to eat just potatoes every mealtime.

Then the liberators came. More English, that is. They certainly liberated us – of everything we had! We had to clear out of the rooms. The Polish prisoners were now set free and one of them stole my sister's fur coat. I tried to rescue my good hat, but then that went the same way. Before the English came we got allocations of bacon and honey, but they took that away from us, too. The English drove us out and ordered us to live in the broken down hen-house.

The farmer we were staying with grew a lot of potatoes and had a big vegetable garden. When we asked him if he would sell us a few potatoes he said. 'You refugees have no right to be here anyway!' So he gave us nothing.

Once my daughter Ingrid was going along by the garden fence and picked three sugar-peas. The farmer's wife saw her and tore them out of her hand. She came marching up to me and held them under my nose. She shouted, 'You're just a lot of thieving scoundrels!' I didn't apologize. It all seemed so stupid. My sister went to the neighbouring farm and asked the farmer's wife if she could buy potatoes. She was told, 'If you don't clear out of here this very minute, I'll set the dog on you!'

There were seven of us, and we all needed something to eat but there was nothing to be had. Then they imposed a ban on all movements. But we were determined they weren't going to starve us out. Potatoes lay in heaps in the barn. We have an old saying: 'You're never too daft to look after number one.' When the farmer went in for his dinner, we stole up to the barn door. We had with us a long, sharp stick. Then one of us held the door back and the other speared the potatoes. At least we got potatoes to eat! We also gathered sorrel in the fields and made soup of it. We also made salads with dandelion leaves. We managed to keep hunger at bay. It certainly wasn't a rich diet but it had to do . . .

Winter and spring passed and we survived. Then summer arrived. My third child was due sometime in August, in about a fortnight's time. I didn't want to bring it into the world where we were. My husband had once given me his mother's address. I had lost it in all the confusion, but remembered that it was just outside Bremen. There were no trains running at this time. How was I to get there? They were supposed to be putting on trains between Soltau and Verden. So the first thing was to get from Lüneburg to Soltau, which was about 50 kilometres. I would have to hitch a lift.

So, hand in hand with my little son, we set out. We were given a lift to the next village by a farmer. Riding on a tractor was a big thrill for my little boy. But not for me in my condition. There was just no way of getting beyond that village.

We went to the police and one of them said that British Red Cross trucks sometimes came through that way. He would get one of them to stop. We had been waiting for about half an hour when a truck arrived. The driver stopped and let us get in the back. We had been travelling quite a way when he stopped at a crossroads. He pointed to the road-sign and motioned that he was going to Münster Lager. There was nothing else for it. We had to get out.

The road-sign said 'Soltau 12 km'. Dusk was already falling and there was not a soul in sight. We sat down by the roadside and darkness began to fall. My little boy was crying, saying, 'Come on, Mummy, let's go home!' I started to feel a bit peculiar, just as though labour pains were starting. Perhaps riding on the tractor was to blame. What was I to do, out here in the middle of the forest? I told myself to remain calm. Behind us, there were rustling and cracking noises coming all the time from the woods. Probably wild boars. It was not exactly pleasant to be there on my own, with just my little boy. But he was already asleep.

It must have been around midnight when I saw a light in the distance. I stood in the middle of the road, waving with both arms. I hadn't reckoned on it being Germans because of the curfew. But it was. They stopped, and I saw that their car was loaded with all sorts of cloth. They were astonished to find a woman about to give birth, and a child, in the middle of the forest. They got out and made room for us, so I climbed into the car with my little son.

When we arrived at Soltau I went in search of a midwife. That was not so easy because the English had turned a lot of people out of house and home. I couldn't find a midwife, and there was no maternity home. But then two men were kind enough to take me to the police station. The police had set themselves up in a large private house. The officer said, 'Why don't you go over to the Nissen huts. You can stay there for the time being.'

So off I went. The Nissen hut was full of people; men, women and children all together. I squeezed in and lay my coat on the straw, covering up my little son, who was already asleep once again. I sat down beside him, wondering whether I was already in labour. Thank God, the pains had suddenly disappeared. I was really relieved about that. It wasn't a very pleasant prospect, having a baby there amongst all those people.

I must have fallen asleep eventually. I woke again at about five o'clock in the morning and got up. In the yard there was a pump where I could freshen myself up. We made our way to the railway station, because there was supposed to be a train leaving for Verden at around six. It arrived at last, about half-an-hour late. I was determined to travel on it, but when I opened the carriage door it was chock-a-block with people.

There was a lady-guard at the head of the train. I went to her and begged her to find me a place. She snapped, 'You'll just have to get the next train. There might be one this evening.' I wasn't taking that. 'Look, you either take me, or I put in a complaint. You can see for yourself what state I'm in!' It worked! The only thing was we had to stand all the way.

Once we got to Verden, I asked about the next train to Hoya and was told, 'Around midday'. In Hoya we had to cross the River Weser, but the bridge had been blown up. They had put up a temporary bridge in its place but there was a checkpoint set up here. They wanted to see our travel permits. We didn't have one. The guard said there was a command post about a kilometre away. I should go there to try and get one.

We turned back and on the way we met a farmer with a horse and cart, carrying manure for the fields. He was allowed to go to and fro across the bridge without a permit. He said to me, 'Get in the cart and I'll cover you up with sacks.' That's how we got over the river. We had found a guardian angel yet again.

It was still about six kilometres to my mother-in-law's. This time there were no cars to give us a lift. So, once again, we went on foot. My little boy got so tired that he kept lying down at the roadside to sleep. I would gladly have joined him. Then two women pushing a cart came along. They were on their way to the woods to gather firewood. They were kind and put the boy in the cart on top of some sacks. He fell asleep straight away.

It was evening by the time we got to my mother-in-law's. It was very crowded there, full of evacuees, but at least we had a roof over our heads. No one could go outside at night because of the curfew, and the telephone didn't work. I could get no rest and made up my mind to find a midwife the next day. My relatives didn't want to let me go. It was the beginning of August and very hot. But I went anyway, and it wasn't long before I found a midwife. Walking around so much had brought on labour pains again. The midwife examined me and said that the contractions had started. She sent me immediately to the hospital. She would stay with me throughout the night because no one was allowed out and there was no doctor available. So there I stayed.

At one o'clock in the morning my daughter was born. A little earlier and she would have been born in the wood with the wild boars looking on. My relations were all worried that I hadn't come back. My sister-in-law set out on a bike for the hospital. She was astonished to find that I had brought a little girl into the world.

Lisabeth Helmerking's adventures were not yet over. With nothing but her suitcases and four young children, she went south into the French Sector and managed to find work in the vineyards and hotels of the Moselle valley. She never saw her husband again. With the sum of money from his life insurance policy she purchased a small piece of land near Koblenz and there, over five years, doing much of the manual work herself, she built herself a house. In later life she sold the house and distributed the proceeds to her children. She now lives in sheltered housing in Cologne.

MARJORIE TOWNSEND, of Lancing, West Sussex, who lived in Manchester throughout the war, had just given birth to her second son when she received the news that all wives dreaded:

'Our little son did his bit for England, too'

Our first son was born in 1940, but when he was only five months old my husband John was sent out to Florida and then to Canada for twelve months to train as a pilot and navigator. He came home unexpectedly one night, in the early hours of the morning, tossing pebbles at the window to waken me up. Our joy in each other was instant and deep. But it was to be a short leave and then he was away, awaiting a posting 'Out East'.

Our second son, Colin, was born on 29 March 1943 – such a lovely boy and so like his father. I was so proud and happy and cabled the news to Burma, where his father had been posted. Next visiting day at the maternity hospital, I saw my mother hurrying up the ward, not with her usual cheerful smile. She had a telegram in her hand. I sensed bad news immediately. It was to say that John's plane had crashed somewhere in the jungle on 29 March, and he was presumed killed.

I would not – could not – believe it. Indeed, I never did give up hope, even when a letter arrived from his squadron leader saying there was little hope of survival as his plane would have crashed at night in the Burmese jungle.

The post – oh how I looked for, yet hated the post. I used to stand at the window when it was due and try to will the postman to bring news, and my heart would sink when nothing came. But I would pull myself together and think, there's another day tomorrow . . . And then, on Christmas Eve 1943, it did come – a letter from the Red Cross saying they believed John was a prisoner of war 'somewhere in Malaya'. I can remember I shouted and yelled in the silence of the house. I must have seemed like a lunatic to my other little son, John, aged two, who began to cry. I hugged him and said, 'It's your Daddy, love, he's going to be safe and come home to us!' And then I rushed off to a phone box to get the glad news to John's parents and mine, and we all had a weep of happiness.

I was to find out much later, after John came home, how the Red Cross heard his name. He had been captured and was a prisoner of the Japanese. It was apparently the practice at the camp to have occasional sing-songs. Unknown to their Japanese captors, the prisoners had rigged up a secret radio relay system in the camp, and these sing-songs were used to convey information to the outside world. One of the favourite songs in use was 'Widdicombe Fair' because, as they sang it, instead of singing 'Uncle Tom Cobbley', and so on, the names of prisoners would be sung. John's name had been one of them and been picked up by somebody in the outside world. All we knew then was that it was being transmitted from somewhere in Malaya. Later we found out he was in the notorious Japanese death camp of Changi.

As the truth about the Japanese atrocities was revealed, I became even more worried about John. No matter what I was doing, the constant fear of his death through starvation or brutality was always there. We were given a vague sort of address to send a postcard. It was to contain 12 words, including name and rank, which the Red Cross hoped to get through. I had a postcard picture of our baby son, Colin, taken at 11 months and I wrote the message on the back.

Eighteen months after Colin's birth I received my first card from John, just saying he had received it. Later he was to tell me how he had gone mad and raced around Changi showing it to everybody and it had done wonders for morale. They had all been told how England was suffering. How they all slapped each other on the back and said, 'If England can produce babies like that she certainly isn't done for yet!' So our little son did his bit for England, too!

But still the atrocity stories came and I never did find out where exactly my husband was. But hope went on. It never dies. I still wonder was it the power of prayer or some form of mind telepathy which joined us over the thousands of miles which separated us. I know I did pray to somebody I called 'Dear God', and often, at odd times, I would ask for His arms to be around John, protecting him and to let him find loving companionship to help him. I know I was not at all surprised that John's first words when, at long last, he returned and we were alone together were, 'You know, I never felt you were very far away, somehow,' and 'I've met some marvellous chaps, wonderful characters.' But, apart from those few words, he never said another word about those terrible years in that camp. No one knows to this day how much he suffered.

While he was away, I used to worry about the children. I wanted them to know and love their Daddy when he came back home to them, so I used to talk to them about 'Daddy' and show them his picture constantly. Then I would wonder, suppose he never did come back? Was I only making it harder for them? But then I would brush those thoughts aside and replace them with the belief that he *would* come back one day.

I was to be amply rewarded. The night John did finally come

home, in November 1945, they were tucked up in bed asleep, but he had to see them. We went upstairs and I wakened them both up. John was now almost five and Colin two and a half. I said, 'You don't know who this is.' Two small voices said as one, 'It's Daddy!', and the ice was broken.

Marjorie Townsend and her husband John went on to have a third son, Martin, in 1946. They now live in peaceful retirement on the Sussex coast. The baby who 'did his bit' for the prisoners' morale grew up to be the co-editor of this book.

FRIEDA REICH, of Frankfurt-am-Main, recalls a favourite pet, and remembers the feelings when, as a young wife, she said goodbye to her husband for the last time:

'Take a good look, you'll not see him again'

In the summer of 1940, at the end of the French campaign, my husband, Wolfgang, was transferred with his company to the Channel coast. One of his letters home told me about a stray dog that had 'joined up' with them near Dunkirk. For the time being it was guarding the company cash-box, but as soon as he could, he was going to get one of his mates to bring it to us in Berlin. My father said drily that the whole family was now going to have to learn French just to be able to communicate with the animal.

The time came and off I went to the Winter Garden Café at Friedrichstrasse Station, where I was to meet my husband's comrade and collect the orphan dog from him. It was a little terrier bitch, about 11 years old, and the soldiers had christened it Puppi. It was ever such an affectionate creature. It only had one failing. Whenever

I was taking it out for a walk and it saw a soldier, it would dash up to greet him with its tail wagging furiously. It never forgot the smell of a soldier. Puppi was with us right up to the end of 1944. Then old age caught up with her and we had finally to have her put to sleep.

In the summer of 1944 my husband Wolfgang, a lieutenant in the army, had been sent on convalescence to Minden in Westphalia, after receiving treatment for a hand injury. There he was to await his next posting. One day he phoned me to ask me to go and see him. He had just received news that he was to go back to the Front. I was working at that time in an office, but office work wasn't considered so important for the war effort. Seeing a soldier who was being posted back to the Front was more important. So I was allowed time off and caught the train to Minden just to have the chance of being together with my husband for a few precious days.

We spent our happy hours together in private quarters where the people were very kind to us. Neither of us spoke of our coming parting, although it was uppermost in both our minds. The house owners could not have been nicer to us. The husband had a business that distributed dairy produce and his wife insisted on baking us a 'proper' buttercream cake to have with our Sunday coffee. What a luxury that was in 1944!

But then came the hour of parting. We travelled on the same train as far as Hanover. Then it was time for Wolfgang to change trains, whilst I stayed on the same train for Berlin. So there my husband stood on the station platform, whilst the train I was on began to move. I saw his figure getting smaller and smaller. As I watched him my only thoughts were 'Take a good look, you'll not see him again.' I knew then that my husband was bound for Yugoslavia, and according to the rumours that were leaking through, things out there were looking pretty black.

At first his army letters came through fairly regularly, and I would always write back straight away. Then his letters stopped coming after the middle of November and a little voice inside me told me that any letters I wrote wouldn't reach him. As time went on, my fears were confirmed. Whenever there was a knock at the door I would start to tremble and it was always an enormous relief when the postman went on by.

In the middle of January 1945, a Party official brought the news that my husband was reported missing. He said a few words, trying to be of some comfort, then he left, probably only too glad to have the business behind him. My premonitions had not deceived me. But like everyone else, I just hung on to those words 'missing' and prayed for a miracle.

Speaking about it today, it all sounds so calm and collected. You just can't put into words the mental anguish one went through then. It wasn't until 1947 that I got definite news. One of my husband's army comrades wrote to tell me that my husband had been badly wounded near Stara Straze in Dalmatia on 4 December 1944. He died of his wounds.

MRS F. HUGHES, of Benchill, Manchester, worked in Ferranti's as a capstan machine operator, until giving it up shortly before the birth of her first child:

'I'm not coming back in the morning'

They said, if you can work that machine, you can work anything. It was like three motorbikes joined together, with all sorts of different levers. You were given two weeks to learn it. I thought, I'll never get the hang of this in two years – I'm not coming back in the morning! But, on going home, I took one look at my Dad's face when I told them and I was back at work the next morning all right. Funnily enough, I actually learned to work it in two days.

We had to work very hard there, but on the whole we were a happy bunch. We sang most of the time. The roof of the building was made of glass and painted black because of the air-raids. Lord Haw Haw announced on the radio that they were coming to bomb Ferranti, which wasn't very nice to hear. In the beginning we used to go to the underground shelters outside when there was a raid on, but after a few weeks we decided just to stay put inside and work on. I remember saying to my friend, 'Won't we be lucky if we're still alive when the war is over.'

Mrs Hughes survived the war, as did her husband, and they had two sons. Widowed in 1979, she still lives in the Manchester area.

HANNA LAMBRECHT, of Langen, near Frankfurt-am-Main, spent her war years in the north of Germany. Her account is a concise and telling depiction of the brutal effect of war on one family:

'Words would not come, only tears'

At the outbreak of the war we were a complete family: father, mother, two brothers who were soldiers, and myself. We lived in Bremerhaven, which suffered throughout the war as it was on the direct flight-path of bombers approaching Germany. So it was sirens day and night for the whole of the war, and I spent most of my youth in cellars and bunkers.

In 1942, when I was just 19, I met my future husband, a chief petty officer in the German navy. Three days after we met he was off on a tour of duty again. After six weeks of intensive letter writing, we got engaged. Times were so uncertain, no one knew whether they were going to live or die. We married in March 1943. My husband got three weeks' marriage leave from the Norwegian front.

Dark clouds were gathering over us. My elder brother was badly wounded in the Crimea and lost both his legs. My first child was born in a hospital cellar in the middle of an air-raid. It was a boy, and for a while I was the happiest mother alive, cherishing and protecting him. But night after night I had to take him out of his warm bed and go with him to the ice-cold bunker. It was too much for his delicate health. When he was only 14 weeks old he went down with acute meningitis and died within three days, on 17 November 1943. On 16 November my husband had come home on leave. It was his first since we got married. He just had time to see his son alive and then we buried him together. I was inconsolable.

Not long after that, on 13 February 1944, whilst my husband was stationed in Wilhelmshaven and I was living with him a telegram came: 'House bombed. Mother injured. Come at once.' My husband got three days' compassionate leave and we left. That evening we reached the spot where our house had once stood. All we found was ashes and rubble, the smoke still rising from them. Sticking up in the middle was the charred frame of our little boy's pram. All around was the darkness and the chill of the night. We held each other close and wept helplessly and uncontrollably. What should we do? Where were they all, Mum and Dad, Granny and Grandad? Were they alive or dead?

My brother – the one who had lost both legs – had a little flat nearby, so we went there and found them all. My mother had severe burns. Words would not come, only tears. We couldn't stay there, it was already full. Neighbours took us in and for three nights lent us their sofa. Then my husband had to go back to the war and I was alone again. My parents' suffering was so great that there was no sympathy left for me.

The day after the bombing I heard that an enemy aircraft had been shot down and that pieces of the aircraft were scattered all over the area where our house had been. I saw the wreckage and in it a human torso, probably the pilot, burnt beyond recognition. They said it was a British plane. I felt nothing. My own tragedy had numbed all my feelings. Later, when working in the garden, I found a human arm lying there between the dungheap and the cabbages. It was a man's arm, quite hairy, with the hand still attached. Probably what was left of one of the crew. That shocked me deeply. I reported the find to the authorities.

On 18 September came the massive raid that just about destroyed Wesermünde. As the bombs rained down I was in the bunker. It was two days before the ruined town emerged from the fire and smoke.

Thousands of human beings and animals suffered a terrible death. The clearing-up operations were hindered for days by the stench of rotting and burnt flesh. Emergency kitchens were set up for the bomb-victims. I felt somehow predestined for this work and reported to the emergency services. Together with other women I peeled mountains of potatoes, boiled soup in huge washtubs and looked after women and babies. That was the hardest thing for me. I couldn't get my own dead baby out of my mind.

By now I had been without news of my husband for weeks. For all I knew I was a widow. Then his letter arrived. From a field hospital in the north of Norway. The mine-sweeper he had been serving on had been sunk by Russian fast patrol boats. Almost all his shipmates had been drowned. My husband had been fished unconscious out of the Arctic Ocean. He was alive.

The war came to an end, but our family's misfortune was still not over. There had been no news from my younger brother, who we knew had been in the fighting in the Crimea. No one dared put our fears into words. Then the terrible news arrived. It was an official packet containing his wallet, his watch, and one of those meaningless official letters saying how he had died in the Crimea for Führer, Volk and Fatherland.

The news broke my mother's heart. She did not speak, she did not weep. She just died, quietly and simply, at the age of 52.

ALFREDA PICKLES, of Shipley, West Yorkshire, found it almost impossible to escape the bombs. Her father was killed during an air-raid, then, on returning from the London area to the relative peace of the countryside, she found that her new neighbours had rather unusual eating habits:

'It was hedgehog pie'

When war was declared we were all issued with gas masks and were told to put them on when the sirens went. (They had not yet made any air-raid shelters for us.) When the first raid began, I put mine on and put my baby Sylvia in the black box she was issued with and started pumping. About two hours later everyone in the street looked out of their cottage windows, all with their gas masks still on, wondering what to do next. It was a real picture. I had Sylvia on a chair and had kept pumping away. She was screaming and I was so worried that I was not doing it right. Luckily the bombers passed over us, but Gainsborough had a few hits that day.

Later on, my husband, who was in the Tank Regiment, was sent to London and as we had friends just outside there, they asked me to go and stay with them. It was the worst thing we could have done. The raids were so bad, as soon as we came out of the shelters we had to return to them again. When we came out one morning, after a particularly bad raid, so many houses had gone that the street was almost unrecognizable, and there were parts of bodies – people's arms and legs – hanging from the telephone wires.

Eventually I managed to get a cottage in Ossett and there was a large house nearby in which lived one of the Gypsy Smith family, with his wife and children. Money was very tight for me and Mrs Smith looked after Sylvia while I went out to work filling shells with gun powder. (Once again I was a prime target as the Luftwaffe kept trying to hit the factory. I must have had nine lives!) One day, on my return from work, Mrs Smith asked me to stay for tea. She brought to the table a lovely-looking pie. I thoroughly enjoyed it, then Mr Smith told me it was hedgehog pie! Did I feel ill! He said that Sylvia had had a lot of it over the months and as she looked a picture of health, I didn't like to say anything.

My father was fatally injured during an air-raid and died shortly afterwards, so my mother came to live with me in my cottage. There wasn't much room, so she sold her own house in Lydd and bought a large house in Ossett, but, sadly, she died not long afterwards, which upset me very much as I was an only child. I was left to cope on my own with Sylvia, and two more babies, as I gave birth to two sons, Frank and Martin, in 1943 and 1945.

ANNELIESE LAUFER-KLAPP, from Berlin, recalls how they made do and mended, in the days when necessity really was the mother of invention:

'We'd rather do it in our trousers!'

Not many people realize that the fashion of trousers for women, so popular today, was created by us in the war. Textiles were in short supply and getting scarcer all the time until they just disappeared altogether. Once we had used up all our evening dresses and bed-linen making clothes for the children, the only thing left was to raid your husband's wardrobe. And we soon found out what a good invention men's trousers are, being both comfortable and warm. (You hadn't been able to get stockings for years.) You could look quite stylish, too, in a pair of well-made trousers.

Shoes were more of a problem. There was no substitute, so bartering was the only answer: 'Woman's size five offered for pair of children's shoes'. Bartering and exchanging went on for everything. (Hence the joke: 'Will exchange slightly used bride for 50 kilos of sauerkraut'.)

I was luckier than most with shoes. We had leased out part of our block of flats to a shoe-shop which was pretty well stocked. It was hit by a bomb and my mother was allowed to pick out as many pairs of shoes as she wanted before damages were assessed. All a bit shady, but at least it meant I came by 20 pairs of children's shoes. But justice saw to it that we were punished. When we were bombed in Sonderhausen the whole shoe-rack was burnt. We ended up making shoes for the children ourselves – out of straw! I was left wearing a clodhopping pair of men's shoes.

One thing I missed badly was real soap. Ersatz soap was available ('floating soap', chalk-soap and pumice-soap), but it hardly cleaned at all and it went for your hands and clothes. I needed soap urgently, too! Looking out of the window I saw my two boys coming home from school, walking stiffly, legs apart. I knew immediately – they had messed in their pants again. When I asked them why, they said, 'The school toilets are so *filthy,* we'd rather do it in our trousers!'

C.M., from the Midlands, faced one of the most heartbreaking problems encountered during the war. How do you cope with falling in love with another man while your husband is away fighting the war? And what happens when you find you are pregnant and the baby is not your husband's? Every wife had to find her own answer and it could not be made without a great deal of heartache and soul-searching. All too often it resulted in a very private, very personal grief that had to be borne in secret throughout the coming years:

'I don't know how I survived'

I was married at the beginning of the war, in 1940, but couldn't really regard myself as a housewife as I still lived with my parents. We were a respectable family. My father was in a good job, working for the same firm since being demobbed after the First World War. I went to Sunday School and was later confirmed, and continued to go to church. We were quite a happy family, but I remember my Dad was very strict with us.

I met my future husband John when he was 18 years old and working very long hours at a large grocery shop close to my home. I used to see him every day and we soon started courting, but my Dad always insisted that I had to be in for 10 p.m. John started to come to my home and I loved to go to his which was in the country, about seven miles away.

It was while we were on holiday in Blackpool, enjoying ourselves in lovely sunny weather, that war was declared. John was one of the first to be called up into the Forces.

I worked at a boys' high school doing secretarial work which I loved, even though the wages were only 6s 4d per week. But it had its compensations. I had long school holidays. With the outbreak of war, I was kept quite busy doing voluntary work, along with the teachers and staff, and this occupied me while John was away.

After some months I was conscripted to a local factory which had gone over to making small arms ammunitions. It was a great change for me and the hours were very long. But, even so, there was a great friendliness and atmosphere between folk. To me there was more excitement in life. I looked forward to John's leave, and I sometimes went to visit him.

Though we were both very young, we were very much in love, and so we got married at the local church which I had always attended. It was a white wedding, with the organ, choir boys, and John in his uniform. Afterwards a reception was held at my parents' home, with the blessings of both our parents.

Time went by, and the war changed everything. Until then I had led rather a sheltered life, but now I had to meet and mix with more people. Things seemed to be happening more quickly and our small town was swarming with either Americans, Fleet Air Arm, or other servicemen. The public houses were always so busy. They were certainly doing a roaring trade and it was so unusual to see women drinking. It just hadn't been done before.

One day an older lady with whom I worked invited me to her home for tea. There I was introduced to a Fleet Air Arm boy who was billeted with her. I had heard her talk about him previously, but didn't pay much attention to it. After talking to him later I learned that she had also spoken of me to him, but he didn't realize I was so young. He was under the impression that I was of a similar age to my friend. So we were both surprised and attracted to each other from the moment we met.

We saw quite a lot of each other from then on and later I was invited to his 21st birthday party, with some of his class mates. After celebrating, and he having a little too much to drink, on returning home he confided to his friends that he had fallen in love, but the girl was married. I knew that the girl he was referring to was me. The next time I saw him I expected him to have completely forgotten about the episode, but he remembered and he told me that he meant it. Quite seriously and sober now, he told me that he was madly in love with me. I knew then that I felt the same about him, but hadn't dared to think about it.

Time went by and the worst happened – we did eventually make love. Then he was moved away to Portsmouth, but he still came back to see me whenever possible. I received long and loving letters from him almost every day. How this war had changed my life – for I soon discovered I was pregnant.

I knew then that I had to make a very hard decision. I knew that if I told him I was expecting his child, he would never have let me go, so I decided I must not tell him. Instead, cruelly, I wrote and told him that our relationship must end and we must just remain friends. I remember his reply as if it were yesterday. He said that his feelings for me could never be as just a friend. He was in love with me. And so that was it!

I was heartbroken. But, above all, the guilt and torture of deceiving John was unbearable. I don't know how I survived. In those days divorce and all that sort of thing was such a disgrace. I just couldn't face up to my father, or going away from home to somewhere strange. Even though I had never confided in my mother, I somehow felt that she knew the truth, for she must have destroyed the photographs and letters that I saved. There was nothing left. I knew, many years later, that she must have taken my secret with her when she died.

I had my baby son and my husband returned home safely. We

bought our first new house, and then John joined the police force. I loved John and was a good wife to him ever afterwards. I had two more children, a girl and another boy. We had a happy married life (apart from the secret I have carried with me all these years). I never told John, I was so afraid of losing him, as I know he could never have forgiven me.

My elder son has been a son to be proud of, both to me and my husband. Since the sudden death of my husband a few years ago, he has been a tower of love and strength to me. I live on my own now, that is why I can reveal it all – my wartime memories of happiness and regrets, which I have never told to a single person. John and I were married for over 40 years and I would give anything to have him with me here today.

I think of nowadays and how different life is. There is the pill and other means of contraception available. I did wrong and I suffered for it. But I was not a bad girl – probably too innocent and too young when I married the first boy in my life. I still loved John – but why did I have to meet someone else? I don't know whether my Fleet Air Arm friend survived the war, or whether he is dead or alive. It would be so nice to know. I hope you won't condemn me too much.

*RIA BRÖRING, from Düsseldorf, North Rhine-Westphalia, was only 17
when the war broke out, but her example is the clearest demonstration that
wartime means the early acceptance of adult responsibilities. What she
saw of the war and Hitler's Germany filled her with apprehension. She saw
columns of weary Jews passing her house en route for transportation. She
heard Hitler's ranting radio broadcasts and became convinced that he was
evil. She lost a brother on the Eastern Front. From the age of 16 she kept a
diary in which she recorded her feelings. To do so was to run a great risk;
if found it would have meant imprisonment, at the very least. But Ria
Bröring was willing to take that risk, and more besides. She distributed
leaflets containing Bishop Galen's famous sermon denouncing euthana-
sia. In 1942, together with her brother, she led a protest with catcalls and
whistles in a theatre where a Nazi propaganda play was being performed.
She was arrested, interrogated by the Gestapo, and subsequently dishon-
ourably discharged from the Hitler Youth. It was a disgrace in which she
can now take some pride. In due course she experienced the bombing of
Düsseldorf, served her compulsory year with the German Labour Service,
and was then conscripted to work on searchlights with a flak unit.
Throughout the war she remained critically detached from the regime she
was forced to serve. Her compassion and good judgement, especially precious in one so young, find ample expression in these extracts from her
diary and war story:*

'Some of us didn't set much store by duty'

Thursday, 23 April 1942
Once again there are huge columns of Jews passing our house. The
suffering of these poor tottering figures is indescribable. They stop
to rest outside our house. They just flop down in the roadway. Many
are so exhausted they can't get up again. Often they are too weary to
carry their bundles any further, and just leave them lying in the
road. Mothers comfort crying children. Old men are helped along
by sons and daughters. Sheer misery stares out of the eyes of every
one of them. Is it not an appalling injustice to rob these people of

their last possessions and then finally of their homeland? Who is going to take responsibility for such guilt and wickedness? A price will have to be paid in the long run. I heard a German woman in the street say, 'Pray God we never have to answer for this.' If only we knew what was going to happen to these Jews. The rumour here is that they are taken off to Poland and then killed – that is if they haven't already died from hunger and the hardships of the journey. How can people who do that to them be called human beings? No, those responsible for this are nothing but animals.

Sunday, 26 April 1942

I have just been listening to the Führer's speech on the radio. It made me so wild I can hardly find the words to describe it. But I have to let my feelings out somehow. This lout who is running Germany is an absolute madman. Megalomania in every word he utters. Today's meeting of the Reichstag [the German Parliament] certainly bears that out. The whole point of the meeting was this: Hitler wanted specific confirmation that he is now the supreme legal authority in Germany. From now on – as he himself says – he will overturn every law and prison sentence that doesn't suit him. For instance, if someone gets a jail sentence and Hitler thinks he is getting off too lightly, he can change it to the death sentence. Perhaps the consequences don't seem too obvious at the moment, but they pretty soon will. The second important point was that German citizens no longer have rights. Up till now if you had duties, you also had rights. But now, as Hitler quite literally said, 'Germans no longer have rights, only duties.' We no longer have a right to take holidays or anything else. If that doesn't get the Germans protesting then they're just a lot of gutless creatures. Hitler's overbearing manner and the blind worship he gets from his Nazi cronies just makes me speechless with rage. I feel such loathing for him and his regime. I can't bear to hear the way the German people are described as 'loyal to the Führer and to National Socialism'. The truth is there is hardly anyone who is loyal to the Nazis out of conviction. I just live for the day when our eyes are opened and we find the courage to shake off this shameful regime.

The first time we managed to catch a bomber in our searchlight-beam was on 7 December 1944. We had been kept at full alert day and night for weeks on end. But the bomber squadrons were passing us high overhead, mostly *en route* for Berlin. Having experienced the inferno of the bombs in Düsseldorf, I knew well enough what the Berliners were in for when the bombers dropped their deadly loads. But I couldn't bring myself to hate those bomber crews. After all, hadn't both my peace-loving brothers been drawn into the war-machine against their will? This time it was a solitary aircraft, obviously detached from the main body of planes. I had mixed feelings when the command 'Searchlight on!' rang out. It was mostly an automatic reflex on my part. The job I had been trained to do was to set the searchlight-beam in lateral and vertical plane from figures that were given to me by the acoustics operator. I did my job, but part of me felt for the pilot caught in our beam, as he twisted and turned to try and escape. As the flak batteries started booming, I felt an urgent wish inside me that he should come to no harm. Before long he vanished from our sector.

Soon situations like that no longer arose. The fact that the war was nearly over started to betray itself in little ways. There was often no petrol for the generator that supplied our unit with electricity. Or, on the rare occasions we did have fuel, the flak battery had run out of ammo. Despite the shortages we still had to put in our full shifts and always be ready at our posts when the alert went. Some of us didn't set much store by duty any more. We used to stretch out on top of the tarpaulins and were so exhausted we even managed to sleep in the freezing cold of a winter's night. But we had to watch out. Some of our comrades were still 'loyal to the Führer' even at this late stage of the war and were carrying out their duties to the very letter. One of these was the daughter of the Gauleiter [Nazi district official] of Stettin. She used to lecture us for not believing in 'Final Victory'. Her family suffered an awful end. Just before the finish of the war she got news that her father had shot himself and the whole family when the Russians marched in.

KATHLEEN BENN, a mother of five, of Tenterden, Kent, lived in the Channel port of Dover for most of the war. She suffered the terrifying experience of being bombed out of her home not once but several times, and it was while sheltering in caves in the famous White Cliffs of Dover that she experienced the ultimate tragedy of war before her very eyes, within her own young family:

'Nobody saw him go out'

At the outbreak of the Second World War I lived in Dover, quite near the docks, with my three children, Jimmy, aged three, Bertram, aged two, and Francis, aged one. My husband Reginald, who was in the Buffs Territorial Army, was called up for regular service previous to war being declared. I shall never forget that Sunday morning when it was announced over the radio. Everyone in our little cul-de-sac came out to talk to one another. The siren sounded and we all thought it was to say that war had been declared, but, actually, enemy planes were sighted coming towards England across the Channel. Luckily no bombs were dropped. Whenever the siren sounded after that, I used to sit on the basement stairs with my sons until the all-clear sounded. Later we had an Anderson shelter erected in our small garden. It was really quite frightening at first, trying to amuse three little boys. But we soon got used to it.

On 13 August 1940, I gave birth to my daughter Sylvia. When she was a few days old there was a terrible explosion. My husband, who was home for a couple of days, said, 'That sounds like a shell.' It had fallen a couple of streets away. He remembered what Dover was like during the 1914–18 war. He picked up our daughter and was going to take her down the basement stairs to the Anderson shelter where our little sons were asleep in wicker cots and a single bed; but, before he could put a foot on the stairs, a second shell fell and the vibration of this knocked him off his feet. Luckily he landed safely at the foot of the stairs.

Thirteen days later I went to Canterbury to stay with my sister. I returned home seven months later to find our home, at 20 Caroline Place, had gone – the whole of our street had been completely flattened during a very heavy shelling raid. The government gave me £9 to buy furniture, curtains, carpets and clothes. I remember getting second-hand beds for 2s 6d each; chairs for 1s each; a table for 2s 6d; a sofa for 2s 6d and armchairs at 2s 6d each.

When we went to town shopping, if the siren sounded, everyone had to take shelter. (For a shelling warning, the siren sounded twice.) No one was allowed on the streets then. Often we spent hours – sometimes up to six or seven hours – in the basements of shops. It was really very frightening as one never knew when the shells were coming, unlike bombs when you could hear the planes coming.

We managed to find another house, 5 Bulwark Street, and were there just seven months when we were bombed out again. The German planes came over and were bombing the guns at Arch-Cliff-Fort, which was situated on the cliffs above our street. The consequence was we were hit and made homeless again. We were given another £9 to replace our belongings once more.

By then we had had so much of it that we used to sleep in the caves. The caves were cut out of the huge White Cliffs of Dover by the Napoleonic prisoners of war. When we used them they were very clean and had been white emulsioned. There were bunk-beds in them, with toilets and wash-hand basins. We took our own sheets, pillows, pillowslips and blankets. We all went there as soon as it began to get dark. It was just like one big happy family. Everyone helped one another and the children played together. But my little Jimmy, aged four years and 10 months, ran out of the cave one day and was killed by the blast of a shell. Nobody saw him go out. It was terrible.

After we lost our second home, we stayed in the caves a lot, until we got another house. We used to go into a café to get a hot meal each day, then have our other meals in the cave: bread and jam, marmalade, cake, and Force Flakes with cold milk. This lasted about three weeks, then I found another house quite near the caves. I then gave birth to another son, Raymond. When he was only two hours old, the vibration from the guns on the cliffs shattered my windows, with the glass flying all over the bed.

There were barrage balloons over Dover and it was quite common for these to be shot down. One had to be very careful as the cable which held them was very dangerous and often used to take the chimneys off houses.

My husband was discharged wounded from the army after Dunkirk, but, as he wasn't 100 per cent disabled, he had to do work of national importance. So, after a while, he drove an ambulance with the ARP. With driving during the blackout, he had trouble with his eyes and was put on the Panel. We had 15s a week sickness benefit, so I went to see Mr Ratcliff, the public assistance man, who gave me another 15s a week. We were paying 8s a week in rent. Mr Ratcliff's office was situated under the Town Hall. Steps at the side led down to it. One day I went by myself to collect the money and was standing on the pavement outside next to a young airman. I heard a plane and suddenly I was pushed to safety by this young man. I fell back through the doorway, but the young airman was killed by the bomb blast. He saved my life.

In none of the houses I had was there a bathroom. I had to bath the children in a tin bath after heating up the water in a stone-built copper, with a fire underneath. We had to cook on a kitchen range – no gas or electric cookers then. And no electric light. We had only gas lamps. When I made cakes, I had no eggs to spare, so I used to put a spoonful of vinegar in and this made them rise quite well. I made pies with 4 oz of corned beef, a tin of beans and a cup of potatoes. Sometimes I used sausagemeat and beans. We rarely had fresh eggs, but we made do with tins of powdered egg. This we found quite good for making scrambled eggs. The only fruit we had were apples. Never saw a banana. But we had oranges at Christmas.

My sister-in-law, who was better off, used to send me parcels of clothes, and when I had any coupons left I gave them to her, as I made all my children's clothes. I cut up skirts and made trousers for the boys; made men's shirts into small ones for them; cut up dresses for my little girl and knitted jumpers for them all. I made all their coats out of second-hand ones. But they were always clean and tidy.

One day when we were sheltering in the caves, the shelling warning went out about seven-thirty in the morning and by twelve o'clock no one was allowed to go home. Some Wrens, who had a depot in the cliffs about 25 yards up the road, brought into our cave great big trays of rice pudding for the children. We felt very grateful to them. But I felt I couldn't stand it any longer so, in 1943, we moved to a house outside Dover, in the country. We didn't have shells there, but with the planes, and then the doodle-bugs, we still didn't feel safe. The ack-ack team, which was stationed just down the road, shot at a doodle-bug and turned it and it crashed into the field just to the left of our house. The soldiers told me it was coming straight at our house before they shot it down.

About half a mile down the road from our house, at St Radigunds Abbey, there was a German prisoner-of-war camp. They used to come and help on the farm. One of them made my children a toy. It was a table-tennis bat, with three chicks on one side. They were fixed with string and a small weight underneath. When it was moved about the chicks looked as if they were pecking.

F.H. was born in 1911 and moved from Leipzig to Breslau (now Wroclaw in Poland) in 1938. From there she was forced to evacuate with her two children in 1945. But evacuation itself, especially in winter, was often as hazardous as remaining in a bomb-stricken city:

'My boy had got frostbite in his little hand'

In January 1945, because of the advancing Russian Army, Breslau was declared a fortress. This meant that all mothers and children would have to leave the town. I had two children, a daughter of four and a baby boy just over a year old. My husband was in the army. My mother had come from Saxony to see us at Christmas, and she was still with us.

It was announced that transport out of the town would be laid on for old people and mothers with small children. Right up to the departure time I was kept busy making dish-towels into bags that the children could carry slung round them. We also had a small rucksack. We wanted to take as much as we could with us. But when we arrived at the assembly point, all that happened was that we were kept waiting together with lots of others in the severe cold for hours on end. That happened to us three times. So we said goodbye to our flat four times in all! In the times in between we lit the stove again, made something to eat, boiled up the little boy's nappies and tried to catch up on some sleep.

The promised transport finally arrived at the pick-up point. It was an open truck. In spite of the warnings that had been given, I was allowed to put the pram on board. If only I had known that earlier, I could have packed all sorts of other things that I could certainly have done with later on. I had packed more blankets than anything else, so as to wrap my little boy up really well. I had hardly packed any clothes for myself. My mother and I each had a medium-sized suitcase, and I had a rucksack as well.

The journey that followed went on for ever. It was bitterly cold and we kept stopping because the lorry was driven by wood gas and it kept running out. It was already late evening by the time we reached our first night's stop in Schweidnitz. I shall never forget our first night in this town. We were put up in a very large room. It was well enough heated, and we lay down to sleep together with all the other people on thick straw that had been spread over the floor. The journey had tired us out so much that we slept well.

Before we went to sleep we noticed to our horror that my boy had got frost-bite in one of his little hands. It was hard and blue. A friendly young girl gave him first aid, spreading a thick layer of black ointment over the hand, which was then wrapped up well. It certainly worked – and fast. The chemist was just as friendly, when I groped my way through the strange, dark town to buy some of the black ointment for myself, so as to be well provided for. It was just as well I did get some. His other hand froze, too, in the next few days.

We had to stay there for two or three days. Warm-hearted women provided us with soup, and the local Nazi leader kept coming to tell us all how sorry he was that no transport could be found. At least he hadn't just done a bunk like so many of them did.

When we did get going again it was in open trucks, as on so much of the journey. One night we were set down to sleep in an unheated cinema. Next door to me was a young woman who had had a baby just before we set out on the road. Her baby must have died very soon after. Another night was spent in a school. My little boy was coughing terribly, but the man in charge said to me I should just go to sleep and a nurse would look after him. Later it turned out to be whooping cough. But I was just so tired I fell asleep. Wherever we stopped, the first thing I would do was to change his nappies, because he had been lying in his pram all day unable to move about. Fortunately he had slept most of the time. My little girl used to copy me, always attending first to the doll she had brought along with her.

On one occasion our night quarters were to be in a private house, but when we got there it was cold and unheated, because the lady owner had been busy packing all night. So we slept on beds with no blankets or sheets. The night in the straw had been much cosier.

Once we stopped in Liegnitz, so I went with my daughter to find an aunt we had there. I had often been to visit her before. But now the snow was so deep that we could hardly find the way. She followed us back to our night's lodgings to say hello to my mother, then went straight back home to put on the water for a bath for us all. But immediately after she left we had to leave and we never even got the chance to tell her. That was very upsetting for us all.

So, after a journey of many different stages, we reached Dresden. That would have been about a fortnight before the big air-raids which killed so many refugees. [13–15 February, 1945.]

We waited for long hours throughout the night on the station platform for a train to be laid on. It came the next day. All the carriages were already bursting with people and prams, and we never would have got on to it but for a young man who pushed us and our pram aboard, despite the protests of the people already inside.

We reached Chemnitz, which was where my mother lived, but we had only been there a few days when the bombs started to fall again. Once more we had to set off on the road. From Chemnitz we went on a slow local train into the Erzgebirge Mountains, where a friend of mine from Breslau had managed to arrange accommodation for us. There, quite unexpectedly, my mother died.

My sister-in-law kindly agreed to take me and the children in. They lived in the Silesian Erzgebirge Mountains, and it was here that we all witnessed the end of the war and the Polish occupation. There was no money in circulation and we had to live by bartering and exchanging goods. Luckily we had brought the silver cutlery with us from my mother's house at Chemnitz, and I made two long and tedious journeys back to Breslau to bring back my mother's clothes. (Each time having to spend a night with my head on a station waiting-room table.) By bartering these we were able to buy a little bread and sometimes a bit of bacon.

I don't know how we would have managed without the fine summer of 1945, though. We were able to go out picking berries and mushrooms, and they let us go over the fields after the harvest, picking up the corn, potatoes and sugar beet that had been left. We were thrown out on the street three times whilst we were there. The Poles wanted the rooms. Then, in the spring of 1946, all Germans were told to leave. It took us eight days to get to a German railway station, all that time in an open cattle-truck, without food, water or toilets. We were told to travel north to Meppen, in Emsland, and it was there, a few days later, that we met up with my husband. He had been a prisoner of war and was released in August 1945.

DOROTHY GRIFFITHS, of Guisely, West Yorkshire. After her mother's death while the family was still young, Dorothy acted as a surrogate mother to her brothers and sisters. She was particularly close to her younger brother Neville who subsequently joined the navy. When war came, her husband had already enlisted in the RAF. She was living with her husband's parents and working as a sales assistant in Marks and Spencer in Bradford:

'Something terrible's going to happen today, love'

Griff, my husband, was paid the 'magnificent' sum of 7s per week – 1s a day – 1s of which had to be paid to me via the post office. From the remainder of his pay, he had to pay 1s a week into Credits – that is, for barrack room damages, etc.

I used to go out once a week on average, usually to visit a Geordie family whose daughter Ada worked as my assistant on Menswear. Her mother had a large family and had been a widow for some years, so she knew what it was to struggle, and she knew what sorrow was. One daughter lost her fiancé in a submarine. A son, Tommy, was lost at sea, and his wife Sally and two children lived with her and her family. Sally had only lived for the time that Tommy would come home. I called to see them a short while after they received the news of his death. Sally was crouched in the middle of their bed, still undressed and wailing incessantly, 'I want my Tommy'. She was just helpless, looking at everyone for help, yet with vacant eyes. It was terrible. No one could help. She was distraught and never recovered. One half of her died with Tommy. The little of her that was left died shortly afterwards. Hearts do break. Her children might as well have been strangers. I can still see her white, thin face and eyes like burning coals, and even hear her voice as it sounded that night. So Grandma (Tommy's mother) had two more little children to be responsible for. Shortly afterwards her daughter Ada, my friend, died of TB, aged 21, in 1940. They were all good, kind people, and the mother, herself a widow, just battled on, with never

97

a moan or grumble, just a wonderful old lady with sadness in her eyes.

In December 1939 – it was not quite Christmas – I went to work and tried to be my usual bright self. I wasn't given to moods and couldn't understand the awful feeling which enveloped me that day. This was just before Ada died, and I said to her at the counter, 'Something terrible's going to happen today, love. I don't know what, but whatever it is, it's bad.' I couldn't shake the feeling off; my chest hurt with the weight of it; I was full of fear, dread and anxiety. I thought about my husband, but somehow didn't fear for him. At 4 p.m. that day, a cablegram boy came in and asked for and was directed to me. He said I had to sign this white slip of paper. I'd never even seen a cablegram before and sort of glanced at it, not comprehending. I had a lot of customers waiting and was trying to put the paper down, but the boy said, 'Is there a reply?' So I had to read it properly. It said, 'We regret to inform you . . .etc.'

My brother Neville, a wireless telegraphist, on the New Zealand ship the *Achilles* had been killed while on duty on the watchtower of the ship, in the River Plate, in South America. He had been on loan to the New Zealand navy. As our own mother had died at the age of 30, leaving five little ones, the oldest 11 (who had since died at 27 years old), I was Neville's next of kin, so I got the message.

On reading the cablegram informing me of Neville's death, I collapsed under the counter. I remember someone helping me upstairs to the rest room. I couldn't talk. The personnel officer gave me a glass of brandy to revive me. She was like a mother to me. She just gave me her shoulder to cry on and held me for what seemed like hours. They sent me home with one of the girls. I'd no tears left.

There was another very sad day in the store. Another of the girls, Mollie Horne, who was expecting her first baby, got the awful news that her husband Jimmy was dead. He was in a bomb disposal unit and the thing that she had always dreaded happened. Taking away an unexploded bomb on a wagon, the bomb went off. There were no survivors. We were all devastated for Mollie.

Then at Dunkirk another of Marks and Spencer's staff, a young 18-year-old boy, Jim Brotherton, was last seen going down in the sea after being hit. His young mother was a widow, and consequently very close to her young son, an only child who had thought the world of her.

It seemed to be one thing after another. The war hadn't really touched any of us there until my brother was killed. He was the first. His death put a more frightening face on things . . . But it was still going to be over soon, wasn't it? But what if it wasn't? We began asking each other the awful question.

Shortly after Neville's death, a letter came from the Admiralty to say that the sailors from the other two ships involved in the Battle of the River Plate, the *Ajax* and the *Exeter*, were returning home. There was to be an investiture, a lunch at the Guildhall, in London, etc., and they were enclosing travel warrants to go down to London for the ceremony.

The ceremony was on Friday, 23 February 1940. Churchill, Chamberlain, and other cabinet ministers were there. It was a very moving sight when all the sailors came swinging along into Horse Guards Parade, with the band of the Royal Marines playing 'A Life on the Ocean Wave'. I wept, as did many more, and today I can't hear that tune without a lump coming to my throat. Queen Elizabeth and King George VI shook hands with as many as possible. The Queen shook hands with me. Churchill was weeping. It seemed strange to see the man who gave us so much drive to see us through the war weeping. But it was the first big sea battle of the war.

Griff's parents, who had accompanied me to London, went back to Yorkshire the same day, after making sure I was booked into a YWCA for the night. I was to meet Griff the next morning. It was my first time in London. I passed the time going to the pictures. Several times I saw myself on the newsreel and on getting back to Bradford I found that half the staff had seen it too. Cold comfort.

Eventually, my husband Griff was posted to York. We got suitable digs, until I found I was pregnant with my first baby. Oh Joy! I couldn't wait to go and buy wool and start knitting, but the landlady didn't want pregnant lodgers, so we had to find ourselves somewhere else.

Griff's next posting after York was Dishforth and the time was approaching for my baby to be born. It was a Friday morning that the labour pains started. I went into the nursing home that day, but was sent out again the following day. I had to stand and wait for a bus – with severe labour pains every 10 minutes. I was ill all the Saturday night. The following Wednesday morning I was delivered of a stillborn son, weighing 9 lbs 1 oz. Five days I'd been in labour and my baby was dead. I was heartbroken.

Shortly after that Griff was on the move again, this time to Herefordshire. He wrote and said he had got digs again, this time with a Welsh lady, who had one small boy. I'd to go down and the lady would meet me at the station. I seemed to be always lugging suitcases about.

Another RAF couple were already there and we got on well with them, but facilities for washing, etc. weren't so good, apart from other much more uncomfortable incidents. For instance, we all ate together, the five adults and the small boy in his high chair. If he needed to go to the toilet, his potty was put in his high chair, still at the table. Whilst we were eating the smell didn't do a great deal for our appetites. When we mentioned this to the landlady, her reply was, 'Oh, you're too fussy. It's a good healthy smell!' All four of us decided she could have it all to herself, and found ourselves another place.

The weeks went by and 1942 came, when I again found myself expecting a baby. I wanted to rejoice but daren't, not wanting to tempt Providence. I prayed and prayed that everything would be OK this time. Once again though we were in the same situation – the kind, elderly lady and her spinster daughter we were living with panicked when we told them the news, and asked us, regretfully, to look for somewhere else to live. We respected their point of view and it wasn't long before we found another place.

Before long it was back home for me to Yeadon, in Yorkshire, to have my baby, with another doctor looking after me, who promised this time I'd have a live baby. Although there were difficulties and set-backs, I went into hospital and had another boy in November 1942. Stephen arrived safe and well. For about seven months I stayed with a delighted Grandma and Grandad.

When Stephen was six or seven months old we went back to Hornsea. Griff had found us a family living in a bungalow near the cliff tops, just out of town. They had a large garden all around the bungalow, with an orchard with apple and plum trees, fields at the back, and a swing strung between two apple trees in the front garden. Honeysuckle straggled over the hedges. Had it not been for the heavy tanks which came up and down the road several times a day, and the bombers heading for Hull several nights a week, it would have been heaven.

Hull, a big seaport near us, was very badly bombed. Sometimes the German bombers would jettison their bombs on their way back after being chased by British fighters, and occasionally we had a narrow squeak. I would sit in the air-raid shelter with my baby night after night. He was breastfed and usually slept through all the gunfire and bombs dropping.

We used to watch our bombers going out, hundreds at a time, at regular intervals. They appeared to space themselves, raying out from a central point. Watching them made the tears come to my eyes. It was very emotional, a mixture of fear and sorrow – and hate for whoever had made this happen. As our planes left the land behind and headed out over the sea, I would say to Griff, 'They've gone over the edge of England and many won't ever come back. They are just going out there to die.' And then we thought of all the innocent people over there who were going to be destroyed by us. When was it going to end? It was all so hopeless – and for what? You felt the futility of it all and the sorrow for all the human beings involved in this hellish war, and wished with all your heart it was over.

Stephen was eighteen months old when Griff sailed away for an unknown destination, which turned out to be India. The bombers still came over. I was back in Yeadon with Griff's parents again and there I was to stay. I'd had a good run and couldn't grumble. Lots of wives hadn't seen their husbands for a few years.

All the time Griff was in India I would let Stephen hold his Daddy's picture at bedtime and kiss him goodnight. I was so afraid of him being a stranger when he came home. After all my efforts to get Stephen to remember Griff, even holding a pencil in his little hand and guiding it to form x's at the bottom of letters, when his Dad did come home there was the inevitable friction. Stephen couldn't understand why this man was in Mummy's bed. After all, he was only 18 months old when Griff left and three when he came back. That's a long time in a little boy's life. So there were misunderstandings more than once.

I know there were many 'Dear John' letters between couples at that time. Separations caused most of that, and 'there but for the Grace of God might have gone I' had it not been for my baby. He was all I wanted, sufficient to keep me waiting happily. A friend further up the street, a lovely person, with no thought of finding someone else – I know that to be true – went out one night with another woman her own age, and the next we knew she was pregnant. Her husband, too, was in India. Whilst everyone was ready to snub her, I felt so sorry for her. She'd been so lonely, and not having any children made it worse. I think, in wartime, having a child was the saving of many marriages which otherwise would have foundered. Someone 'very kindly' wrote and told her husband, which she wanted to do herself. After much pain and heartsearching on both sides, they stayed together, but very unhappily so.

I expect the same thing happened in Germany. At that time there was so much propaganda. It was only when we heard of the bombs that we had dropped on places like Dresden, Cologne and Hamburg that we realized they were suffering too; they were human, just like us. The German soldiers, too, were all somebody's sons, husbands, fathers, brothers . . . What a waste.

A few years ago, Griff and I visited Cannock Chase, in Staffordshire. There is a war cemetery there, a German war cemetery, and it is beautiful. If a burial place can be called beautiful, then it is. It is made in a natural bowl, all surrounded by greenery, trees, bushes, tall cypresses and poplars. The graves are well tended, all with rose bushes or plants of some kind. All with headstones. It was so peaceful and holy. Anyone who could come away from there without shedding tears for those men, and the families they left behind, must have hearts as cold and hard as those headstones. It's such a pity that these feelings can't be uppermost before a war begins, not only when it's all too late and futile.

IRMGARD MÜLLER, from Rosbach, was 25 when she married a flight-sergeant in the German Luftwaffe. He spent most of the war on the Eastern Front. She worked as a schoolteacher:

'Something glinting among the ashes'

A good friend of mine lost all her relatives when there was a heavy raid on Mannheim. They were all buried beneath the rubble of their house. She stood in front of the mountain of rubble, emotionally devastated. Suddenly she noticed something glinting among the ashes. She bent down to pick it up, her whole body trembling. It was a pendant that her mother had been wearing. Even the gold chain was still attached. It was all that was ever found of her mother.

The sirens had been going almost every night recently. Every night we could hear the drone of the heavy bombers *en route* for yet another German town. At that time my husband was stationed at Magdeburg, which had recently been the target for a very heavy air-raid. I had been so worried about him. But were miracles still possible? On my way home one day, towards the end of January 1945, suddenly there he was striding towards me, unexpectedly home on leave.

He only had a few days to spend with me, before going back again. He was keen to spend our time together in his home village, about 50 kilometres from where I was working. Journeys of any sort were hazardous in those days, but we decided to risk it. The train took eight hours to cover the short distance. We reached Giessen at just after midnight. From there we still had a walk of five kilometres. It was a freezing cold night under a starry sky. Giessen was a ghost-town. It had once been a beautiful place, but recent raids had reduced most of it to rubble. In the silver moonlight, isolated chimney-stacks jutted into the night sky. The mountains of rubble lay mercifully hidden beneath a blanket of snow. We knew that under one of these piles a dear friend was still lying.

The little village where my husband had grown up had been spared. The flat was freezing cold, but we were just happy to have arrived. We never turned the wireless on during the time we were there. We wanted to shut out all the depressing news. But the war wouldn't let us escape. Neighbours told us terrible stories about what was happening to the refugees from Eastern Prussia, fleeing to the west on the icy roads, and in the overladen ships. I shall never forget the oppressive atmosphere of those few days. We knew only too well that this was going to be his last leave, and that there were terrible times ahead.

He was told to report back before his leave was up. Before joining his own military train, he came to see me off. It was a bitterly cold winter's morning, the station half hidden in the fog, as he stood on the platform. I waved from the window for as long as I could, but soon the fog and the steam from the train enshrouded him. I pressed myself into the corner of the compartment, feeling a deep sense of hopelessness and powerlessness. I was left numb by this parting. It had been harder than any of the other times we had said goodbye. It tore me apart.

Irmgard Müller's forebodings were to prove correct. Her husband rejoined his unit, only to be captured by the Russians and did not return until 1949, after four and a half years in a labour camp.

EDNA HUGHES, of Liverpool, Merseyside. Edna lived in Liverpool throughout the war, but, despite the bombing which severely affected her own family, as well as their friends and neighbours, she succeeded in maintaining her sense of humour:

'No, I'm Church of England'

I was working in Coopers, in the centre of Liverpool, when war broke out. We were invited to join first-aid classes run by the Red Cross. I also joined the ARP. We were all issued with gas masks and to test them we had to enter a van into which gas had been leaked from a capsule of Phosgene. It has a burning sensation on uncovered skin, but the masks seemed to stand up to it, thank goodness.

During my time as an air-raid warden I had to go out as soon as the siren sounded. We helped people into the shelters and took care that no lights were showing. The tops of posts and stone pillars were painted with a special paint which we had to examine to see if there was a change of colour to a greenish hue. Perhaps that meant that gas had been dropped. But, of course, that never happened.

I think I was the first person to make what we called a dug-out, in our house, during the nine months or so before war was declared. I obtained a tea-chest and began to stock up with all kinds of tinned foods, fresh water, also tea, coffee, cocoa and sugar, which I believed would be very scarce. The place was ready for a siege. I also hung a heavy wool blanket across the door because I believed we would have gas attacks. I'm afraid everybody was highly amused at seeing my preparations. Even our insurance man and the rent collector were tickled pink as they peeped behind my barricades.

As time went by, with nothing happening, my mother would say, 'Come on, Ed, let's open another tin of corned beef, or salmon.' And, alas, when war finally came the tea-chest was empty, and the blanket across the door was proving to be a nuisance when going to put money into our gas meter. So that was taken down, washed, and put to better use.

Well, when war was declared, as a member of the ARP, I was issued with a tin hat, torch and navy-blue uniform. I was often called out at night, always after twelve, and still had to go to work in the morning. At first, I must say, it was very exciting. One felt as if one was doing something constructive and useful.

I lived in a small square of 14 houses, all with our own gardens, on top of a hill by St George's Church, Everton, and I believe the large house on the corner of our square was one of the first to get a direct hit. All of the family except one old chap were in the shelter. He decided to stay under the stairs and, of course, he was killed outright. People came from far and near to see that heap of rubble.

After that tragedy, you knew the future was beginning to look grim. My young man was called up then. Not being fit for the army, he joined the fire service. As he had been an insurance agent, he asked me to take on his job, so I left mine to start collecting premiums and, as I couldn't ride a bike, I walked the round, which was scattered all over Liverpool.

Of course, we were married by then. After our wedding we went across the road to the grocer's to pick up our meagre rations and then wended our way to a flat we had managed to find. We lived in a very large house that had been converted into flats. Ours was on the second floor. Our landlord, his wife and daughter lived on the premises and, while we were getting married, he built the most beautiful fire for us and laid on a supper for two. A welcome start to our honeymoon.

The raids were very heavy by now and I sheltered with the rest of the household in a cellar that wasn't reinforced or anything. I felt they would never get us out alive if we had a direct hit. My husband used to come home with his face all black with smoke and his eyes red-rimmed with lack of sleep.

Every night at about six o'clock, the main road, which was Prescott Road, was absolutely crammed with people – walking, cycling, in cars, with pillows, blankets, and sleeping bags, all dashing to the open fields to escape the bombs.

One night, during a very heavy raid, I had been sick and my doctor told me to stay in bed and not go down into the cellar. I was frightened, being so near the roof, but my neighbour, another young married woman who was in the other flat, offered to stay with me. While the bombs dropped she put the loudest music on the gramophone, as bombs whistled down all around us. Houses and shops were all hit that night, including houses just across from us. We were at the Nesham Park end of the road and we looked out of the window to see chandelier lights floating down from the sky. We were told they were Molotov bread-baskets. A stick of eight bombs dropped on all the stone fountains on a wide path in the Park.

Being newly married, I was lucky to find a good butcher and greengrocer. I was a bit flummoxed when I had the chance to buy a couple of oranges. I was asked if I was an RC, to which I replied, 'No, I'm Church of England.' I wondered what on earth being a Roman Catholic had to do with anything. 'Regular customer, you fathead!' the grocer said.

There was one dreadful night when I had left it too late to go home and the raiders were upon us. It was the night when Jerry had it all his own way. There was no return gunfire from us and the planes dropped everything on us. We were in the coal cellar under the lobby, which I had whitewashed in preparation. We had neighbours in from both sides. Old Grandma Naylor sat on the top step so she could get out quick. My young brother and sister, mother, and me spread out up to the coal grid which opened out to our garden path.

With pandemonium going on outside, someone suddenly shouted, 'Oh, look, there's a cockroach!'

And so it was – the biggest, blackest, shiniest cockroach I have ever seen.

My brother Bill said, 'It's all right, I'll get him with this hammer.'

We all stood up as Bill advanced with his weapon and struck out – and missed. I can honestly say, not one of us wanted to sit down again. Noises outside were forgotten and for another hour we all stood up, waiting for the all-clear to go.

We put a better light in Mum's cellar after that, but nobody felt happy about using it. But I suppose it was still the better of two evils.

I think the worst night of my life was 3 May 1941. We had been bombarded all week. A landmine had fallen on a house where they were holding a wedding party. Everybody was killed. Many houses, including ours and my mother's, were ruined.

An ammunition train was exploding every few minutes and every bang brought soot down the chimneys and shattered more windows.

I set off to see how my mother, brothers, and sister were. I had no idea what the situation was really like until I started out. I had to walk about a mile over such devastation and rubble that I cried all the way. They were carrying the bodies out of the house where the wedding had been held, quite close to my old home.

My Mum was lying on a sofa covered with soot and splintered glass. The house was completely unsafe, so we just got a few things together and went like refugees to my flat, where we were all able to have a much needed bath and rest.

I was now pregnant and found I was able to get a bit more in the way of rations. I was pushed to the head of the queue for oranges and bananas by the women of Liverpool. I was always a bit shy myself. I was still walking up hill and down dale collecting insurance until I was eight months pregnant and felt as fit as a fiddle. My sister-in-law took over and I had to cancel all my engagements after that.

It was August 1942, when I had to give up my collecting job. The raids had ceased in our part of the world, except for the occasional alert. You had to take cover, but it usually turned out to be one of ours. For me, the fear was always worst at night when my husband Charles was on duty.

My Mum couldn't go back to her own house which was too badly damaged after the blitz, so my elder brother took her and our sister into his home until a place could be found for them, and I had two brothers living with Charles and me.

When the air-raids started, a lot of people had packed up lock, stock and barrel and gone to live in safer places, so quite a few houses were available for those who had been bombed out of their own homes. My Mum was soon installed in a six-roomed house, undamaged by bombs. Bill bought a couple of hens, also a few chicks to augment our rations.

It was after getting the hens that Mum was given the nickname 'Chick', which we all called her. She was good-humoured and very even-tempered, and was quietly waiting for any symptoms of labour from me. By then, the baby was letting me know it was there all right, with plenty of kicks and movement. Plums were in season and there were some to be bought, especially if you were an expectant mother. I was enjoying a plum when I felt the first twinges. It was the evening of 9 September 1942. 'I think I'll go and lie down for a while,' I said to Chick.

'Oh no, you won't,' said my Mum. 'This sounds to me like it could be on the move.'

'There's another week to go,' I protested, but to no avail. I could see Mum wanted me off her hands without delay.

Everywhere was blacked out. There were no taxis, no people with cars like today, and we couldn't find a telephone. They used to have them in post offices then, but they weren't open.

Being about a mile from the hospital and as my twinges had now stopped, we set out to walk. My Mum's friendly neighbour offered to accompany me. I'll never forget that journey. Worse pains started and I had to stop and lean against the shops, or anything I could find, for support. Eventually we arrived at the Royal. I don't think I cared what happened after that. My friend handed over my attaché case with the baby's things in it, and my entry card, and I was carted off. I had had a very easy nine months, so who was I to complain about what was happening now?

Very soon afterwards I gave birth to a lovely baby daughter. They brought the baby to me, with a lovely cup of tea, and all the pain was forgotten.

IRMGARD KONRAD was born in Breslau and is now a citizen of East Berlin. Her story is one of a young Jewish woman in love with a German Aryan young man during the Third Reich:

'I turned up wearing the Jew's Star'

My father was Jewish. You understand what that means? Perhaps you learned all about that at school: Nuremberg Laws and the Holocaust. What was it like in practical terms, though?

Dad died in 1924. Perhaps it was just as well that he didn't live to experience what happened. My family had moved to France before the war. First my eldest brother, then he sent for my mother, and then the rest of the family. I didn't want to go. I was already going out with Fritz. But we couldn't even think of getting married; it was banned by law 'for the protection of German blood'. So Fritz lived with his parents, and I had my own little room. Was love stronger than fear? Of course it was – and in any case no one could possibly imagine the full extent of what happened later.

In an odd kind of way I felt secure enough in our little community. Fritz was his own man, the sort who had written on a wall during the last election campaign in 1933 'Vote for Hitler, Vote for War!' A working-class youth. A man who could defend himself and not just sit on the sidelines. He gave me courage.

The first time the Gestapo called I was just 17 years old. They soon let me go. Probably thought I was just a silly young thing. Fritz didn't get off so lightly. In 1936 he got two years imprisonment for 'high treason'. When he came out in 1938 he was classed as 'unworthy to bear arms'. Better than being cannon-fodder, we said to ourselves, as the call-up orders started arriving all round the neighbourhood.

But even being 'unworthy to bear arms' only kept him with me until the end of 1941. Once the days of the blitzkrieg victories were over, they drafted even the 'unworthies'. Do you know what the 999 Company was? It was a punishment battalion, a suicide squad.

That's where my Fritz ended up. He was sent first to Stuttgart for basic training, then it was off to the Eastern Front. I never heard anything more from him. The 999 Company were not allowed letters home.

I was wearing the Jew's Star by now, and I would just have made things dangerous for him. As long as Fritz was there, he helped me, he shared the wearing of the Star. We had learned when we were out walking how to hold hands or to carry my handbag so that the terrible Star couldn't be seen. That was forbidden, of course, but there was no other way we could have gone out together in public. Just imagine! Still, we would have gone mad staying indoors all the time. We were young and wanted to have some fun together.

I must just tell you what a shock my boss got, when I turned up wearing the Jew's Star. I had been thrown out of my beloved bookshop job when I was arrested in 1933. I would love to have made a career with books, too. But I put an advert in the paper and found quite a good job. My new bosses were 'dyed-in-the-wool Nazis', of course. Messrs Floegel and Grammatke really were staunch Party supporters: always flags out and the radio on so that the staff could hear the Führer's speeches. I'm sure they believed absolutely everything Hitler told them. They were in the picture-framing business. Prints at first. 'Utta of Naumburg' and the like. Then more and more portraits of Nazi big-shots. Hitler and Goering sold especially well. So far as Floegel and Grammatke were concerned I was a solid German worker. And I was certainly quick and skilful, and always willing to work overtime, especially as Christmas approached, when business was booming and customers were always calling at our premises in Sonnen Strasse. Then came the bombshell that I had to drop on them. That was when I had to wear the Star. I was supposed to inform my employers of that. I can still see their astonished faces today, when they heard that their model German working girl was really born of 'that lazy race of parasites that were feeding off the body of the German people'. They didn't say a word as I packed up my things; they just stared at me.

Then Fritz was sent away, and I had to join the Jewish work squad. By now, even half-Jews like me, were being roped in. My work was 30 kilometres from Breslau, in Sackrau. We had to travel there by train every day. You're probably thinking, well at least it wasn't the concentration camp. That was my first reaction, too. At least we hadn't been transported. At that time the walls of Jewish shops bore messages like 'Gone to Auschwitz'. No one could imagine the real horrors, but we knew well enough that the concentration camps and Auschwitz stood for something terrible. We lived in constant fear of them. You know, the uncertainty can wear you down so much that you actually feel relieved when your turn comes and they transport you. At least you're rid of that nagging fear that is always with you, slowly driving you mad.

Every morning when the Jewish girls arrived for work there were stories of missing mothers, grandmothers and other relatives. And the insults we had to suffer! Jews were not allowed to use the seats on trains. They were not allowed to wait in the station waiting-rooms, even though it was cold and raining. And there was a lot of waiting in those days. Wartime transports and hospital trains bringing back the wounded from the east always had priority. There were lots of hospital trains. Today when I see pictures from South Africa and hear of all the bans for the black people under Apartheid, then I think of the stations and the trains when we were on the work squads.

My turn came in 1942. Transportation to Auschwitz. Then on to Ravensbrück, north of Berlin, to the women's concentration camp. I was a small, sturdily-built Jewish girl and must have looked strong enough for work, so I escaped the gas. That was the time when the tide was just turning against the race that had wanted to rule the world. There were shortages everywhere. Labour was also in short supply. So concentration camp inmates were brought in to do the donkey-work. The Nazis called it 'extermination through work'. I was sent to a branch of Siemens to work for the so-called Final Victory. I tried to work as slowly as possible. Others did, too. Always on a knife-edge between barely surviving and doing as little as possible for this war. Was it only us inmates who worked like that? We weren't allowed even to speak to the 'normal' workforce. So I can only speak about my supervisor. I called him Father Grosse. He used to slip the drive-belt on the machine I was working at. I got a break, while he would say to the SS guards that the machine needed repairing.

Back to the war. English and American planes were now flying overhead. In daytime, too, in 1941. We half-Jews were shut up in the boiler room whenever the air-raid siren went off. We were working in an armaments factory, so we must have been the target. But was I afraid of the bombers? Odd as it may sound, no. I wasn't afraid of those men in their planes up there above us. The droning in the heavens gave us hope – that the war would soon be over. Our sufferings, too.

LEONORA PITT, from Walsall, West Midlands, experienced life in the services for herself, before returning to civilian life, to discover that living with the 'in-laws' was not the ideal way to begin married life:

'I came back to our empty little room'

When war was declared, Mum said, 'God help us!' and cried. Dad said, 'I knew it would come!' My brother decided to join the RAF and me, at 14, I just felt excited.

Gas masks were issued, along with identity cards and ration books, petrol, and clothing coupons. Steel cages, known as Morrison shelters, disguised as tables dominated living rooms. The sirens would go at 7 p.m. and we'd grope our way to the air-raid shelter in the blackout, loaded with pillows, blankets, books, torch, flask, my piano accordion, and, of course, Mum's handbag, with birth certificates, rent book, insurance policies, and anything of value.

I still recall the heat that met us at the door of the shelter. The smell of unwashed bodies and Mrs O'Conner's wintergreen ointment. We'd have a sing-song, with 'Roll Out The Barrel', 'Red Sails In The Sunset', and me playing the accordion. As the night wore on, men would produce bottles of beer, and women a drop of gin or whisky. Every so often silence would fall as we heard the crump of a bomb and the ack-ack retaliating. Sometimes I'd creep out into the cold night air and gaze up at the beautiful starlit sky. Then I'd hear the drone of a plane and on would come the searchlights. I'd catch a glimpse of silver wings caught in the beam. The ack-ack would fire its guns and the tracers would stream across the sky. Walsall was nine miles from Birmingham and 40 from Coventry, so we always caught the stray bombs and shrapnel.

Things got more difficult as the months went by. Water and gas got cut off due to bombed gas and water mains. Industry was disrupted with electricity cuts. Permanent waves were a hazard as electrically heated tubes were put on your hair in those days and a power-cut left you wet, cold, and with half a perm.

I worked at an iron foundry, along with my Grandad, Dad, uncle and brother. This was where I met my future husband. One dinnertime we were sitting outside when a German plane came over on a daylight raid. We reckoned he was lost. The pilot must have seen the flames of the cupola (the oven where the work was hardened off). I don't think I've ever been so scared since. I saw the pilot, complete with leather helmet, and German markings on the wings of the plane. The bomb doors were open and I could see three bombs. As he flew over very low, he released the bombs. Someone must have been watching over us, for, as he was flying too low, the bombs didn't go off. One landed on the gasometer itself. This was a Red Alert for the whole town, as the gasometer then became a bomb. Brave firemen and the Home Guard worked through the night to remove it and make it safe. We heard that the plane had been shot down before reaching the coast. We all felt we'd had a narrow squeak.

My boyfriend Tom and I used to go dancing, cycling, and to the theatre or cinema, to see Abbott and Costello, Judy Garland, *The Way to the Stars*, *The Glass Mountain*, etc. Films like that kept us going.

Stockings were in short supply so girls coloured their legs with tan cream, or (if you were skint) with gravy browning – very nice until it rained! A friend would draw a line down the backs of your legs, with an eyebrow pencil, for the seam.

By this time my brother had joined the RAF and was posted down to Ruislip. My boyfriend volunteered for the navy and passed A1, so I volunteered for the WAAF. I too passed my medical and was called up in two months. (Active service or munitions work was compulsory for girls then.) Tom's call-up was deferred as his war work was too important. So there we were – I went, he stayed!

I went as a barrage-balloon operator, but the trade was closed, so it was the cookhouse for me. I did my training at Innsworth in Gloucestershire, then went on to Morecambe to pass out. The excitement and newness of everything carried me along for the first three months, then I began to get homesick. But, most of all, I missed Tom. I was madly in love by this time, as only a 17-year-old can be.

We had our inoculations and boy did I feel ill! I also had four teeth filled. I was miserable and lonely. Tom wasn't a good letter writer which didn't help. Then rumours went around that we were being moved. Good – I'd always wanted to travel!

Midnight came and we humped our kit to the station, complete with packed rations. We boarded a train and I took my last look at the sea. (It was the first time I'd been to a seaside town in my life.) About four o'clock in the morning we stopped at a little station. We all tried to guess where we were. There were no station signs and no lights. Six RAF lorries were waiting to take us to the camp. Dawn was breaking and we were given a hot meal and cup of tea, then we were allowed three hours sleep. We slept on mattresses in one big hut. Next morning we were paraded and given our huts. But where were we? We were in Fradley Lichfield – only 10 miles from my home. Me who wanted to see the world, or at least England! I guess they thought they were doing me a favour. Actually I was really lucky as I could get home most nights by hitching a lorry outside camp. Most times they were going through Walsall.

I shared my Nissen hut with 19 other girls and the flight sergeant. You had one bed, three biscuits (small mattresses), two sheets, two blankets, quilt, one pillow, one locker, one equipment hook, and lights out was 11 p.m. You were responsible for *all* your bedding and kit. If you lost anything or broke anything you paid for it out of your pay of 7s 6d per week.

Domestic night was Thursday, as was FFI (Free From Infection night). You had to stay in your hut and do your cleaning. Then about 9.30 p.m. you stood by your bed, barefoot and naked, except for your knickers. Can you imagine 20 girls standing to attention in airforce-blue knickers, complete with elastic round the legs? Then you would be examined – your hair for lice, your feet for blisters, your teeth, and then the examination for VD. I hated it. I used to feel so degraded. There was the male medical officer, a nursing sister and the flight sergeant, strutting along looking at us as though they were at a cattle auction.

My work was mainly in the cookhouse, but you still had to parade, do PT and read the DO's (Daily Orders). DO's used to confuse me: 17.30–23.59 – by the time I'd worked out the time I'd find I was late!

The breadroom I loved. This was a room 12 ft square. Every morning the bread van came from Lichfield and, as it couldn't get near the breadroom, the bread was thrown two at a time across the cookhouse, through a window, and stacked on the shelves. (Woe betide you if you lost your timing and dropped a loaf!) Then you could spend a warm, cosy morning slicing bread on a bacon machine.

One day while in Lichfield, a gang of us heard a brass band playing 'Over There'. Yes, the Yanks had come. There they were, marching through the city to Wittington Barracks, two miles east of Lichfield. They soon took over. They had bigger lorries, bigger tanks, better uniforms, bigger mouths, and, rumour had it, bigger . . . !

Our lads disliked the Yanks. Walsall was put out of bounds because of the fights that took place in the town-centre pub. They were a menace. We'd get one of our lads to walk us the four miles back to camp as there would be a Yank lurking behind every bush. From some dark corner, you'd hear a voice say, 'You will take me back to America after the war, won't you?'

'Sure thing, honey . . . Just lift your skirt a bit higher.'

They wooed the British girls with nylons, candy and gum, and always had plenty of whisky. They had charm all right, but discipline was slack, and they didn't show much respect for their officers. In fact, if we had saluted our officers as they did we'd have been put on a fizzer (charge).

Tom and I arranged to be married at Easter, but I went down with whooping cough (caught off Tom's small niece) and pneumonia. I spent three weeks in the district mental hospital, part of which had been taken over by the RAF. There were civilians in our ward. One woman of about 50 had stepped out of a train on the wrong side and had broken both her legs. She was so worried. Her husband and three sons were away and she only had three land girls and one old man to run the farm.

Tom arranged the wedding for 1 May 1943. I borrowed my wedding dress of white velvet, long veil and tiara of artificial orange blossom. My friend Muriel, also in the WAAF, bought a second-hand, pale-blue, long dress, short blue veil, Juliet cap and gloves to match. I had to have my parents' written consent as I was under 21.

I spent my wedding eve at the local fairground with Muriel, whose folk were fairground people, so she had relations at every travelling fair. She came from Lancaster. We ended up eating fish and chips at two o'clock in the morning in an aunt's caravan, after going on everything from the dodgems to the haunted house – all free – gratis!

We slept three in a bed that night, Mum, Muriel and me, as my brother was home for the wedding. I awoke at my usual time, about 6 a.m., lit the fire, brewed the tea, then put the kettles and saucepans on to heat the water for a bath. This was a hip bath in front of the fire. I woke everyone at 7 a.m. with a cup of tea. I'd already put the bacon in the Dutch oven in front of the fire to cook. We all had bacon sandwiches for quickness.

My bouquets arrived – cream tea roses and lily of the valley. Muriel's was of anemones. As time drew nearer to ten o'clock I got more nervous. What if Tom had changed his mind? I stared into the mirror – five feet five inches, with mousey hair and hazel eyes. Whatever did he see in me? What would tonight be like? He was 26 years old, had been engaged before, and admitted to being a flirt. Should I get changed and go back to camp? Marriage was for life. All these thoughts chased through my head. Then Dad called upstairs to say that everyone had gone and the taxi was back. Dad said I looked lovely and kissed me. I was still his girl and if I needed him he'd always be there.

Neighbours lined the pavement to wish me well, calling out,

'Good Luck!' Soon I was walking down the aisle on Dad's arm. Tom was waiting for me, looking very handsome in his pin-striped suit. All was well, my fears forgotten. We came down the aisle to the Wedding March. There were no church bells. Church bells meant invasion. There was no confetti either.

The reception was held in the oak room of the local picture house-cum-restaurant. We had ham salad, trifle, white wine (one glass only for the toast), a two-tier cake covered with iced card-board, which was removed to reveal a fruit cake underneath, but it looked authentic in the photographs.

We left at 2 p.m. for a honeymoon in the Lake District, but it was midnight before we got there. The train was delayed at Preston. All I can remember of the journey was tea and a pork pie snatched on various platforms. At the hotel we had sandwiches and a drink before going to bed. A night of mad passion followed. The proprietor used to ask every morning, 'Are you two still living together?' This used to make me blush.

Staying there was a girl and a Polish boy, and he would insist on putting leftover bread in his pockets. She would say, 'No, Jan. It'll still be here when we get back.'

I saw my first Sunderland Flying Boat on Lake Windermere. They were built there. The lake was cleared of boats when they were test-ing them. We hired cycles and explored the countryside. Coming along the road one day we saw a *blue* horse. We couldn't believe it, until we discovered that Reckitts had a factory there and everything was blue, even the flowers and grass. It was so funny.

The week fled by and I was soon back at camp. I missed Tom dreadfully. I just prayed that I could have a baby and so get out of the Forces. I was teased a lot at camp. I was proud of my wedding ring and looked on it as a protection, until a fellow said, 'Aw, come on, a slice off a cut loaf ain't missed!' I was shocked. I wanted no one but Tom.

Life went on as usual at camp. We'd hear the bombers come back in the wee small hours. Our hut was in direct line with the flight path. Sometimes the planes came in so low you would instinctively duck. One day a plane landed; it was on fire. They managed to get the pilot out, but he was already ablaze. Fire engines were always at the ready when planes were landing. Suddenly there was a terrific blast and débris shot everywhere. One of the aircrew was hanging dead from a tree – a fellow not much older than me.

War had become very real to me since 1939. Some of our Wellingtons took part in the famous one thousand bomber raid. Nearly every day someone who you had chatted to one day would be missing the next.

I was delighted when I discovered I was pregnant and the wheels were set in motion for me to leave. After a visit to the MO, three weeks later I had an honourable discharge on compassionate grounds. I left the WAAF with £5, 120 clothing coupons and my personal clothing. Uniforms, gas mask and PT kit, all had to be handed in and accounted for. ACW2 Pitt had become Mrs Thomas Pitt. A new way of life had begun. No more getting up at 6 a.m.; no more parades; no more discipline. I was somebody again – not just a number.

You were allowed vouchers to set up a home, so we purchased one utility bedroom suite. This consisted of a double wardrobe, tallboy, dressing-table and bedsteads and springs. You had two designs to choose from in light or dark oak – likewise with the dining-room suite of a sideboard, four chairs and table. The suites cost £15 and £10 respectively. We were lucky because someone had given us a pair of sheets and one blanket as wedding presents. Different friends and relations chipped in with all sorts of things, such as odd cups and other household utensils, all second-hand.

We lived in the front room of my mother-in-law's house. We all ate together. From the beginning it became clear to me that she disliked me. What had I done? I didn't know her that well and had always been polite. I soon found out why. Tom had been engaged for three years to the girl next door. She was apparently a paragon of virtue, while I was flighty and too young. She told me the marriage wouldn't last and Tom would soon find out his mistake. From that day on my life was hell. I was pretty hopeless around the house and when mother-in-law was around I became even more ham-fisted.

Monday was washing day and this meant filling the copper, lighting a fire underneath, transferring the water to a wooden tub, then pushing the clothes with a dolly. Then the tub was refilled with cold water and the water blued with a dolly bag (probably from Reckitts of Windermere). The clothes were then wrung through a big mangle with wooden rollers. The boiler and tub were emptied by hand with a bowl. Everything was put away and the washing pegged out on the line. Everything then was made of either cotton or flannel. Tom and his Dad both had very dirty jobs and wore white shirts only for best. The kitchen floor was then scrubbed and reddened with raddle. If it was raining the clothes were draped on a wooden clothes-horse and nobody saw the fire all day.

Tuesday was ironing day, Wednesday the bedrooms. There was no vacuum cleaner, just a sweeping brush and mop and a damp cloth to do the carpets. Rugs were shaken and the carpet put over the line and beaten. On Fridays the floors were polished and the silver and brass cleaned; windows were washed and polished and cupboards cleaned out and relined with paper. The worst job was blackleading the grate and cleaning the flues.

Dinner had to be taken down to the men every day, in four aluminium basins wrapped in cloth; two dinners and two puddings in a wicker basket, similar to a cat basket. Tom's Mum did all the cooking and I did the housework. I didn't mind whatever happened during the day, it was forgotten as soon as Tom got home and we could shut ourselves away in our room.

I remember we made our own 'Monopoly' game. I painted the board and we printed property cards with a John Bull printing set. It lasted for years. I made baby clothes and knitted. We had no TV then, or radio, but we had a gramophone which we bought off a friend, along with some records, and we would sit in the firelight and listen to the Inkspots and Bing Crosby. Mendelssohn's Violin Concerto was my favourite, with Yehudi Menuhin playing – much better than Fritz Kreisler.

Our daughter Margaret was born in the local hospital on 7 April 1944 – Good Friday. The pain was forgotten in the joy of seeing Tom holding his daughter. I have to smile when I remember my Mum telling me that she had told the neighbours they could all put their notebooks and pencils away – I'd been married for 11½ months! Nobody got married at 18 in those days unless they were 'up the spout', as we used to say, especially if the bloke was 26.

Well, gone was the young, carefree girl whose only worry was being late on duty. Now the baby's every whimper and spot sent me scurrying round to the welfare clinic, and if she slept too long I'd have to look and see if she was breathing. But oh the nappies and the washing – they seemed never ending! (I should have worried – I had five more children in the following years, including twins!)

My days seemed filled with housework, washing and looking after the baby, then, when Margaret was two months old, the blow fell. Tom received his call-up papers. I was devastated. Tom wasn't too happy either. He was drafted into the army within two weeks. There I was with my world turned upside down again, waving goodbye to him as the train pulled out of New Street station. I stood there with the baby in my arms, the tears streaming down my face. I had felt so safe as Tom had been deferred since his medical in 1941. I came back to our empty little room. I couldn't stand it and most days or evenings I went down to my Mum's, bathing Margaret, getting her ready for bed, then tucking her up in her pram. The half-hour walk used to put her to sleep. Dad and Mum were always pleased to see me. I would always have to be back before ten o'clock as my mother-in-law would do her nut and threaten to lock me out. 'Gallivanting off every night, keeping a tiny baby out in the night air!' I never answered back, but, for some reason, this made her even more mad.

Tom came home on his first leave of three days after his two months' training. They were heaven. He was stationed about 40 miles away but got home fairly often. Margaret was only a few months old when I found out, to my dismay, that I was pregnant again. Tom was due to be sent overseas. I confided in my sister-in-law and I asked her to promise not to tell my mother-in-law until I told her myself. I thought I could trust her, for she was 18 years older than me. That night as I lay in bed I heard mother-in-law ranting (there's no other word for it) that she wasn't going to put up with another snivelling brat. 'You might know this would happen, dolling herself up every time he comes home on leave, kissing and throwing herself at him. It isn't his fault!' I cried all night. Where was I to go? She was going to throw me out. Father-in-law was a meek little man so there would be no help from that direction.

The next day I went down to my own Mum and Dad. I told them I was going to have another baby and could I come home. Mum thought Tom could have been a bit more careful, but said yes, they would have me. Over the next week Dad distempered the bedroom and the front room and on the Saturday I moved. I couldn't help feeling bitchy. I was going before I was thrown out.

I wrote to Tom and told him I was moving. He was most annoyed and accused me of being a Daddy's girl and not being able to stand on my own feet, and running back home. Our first quarrel. I don't know to this day what his Mum said to him, but I didn't tell tales. He thought the world of his Mum and Dad. I didn't tell him about the coming baby. He was on all-night exercises and during this time developed sciatica. It was due to sleeping out in the open and getting wet. He was immobilized for weeks and had to have treatment at Droitwich Spa. Mother minded Margaret for the day while I went to visit him in hospital. Our quarrel was forgotten. He was happy about the baby.

Here was I, 20 years old, with one and a half babies and £2 a week army pay (Tom got an extra shilling a week because he was a good marksman). As well as food, coal was rationed. One hundredweight of cobbles cost sixpence. Mum and I used to fetch it in barrows from the local coalyard. I always seemed to get the one that the wheel came off. I used to pay Mum £1 15s a week and this covered rent, gas, coal and electricity.

I didn't see Tom for two years. He was sent down south. His job was escorting prisoners of war to farms in Cornwall. The night my second daughter was born my brother was home on leave and he got me to hospital. My second confinement was easy. Mum was able to cope with Margaret during the week I was in hospital. It cost me nothing as I was a soldier's wife. It had cost me £10 to have Margaret in the same hospital before Tom was called up.

The children had National Dried Milk. Cod liver oil was free and concentrated orange juice was sixpence a bottle. You also got cheap milk at twopence a pint. I used to get an extra tin of dried milk, save my butter and make sweets, peppermint or rum flavour – very chewy. These I used to send to Tom, along with books. Irene was 18 months old before Tom saw her. I learnt then what a lucky escape he had had while in hospital. His platoon had gone to France in a glider. It came adrift and came down in the Channel. Everyone was lost.

A friend of my brother's bought me half a parachute, some parts of which were singed, and I made petticoats and a blouse, and a christening robe for Irene. Over the skirt I put pieces of my wedding veil that were prettily embroidered. It also made pillowslips for the pram. Dad bought me a new high pram, strong enough to carry two. He made a padded seat to fit across to sit Margaret on. Margaret's pram I swapped for a book of tea coupons.

The babies got me down sometimes. I remember one night when Irene was cutting her first teeth, and Margaret her double, and me a wisdom tooth – all three of us were crying at once with toothache.

Sometimes Tom would arrive on leave in the middle of the night. I'd feel someone getting into bed and I'd say, 'Is that you, Tom?' Daft question. He would say, 'It'd better be me!'

No one locked their doors. The moment fellows arrived home on leave they would be asked, 'When are you going back?' We just wanted to know how long we had them for.

Tom was then posted to Newcastle-upon-Tyne; first at Pity Me, then at Wide Open, near Gosforth. He became a military police-man, training motorcycle riders.

VE day came and everyone went wild. Our spirits lifted when lights were allowed; it was like fairyland. No more worrying about bombers, the moon, and air-raids. Blackout curtains came down and were made into aprons and cushion covers, brightened up with ric-rac braid.

Tom was told that providing he returned to his old job he could be released a year earlier. So, naturally, I said, 'Come home.' The first few weeks were difficult. He'd been away for three years and Margaret would run to my Dad if Tom corrected her, and Dad felt resentful now that Tom was in charge. There was a lot of friction and squabbles. The food situation wasn't much better. Potatoes were in short supply and sometimes bread was rationed. I had a friend at the local abattoir who would bring me skirting (fat lining off cows), then we would live like lords. I'd render it down and we would have fish and chips, doughnuts, pastry and cakes. It wasn't as bad as it sounds. It was another three years before tea and sweets were off ration.

I found I was pregnant *again*. It was to be 13 years before we had our own home. But that's another story.

Tom and I were very happily married for 40 years. We celebrated our Ruby Wedding, with family and friends, three months before he died of cancer in 1983. We had six children, two girls and four boys, including twins. (No, I'm not a Catholic – just a naughty Baptist!) I have seven grandchildren and one great-granddaughter. There are 22 of our immediate family, including sons and daughters-in-law and their children. At our local beauty spot on Cannock Chase, we planted Scots Pines, one for every member of the family, in memory of Tom, and once a year we all meet and picnic there. Ours was a true love story and I don't regret a moment of my life.

The following two letters were sent to us by Maria Herbrand, of Niederkrüchten, North Rhine-Westphalia. The poignant events which gave rise to the correspondence are evident enough to require no comment. Like many wartime stories, it had no happy ending for the mother, though it is just possible that the baby in the pram survived:

'It proved impossible to find the child again'

Rheindalen
Bahnhof Strasse 41
11th Feb 1946

To:
Radio Announcements Department
Missing Persons Bureau
German Red Cross
Hamburg/Altona Allee 131

Dear Sirs,
    Re. Missing child Dieter Brüderreck, born 16.9.44
I am writing on behalf of the mother, at present in the Soviet Occupation Zone, who is looking for her little boy, Dieter.

The child went missing on 6 February 1945, on the railway line between Reetz and Tornow, when the pram he was lying in rolled off the train. In all the confusion – the Russian Front was advancing rapidly – it proved impossible to find the child again, although the mother got out at the next station and walked back as far as she could down the line.

If any child matching the description is brought to your attention, could you please pass on the information to me?

With many thanks in anticipation,

Yours faithfully,

Maria Herbrand

Extract from letter of 10 March 1953 from the baby's mother to her friend Maria Herbrand:

. . . Despite all our efforts we never managed to find our little Dieter. Missing persons announcements were given out on Hamburg and Berlin Radio, but all to no avail. Your two sons will be quite big now. Little Axel must be eight years old. How time flies!

To you, Frau Herbrand, and to your family our warmest greetings and best wishes.

Your,

Frau Anna Brüderreck

FLORENCE MORRIS, of Burslem, Staffordshire, remembers how feeding hungry teenagers, under wartime rationing, could be a real problem:

'Did you enjoy your onions, Floss?'

The most terrible part of the war for me was the food rationing. I had twin daughters, aged 14, who had good appetites and were always hungry. While I was at work the twins would put all the whole week's rations into one big frying pan and eat the lot.

At home we'd grow as much food as we could and a funny thing happened to me in this regard. I'm very fond of flowers, and also of onions, and one day a friend rang my doorbell and pushed some small bulbs into my hand. As we worked different shifts, I didn't see her after that for quite a few weeks, until one day she shouted over the gardens to me, 'Did you enjoy your onions, Floss?' Well, I thought it was flower bulbs that she'd given me and I had put them in bulb fibre and was patiently waiting for daffodils or tulips to appear. You can imagine the jokes there were about that – much to my disgrace!

With the twins ready to leave school, and my husband away in the army, I was termed a single person and had to enlist for war work. I worked in the foundry at Longport night and day, on 12-hour shifts, drilling holes in tank tops, with an electric drill, on to white dots that a draughtsman had marked out. It took three men to put the tank top into position. They were made at Bamfords in Stafford and were bullet proof and very heavy. The foundry works has gone now and a traffic roundabout stands in its place.

After the foundry I had to work at Radway Green in the bond weighing department, putting 303 shells into steel boxes to be sent to the Swinnerton Powder Munitions factory to be filled. During the night shift there I found I couldn't eat a big meal at midnight so I took my own bread and dripping for a snack, but the London women, and the Irish ones, would sit down to whole plates of potatoes, etc. While we were there we had ENSA to entertain us and it was funny to see a very serious man playing the violin and a lady trying to sing a song with no one bothering to lift their eyes from their plates to look at them.

I left munitions because the twins were still only 14 and I would not leave them alone to do the night shift. I went to work in a baker's, making sandwiches for miners as there were no canteens for them then. We made them with ham or cheese fillings and in one packet, for a joke, I enclosed a note, with my address, saying, 'If you enjoyed these snacks, please throw a piece of coal into my front garden.' Within two days I had quite a pile of coal there and, as it was on ration, my neighbours were most curious to find out where it had come from. 'The Germans are dropping me coal instead of bombs,' I told them, and we all shared it.

We lived near to a Corona lemonade factory then and once, when I was walking along the main road with the twins, the sirens went off and a German bomber came so low over us that we could see the helmet of the pilot in the cockpit. He had dropped his bombs on the pop works. He was two fields away from what must have been his proper target, the Rists factory which the government had taken over.

We had our bright times too, though. I loved to dance and when the pilots came to our private dances I loved to see their dress uniforms and the lovely kilts of the Scottish ones. They would come as guests to Swinnerton Hall. The Americans lived and took aircraft up from there. Because they were stationed in the Potteries, the American pilots wanted nice bits of china to take home to their mothers or wives, but the nice decorated pieces were for export only. There was only utility white available to buy. But I said, 'If you can get me a tin of treacle or syrup, I'll bring you some decorated china.' Sweets were on ration and I thought I'd like to make some treacle toffee like my mother used to make. Well, the next day one pilot went to his Jeep and brought out a tin as big as a petrol can, full of what he called molasses. I was able to make toffee for all the children in the Avenue.

Clothing was on ration, too. We had to give 20 clothing coupons for a coat, so I begged a few American blankets as theirs were a lovely soft grey. The British soldiers had only khaki ones which weren't half as nice. I had Mother's sewing machine and I made short swagger coats, which were then in style, and gave them to friends who had big families, and I kept one for myself.

HEIDI PRÜFER, of Cologne, North Rhine-Westphalia, was widowed early in the war, and was left to bring up her four children on the proceeds of her small shop in Cologne. As the air-raids on the city became worse, she decided to have the children evacuated:

'They're even laying carpets in the cowsheds'

The war had made me a widow, and in the autumn of 1944 I was left alone, with my children scattered to the four winds. How can anyone understand the misery of a mother torn apart from all her children? But that was the price we had to pay for their security. Evelyn, 12 years old, was evacuated to a farm. Rosemarie, 11, was away in Grünberg, in Silesia. The two boys, Wilfried and Günther, aged seven and six, were with my parents in Neuwied. How the children missed each other. Evelyn would write, 'Mummy, please tell me how long Rosemarie's hair is now.'

At the end of September our house in Cologne was hit by incendiary bombs. In the general commotion I lost my head, rushed back into the flat and, seizing a cake I had baked the day before, I wrapped it in a dish-towel and took it with me. The survival instinct? Perhaps. Anyway, I left all our valuables and papers just lying there. The hours we spent in the cellar after that were terrible. People were hanging on to each other and screaming out loud in sheer terror. Our house was completely burnt to the ground. It was only thanks to people outside that we managed to climb out of the cellar again. Covered in soot, and with tears cascading down my cheeks, I wandered through the smouldering town. I had lost everything now.

I used to run a small stationers and I re-opened for business soon afterwards in makeshift premises in a bakery in Blumenthal Strasse. Friends had provided me with furniture. Every day I would travel between Cologne and Neuwied, where I was now living with my parents. The 31st of October 1944 has always stuck vividly in my memory. Our train was just approaching Cologne when we were attacked by low-flying aircraft. We escaped the bullets by diving into a ditch. Luckily they didn't manage to put the train out of action, and we were able to continue our journey into Cologne. But here there was another unpleasant surprise awaiting me. The British had been bombing civilian targets again, and, although my little shop wasn't completely wrecked, all the doors and windows had been blown out. Looters had been at work after the raid, and all the bits and pieces I had managed to scrape together were gone. I was back at square one! Only this time I just didn't know where I was going to find the strength to carry on. I was filled with a mixture of grief and sheer fury. It was whilst I was in that frame of mind that I vowed I would never speak to a 'Tommy' ever again. It was a vow I took back later, when, in the late fifties, I travelled to England and found that they were good people.

I was still living with my parents at Neuwied when Christmas 1944 arrived. I had taken my father's advice and fetched all the children back from evacuation. He thought we should request to be evacuated all together. We had lost everything in the bombing of Cologne – our home, our furniture, clothing, and all our household effects. Christmas dinner was meagre that year, but being together again seemed to make up for everything.

In January 1945 we all boarded the train that was to take us to an evacuation address in Thuringia. There was no heating on the train. The water in the pipes was all frozen. Babies started crying. On the journey we were attacked by low-flyers.

It was already dark and freezing cold by the time we reached our destination of Walldorf an der Werra, but at least we should be safe from the bombers here. We disembarked at the station, too weary to talk, and were greeted by the local Hitler Youth, who sang songs and played guitars as we walked into the little town. The refrain 'We're marching to war against England' rang out over the sparkling, snow-covered countryside. It was so cold that little icicles formed on the hairs in your nose. How senseless it all was! What a mockery to sing those songs! Had they still not had enough?

We stopped off at an inn, and got the chance to have a wash in a zinc tub. My two daughters, 11 and 12, were embarrassed about getting washed in public. We couldn't remain at the inn, however.

We were taken to a school. The largest of the classrooms had been laid out with straw, and there all the people from the train bedded down, men and women, old and young together.

Over the next few days the evacuees were allocated to different families in the neighbourhood. No luck for us, though. No one shouts 'Here' of their own free will when you are a widow with four children.

Wilfried, my second youngest, had in the meantime made firm friends with a fat lady who had a loaf of bread hidden in her coat pocket and kept giving him pieces. He couldn't resist bread, and refused to be parted from her.

The Gauleiter [Nazi district official] said to me, 'Make out you've only got two children, and then we'll take it from there.' And that is how we managed to get a room in a house owned by an elderly couple. I took the two girls with me, whilst the boys had to go somewhere else. Later I made my little confession, and was allowed to have the boys join us. There was just the one room, a bit on the small side for the five of us. There was no proper bed and just one of those cylindrical iron stoves, which had to serve us for heating, cooking and washing.

Survival training began with bread-making. What a joy it was for the hungry children as they watched the dough rising over the top of the baking-dishes. But the children were never full, and it was a strain living there in a completely strange environment, amongst complete strangers. They never made us exactly welcome and seemed to regard taking us in as a bothersome duty.

One of the jobs for the children was going round the surrounding villages bartering our few remaining clothes for food. The country people always said, 'We haven't even enough to feed ourselves.' But the word amongst us 'townies' was: 'They're even laying carpets in the cowsheds!'

In April 1945 in Walldorf an der Werra the sound of gunfire and explosions could be heard. White flags started to appear. We were all frightened. Then we saw our first Americans. They were searching the local people for watches and then 'confiscating' them. But bicycles seemed to give them more fun than anything. They would ride round and round the village square to roars of laughter from their comrades. They were always asking for the 'frauleins', with the result that for weeks all the girls and young women were kept out of sight. The children had no fear of them at all. They used to trot back home with sweets they had been given. According to them, the coloured soldiers always gave the most. The children hadn't seen oranges, bananas and chocolate for years. They had never even heard of chewing-gum.

The war was over! Though only 39, I felt totally drained and longed to see my parents again. There had been no news for almost six months now. Rumours were growing that the Russians were coming. The thought filled me with horror. We had been getting the most dreadful reports. In May 1945 there were still no trains running, so we managed to get hold of three old prams to carry our belongings. Preparations were made and at the beginning of June, on Corpus Christi Day 1945, we set off. Travelling on foot, we barely covered 30 kilometres a day. Prams are not ideal for long treks like that. The wheels kept coming off. My daughter Evelyn proved to be the best mechanic among us. The boys were always in tears. Their shoes were not up to it, and their feet were hurting. So now and again they would be given a turn in the prams. After a few days we reached Friesenhausen, a village near Fulda, where a distant aunt of mine lived. We stayed with her for a few days, but then I became restless. Were my parents still alive?

On we marched to Fulda, and from there we were able to get a train to Mainz. In Mainz we waited for 20 hours at the station without food or water. Then a goods train was laid on. With a struggle we managed to heave our prams aboard one of the wagons. The train pulled out – and left us on our goods wagon standing there! We stood there watching the rest of the train disappear and I burst into tears. They had simply left us behind!

After a long wait, an open-sided rail wagon appeared and we travelled to Koblenz in that. We were all packed tightly together: soldiers, refugees, evacuees. All of us on the move, returning home, uncertain whether our families were still alive, or whether our homes were still standing. We stopped occasionally at stations for a drink of water. I noticed one of the standpipes had a sign hung on it:

Whilst at this tap you stand and queue
Admire what Adolf's done for you.

A peculiar sense of humour! It didn't even raise a smile from me. I felt sick and weary, and my only thought was to get the children back safely to my parents. Pray God they were still alive.

Koblenz was in complete darkness when we arrived. The curfew was in force, so we were not permitted to leave the station. The French Zone began at Koblenz and one of my more cheerful fellow-travellers told me, 'If you haven't got ID cards, the French will send you straight back again.'

The next day we boarded one of the improvised ferries and crossed the Rhine to Vallendar, on the other side of the river from Koblenz. We were all filthy dirty, and, once we got to the opposite bank of the Rhine, one of our prams decided to give up the ghost. We got a lift on a gas-powered truck and it took us right to the door of my parent's house. My mother almost fainted with relief at the sight of us all. Thank God, we'd all survived! What more could we ask?

PAT CRAIG DE SOUZA, of Birkenhead, Merseyside. Pat nursed in one of the big teaching hospitals in London prior to her marriage in October 1939. She then joined a bank as a clerk, with special nursing responsibilities. With her husband away in the war, she lived alone in a flat in Hampstead, London:

'Please God, let it go over our house'

Each night at about 6.30 p.m. the German bombers would arrive and the alert would remain in force until 6.30 a.m. In the flat above me was a German doctor and, as soon as the alert went, he would come knocking at my door and inform me, 'The siren has gone.' I, in turn, would reply, 'If you're afraid, go down to the shelter. I have my dinner to cook.'

In the basement flat was an old Cockney lady and her two daughters and sometimes I would go down to see them. It could be quite amusing. One would hear the whistling of a shell and the eldest daughter would shout, 'Duck, Mum!' Mother ducked, with a glass of beer in one hand and a pair of metal-rimmed spectacles in the other. Yes, she did duck under the dining-room table – all save her bottom and legs! This happened quite often.

I never went to a shelter at home, although I had to during the day at the bank. At home I felt I would rather go down with the building than have it come down on me. The back of my flat was in line with the East End, St Paul's, and the City, and when there were big fires, especially when the London docks went up, it was a terrific show from my kitchen window. It was really nerve-racking living alone. Each night I would write to my husband, but I used to think that by the time he got the letters I could be in Kingdom Come!

In 1943, my eldest son was born – a big responsibility in such conditions. I dared not put him in a cot so I got a very large basket from Covent Garden market and lined it with cotton wool and draped it with a lovely evening shawl. This I could take into bed with me, so I felt my baby, Tony, had some protection.

I can remember standing with Tony in my arms one day and this V1 bomb coming straight towards us. I just stood there transfixed and prayed, 'Please God, let it go over our house.' And it did. It fell in the next street. Another night a landmine destroyed half my road, but my end escaped.

B. V. was born in Danzig, but lived in Berlin throughout the war. She suffered not only the terrors of the air-raids on Germany's capital city, but, when defeat came, she also had to endure a traumatic experience, dreaded by every woman, at the hands of the victors:

'They dragged me off to an upstairs room'

Although I was born in Danzig, I had been living in Berlin since 1937; but the terrible air-raids between 1943 and 1945 made me return back home to Danzig with my two sons, aged two and four years old, to live with my parents and sisters. Things were pretty quiet there. The Russian planes left us in peace to sleep most nights. It was only when we saw the endless columns of refugees trailing through the city with their carts and all their belongings that we realized things were bad. This was a foretaste of what we were in for if the Russians broke through. They were getting nearer all the time and we could now hear the thunder of the guns quite clearly.

We held a family council and it was decided that the best thing would be for me to leave for Berlin with the children, while it was still possible. My husband was still working there. He was a chemist who had been drafted in to work in the laboratory of an armaments firm. I hadn't had any word from him for a long time because of the constant air-raids on Berlin. I decided to set off anyway. But getting away wasn't so simple. A friend gave me her place on a train that was reserved for employees of the railway and their families. It was the very last train to leave Danzig.

My sister, who was working down at the harbour, had also managed to get me a place on the ship the *Wilhelm Gustloff*. I couldn't make my mind up which place to take, but decided on the train, whch was just as well when we heard of the terrible fate of the passengers of the *Wilhelm Gustloff* when the ship was bombed. (My sister didn't manage to get away herself. She was captured by the Russians and sent to the Soviet Union for two years.)

So it was the train we boarded on 23 February 1945 and set off into the unknown with pounding hearts. The train journey to Berlin lasted for days. My son Dietmar had to celebrate his sixth birthday on 25 February on the train, with no special celebrations. There was just a single small stove where we could warm things up. Once the train stopped in the open country. There was an air-raid on Berlin. We could see the 'Christmas trees' (marker flares), dropped by the bombers, burning over the city and could imagine what was happening there.

After three days we reached the outskirts of Berlin and the train stopped in open countryside where we were told to get out and walk. I stumbled my way along the track with a frozen, tearful child clinging to each hand, and was in mortal fear every time a train approached. As soon as I saw a telephone-box I phoned up the laboratories and they were able to confirm that my husband was still alive and that our house was still standing. At last my greatest fears were at an end.

After wandering about all over the place we finally reached home, where my husband was overjoyed to see us. From that moment on there were air-raids day and night on Berlin, and we hardly ever seemed to get out of the shelter. My husband was working quite close by and whenever there was a daytime raid he would come running back, sometimes while the bombs were actually falling, so that we could be together, and to bring down the bedding. If we got hit then at least something would be saved.

In May 1945 came the Russian siege of Berlin, which we sat out in the cellars. They set up a rocket launcher (we called them Stalin's Organ) in the garden, just ten metres from our house, and bombarded the government buildings in the city centre with it. What a terrifying sight it was, belching great tongues of flame.

The first Russians who came down to the cellar, to all our horror, dragged me off to an upstairs room. Three of them raped me and there were others waiting their turn. In despair I waited my moment and then jumped off the balcony into the garden. I hid myself away in the cellars and did that every day afterwards when they came.

Between May and December 1945 I had to be treated for gonorrhoea which they had infected me with. I shared the fate of many women. The Russians had confiscated all the effective medicines, so that's why the treatment took so long. I kept getting recurrences. The emotional anguish it caused for both me and my husband was enormous. Whenever I saw a Russian after that I just fled in panic. It was a terrible time and has certainly left a scar on my memory. I still relive it all today.

MURIEL HAWKINS, from Kilmersdon, Avon, England, was a young bride of 21 and had been married for only a year when war broke out. Although she had as yet no children of her own, she very soon became mother to a constant stream of evacuees:

'Day after day just plodding on'

If you had a spare bedroom you were listed to take evacuees, so very soon I had a ready-made family of two brothers of eight and 12 years, sent from the East Coast because of fear of invasion. They were nice boys and were just getting settled in when some small bombs were dropped on our nearest town three miles away. I never did find out how their parents heard of it, but down they came at the weekend to see. The father wanted to leave them. He was right, there was far worse to come. But I could see the mother's side of it, so after tears and talking, they got up on the Monday morning and took them home again.

As my own baby was born in November, I didn't get any more evacuees until after Christmas. By then Bristol was a regular target, so I got a little girl from there. She was with us for a year, going to school and making friends, then she moved in with another little girl in the next village.

I was lucky in that my husband was exempt from call-up because of driving a large lorry. That meant he was occasionally at home, but mostly I would never really know where he was. He could be in towns helping out, or at army camps, or aerodromes, or hauling wood for the pits – anything that was needed. Whenever he was home for the night he had to be with the Home Guard on lookout for fires or the invasion of enemy troops. Looking back, how did one manage with so little sleep, with food so short, and living in fear all the time of what might happen?

'Dig for victory' we were told, but at times one wondered exactly how that could help win the war. We had six hens that we fed on boiled-up rinds from the vegetables and greens. They rewarded us with eggs occasionally. Our milk was fresh from the farm so we carefully skimmed off the top each day and put it in a screwtop jar. When the jar was about half full we would shake and shake it and were rewarded with about two ounces of butter. The little butter-milk left we mixed with flour and sugar and fried – frying-pan cake! It was beautiful spread with jam.

We had no indoor tap or sanitation, which had its problems with a house full of people, but I learned fast! One good thing about a village pump was that you met everyone and heard good news and bad, and could be in touch should anyone need help.

For myself life seemed to be day after day of just plodding on, doing my best with what there was, and praying day and night for the beastly war to end, and everyone to be safe again.

Our next evacuee was a young woman from Bristol expecting her first baby. Her husband worked at night in an aircraft factory. She was with me a month when her little girl was born. Her husband came at weekends. They stayed for another month before going back home. I had my own baby and helped at the birth of this one. Life was so busy that I never had the need to wonder what to do with myself. Next came two girls who worked in an arms factory about ten miles from our village. They stayed all winter, going by coach in the morning at six-thirty and returning at night at six o'clock. It was always dark for them as the factory was underground. Then two land girls came from Yorkshire to work in the woods. Very nice girls. But six months, they said, was long enough for them, so back they went.

My sister's husband was called up and was overseas by this time, so she wanted to come and stay. With her little girl, she stayed until the war was over. We were a comfort to one another, whether it was by day trying to lead as normal a life as possible, or sheltering under the table at night with our children. I was indeed very happy to have her.

How I ever managed to feed and care for such a lot of folks I will never know. I remember very well feeling so tired with it all that I couldn't have cared less about victory celebrations. I was just so wooden by then it didn't seem possible it was at an end. I often wonder what happened to all our evacuees. I have only seen one since, that was one of the arms workers. Did they all survive the horrors? I hope so.

What I thought was so lovely when the war finally ended was being able to put my baby to bed in peace, throw away the blackout curtains and have the windows open at night. My husband was home again, none the worse for it, only very tired, and his eyesight was very poor for a time because of so much blackout driving. We have had a good marriage. There were two more children and now eight grandchildren. What a blessing I have been given.

GRETE EMDE, *of Mönchengladbach, North Rhine-Westphalia, recalls the difficulties of evacuation with small children, and the heartache of having to deny a sick child what in peacetime would have been the simplest of requests:*

'She keeps asking for an egg'

I was a housewife in the war and we lived in Düren. It was 97 per cent destroyed in the war. [Düren is a small industrial town some 25 miles south-west of Cologne.] My two daughters were born in 1939 and 1941. My husband was a schoolteacher and taught English, French and Religion. He was never a soldier, even though he was called up on 1 April 1941. He worked first as an interpreter, then got further training and was sent to Toulon in France. He was captured there by the Americans and they sent him as a prisoner of war to England. He didn't get back home till Christmas 1947.

My children and I had a lot to put up with while he was away. You had to stand for hours queuing for a loaf or a piece of fish. Everyone had ration cards. They had to completely evacuate all the 40,000 people out of Düren. I was sent to Bad Wildungen, in Hessen, with my two children. They declared it a hospital town so that they would not drop any more bombs on it. It was just like a miracle for me, but we went hungry here as well. I had to pull my belt in really tight so that the children wouldn't hear my tummy rumbling whenever I fed them.

When one of my little girls had a really bad attack of measles, the doctor told me to prepare my daughter for heaven, for she was going to die. I prayed constantly that God would spare my child.

One day the fever subsided and she kept asking for an egg, so I went to see a cousin of my husband's who had a little farm in the neighbourhood. She asked how my little girl was, so I said, 'She keeps asking for an egg.'

But she just said to me, 'I need all my hens' eggs for myself, so the answer is No.'

Then I went to the biggest farm around there. The farmer's wife knew my husband's folk very well. He came from that area, you see. She picked up a pear that was lying on the ground and said, 'Give that to your sick child.' She wouldn't give me any vegetables either. She just said, 'Pull yourself some young nettle leaves. You can make good spinach out of them.' I did what she said but the children wouldn't eat it.

When I was still in Düren I had to have a thyroid operation because of all the bombing. I was on the danger list and my husband got special leave to come from France to be with me for two days. But God spared my life.

There were a lot of evacuees returning to Düren after the war. We got back in an open railway coal wagon and found the town was nothing but ash and rubble.

My children and I were given numbers 221, 222 and 223, there were so many of us returning then. I had nowhere to live; we had no furniture, no clothes, except what we were wearing. They gave me two bomb-damaged attic rooms. There was no glass left in the windows and the roof was leaking. They told me to buy myself three paper sacks and ask a farmer for some straw and that could be our beds. We were told that we'd just have to manage as best we could.

Eventually we were all issued with a box to store potatoes in. We were each supposed to get an allocation of 50 kilos, but I never got my share because I didn't have a carpet or clothes that I could give in exchange. When I spoke to a farmer in the ruins of our street one day, I told him my husband was still a prisoner of war and I was stuck up there in a bombed-out attic with two hungry children. He answered, 'You'll get your potatoes, but only if you'll sleep with me one night.'

I said, 'Get lost, you filthy swine!'

I can't write much more, it was all so terrible. Remembering these days is very upsetting for me. I am now 84 years old. My husband died over 20 years ago and my youngest daughter – that's the one who wanted the egg – died of cancer when she was 40. My other daughter lives in Schleswig Holstein. She married a pastor and has two daughters, who are my great joy.

WINIFRED WATKINS, of Willenhall, West Midlands, found that being a young mother with no home of your own in wartime could bring real problems:

'I thought, some fireworks!'

My first son was born on 8 September 1939, five days after war was declared. I was taken to hospital and was on the danger list with septicaemia for 10 days afterwards. When the air-raids started most of the patients had to be evacuated to other wards. We felt really sorry for the nursing staff who helped to keep us calm during that terrible time. I would lie there and think of my poor baby who was at home with my mother-in-law as, because of my illness, I couldn't feed him. I was in hospital for a month and they were the longest four weeks of my life.

When I came out I lived with my mother- and father-in-law. Although I loved my mother-in-law, I couldn't get on with my husband's father, so one morning before they were up, and after my husband had gone to work, I washed my baby and, not having a pram, I carried him in my arms all the way from Willenhall to Bilston, a distance of about two miles. I will never forget that walk for he was 11½ lb when he was born and I was still very weak. By the time I got to my Mum's the sirens were going again for another air-raid. I must have had God on my side for I arrived safely. But my Mum, God bless her, nearly had a fit when she saw me.

Luckily there happened to be a tiny old house vacant in my Mum's street and on the spur of the moment I took it, not knowing or caring what my husband would say. I thought anywhere was better than lodging in his Mum's modern bungalow.

Eventually we settled in, but it was situated near Sankey's works and so we suffered badly in the air-raids. Our neighbours had dug a hole out in the yard and made a good shelter, but my husband worked nights and I was left to cope with the baby alone. I put his bottle on the table one night and it was blown off during a raid. I used to scramble under the table with him until my neighbours came and got me. We had good neighbours.

When he was nine months old my baby got pneumonia. We were still in that old house and the doctor said I must keep the room warm. But coal was rationed and I was at the point of screaming through lack of fuel when the coalman from across the street came over and said they were sweeping the yard for slack for me and everyone was collecting wood from everywhere they could. Thank God, my little boy survived.

We were about 18 months in that house before we got another small one in Willenhall. We had just gone to bed one night in our new house when there was a bad air-raid. A nearby factory had received a direct hit and we had to get out of our house as all the windows were shattered. There was water from firehoses all over the place. At that time I had another baby boy and I can remember the elder one saying, as we went down into the shelter, 'Mum, look at the fireworks.' I thought, some fireworks!

The air-raid warden told me to get down as the bombers were right overhead. I did as I was told and promptly fell on his helmet, cutting my eye.

But everyone was so wonderful during that terrible time. I remember being put to the front of the queue for cakes, etc. because I was pregnant. The food queues looked really comical – just like clinics with all the expectant mums standing in a line.

My husband was a drop forger and he used to get very dirty. He was exempt from war service because he worked in heavy forging, doing tank wheels, and he worked very hard indeed. I used to have a dry shirt ready for him to change into at lunchtime before he went back to work. It was terrible for all those poor men. They worked very long shifts and, with the blackouts up at the windows and the red-hot furnaces, the conditions were terrible, and they were paid very little for the work. Most of the men my husband worked with died very young. They used to say it was worse than being in the army. I can tell you most of us had a rough ride. But once again my wonderful neighbours were a great help. Someone was always ready with a cup of tea to calm shattered nerves.

We never knew if we were going to bed to sleep or to be got up once again in the middle of the night. When my husband was on nights I used to go to bed with my clothes on so I could get up quickly and lose no time in getting my children to safety. We really suffered in those years. I know I was a nervous wreck. I would hate my children to ever go through what we went through.

My husband had to go into hospital in October 1942 and didn't get back to work until January 1943, during which time I just had to manage as best I could. You had to make what little you had go a very long way. It became a work of art. I remember learning the knack of putting marge on bread and taking it off again. I also had to beg for old coats to make into peg rugs which I sold to get enough money to live. There was no social security in those days. Still, I don't think it did me any harm. It was living through those terrible raids that upset me most. I don't want to ever go through that again.

My brother-in-law used to work with some prisoners of war and often used to bring them home to lunch. They were such lovely young German lads. They used to say, 'We didn't want to fight. We were made to.' They were very clever and used to make my children lovely toys.

My second son was born on Easter Sunday morning 1941. My husband had just gone on Home Guard duty, from eight at night to eight in the morning, when the labour pains began. I was so frightened, but fortunately my sister-in-law was next door. This was an answer to my prayer as it was Easter Saturday night and she usually went out. She stayed with me until my little son was born on the Sunday morning. I was in labour all night. The blackouts were up and I lay listening to the drone of the German bombers overhead. I was perspiring like hell and my mother-in-law tried her best to keep me cool by using a fan on me.

My baby was eventually born. He weighed 12 lb. I was in a real state and needed a doctor to stitch me, but my own doctor was away on military service. There was panic stations, but they finally got hold of another doctor around lunchtime and I was stitched without a pain killer. I vowed I wouldn't have any more children, but in the end I did have another. My third son was born in 1944. That birth wasn't as bad as the others – and there was no air-raid!

MARGARETE ONKEN of Bremerhaven was 23 when war broke out. Her husband was in the German navy and for the duration of the war she and her three children lived in the German naval port of Wilhelmshaven. She preferred to stay there, so as to be within easy reach if her husband got leave, rather than be evacuated out to some remote, but safer, area in the east. In the following incidents she recalls her most vivid memories from those troubled years:

'Hollow eyes set in hunger-ravaged faces'

One cold, wet winter's night in 1944, I was cycling through a prohibited area that belonged to the military. That afternoon enemy planes had bombed Bremerhaven and the station as well as other parts of the town had been destroyed. The smallest of my three children was seriously ill and, for safety reasons, had been admitted to a military hospital outside the town. I had left my other children in the care of a neighbour and I was now waiting for my mother-in-law to get back from a visit to the hospital. Her train had been held up, and the railway officials told me there was a chance that she would be on a goods train due into the military station-yard. That's why I had permission to be there.

The terrible state of the roads meant the going was very slow. The cold and dampness chilled me to the bone. I couldn't see the bushes at the side of the road; I could only feel them as I brushed against their black dripping branches. It was deathly quiet, just as if the bombing that afternoon had killed every sound. Suddenly, right by me, searchlights blazed into life, their concentrated, shadowless glare stabbing through the darkness. They illuminated a large square surrounded by green huts. Figures in uniform were moving about, armed with guns. What was going on? It was strictly forbidden to show even a glimmer of light in the blackout.

Then, in the distance, I heard the tramp of marching feet. I carried on in the direction of the sound. I was beginning to feel apprehensive, even frightened. The stamping, hurrying feet got nearer and louder. Now I could make out barked commands. The square that was lit up by the cold glare of the searchlights had high barbed-wire fencing around it. There was a gate, with SS men standing guard. That was odd. If this had been a transport of prisoners of war then ordinary army sentries would have been posted. The next moment the first faces caught the light, then more and more, and soon I could see hundreds of emaciated figures in striped suits, all with hollow eyes set in hunger-ravaged faces; figures tossed up like hideous flotsam and jetsam from the darkness, closely guarded on both sides by SS men.

Jumping off my bike and letting it fall to the ground, I pressed my hands to my breast to still the thumping of my heart. I was filled with a mixture of pity and fear. I was used to bombs and destruction, to grief and death, but what I saw here was more gruesome than anything I had so far experienced. It was human cast-offs I was seeing marching here, that much I knew for certain. Had they arrived with the goods train? The forlorn troop was being hurried across towards the gate. After the last one had passed through, it was locked. Then the lights went out, a few shouted commands echoed through the dark and wet, then the lonely silence returned.

My hands were trembling as I picked up my bike and set off on my way. My mind was in a turmoil about what I had seen. None of the SS men had taken any notice of me. Wasn't that odd? I had been witness to an oppressive, pitiless process that was meant to be hidden from the public gaze. I hadn't been seen, because I wasn't meant to see. A figure suddenly loomed out of the dark in front of me. I gave a shriek, thinking, 'One of them's escaped!' A calm voice said, 'It's all right. You're quite safe.' Then the figure vanished again, dissolving into the shadows. I never found out who it was and it was a long time before I mentioned what I had seen to anyone. The war came to an end not many months later. It was then that I discovered the explanation. They were concentration camp inmates being hurriedly transported after their camp had been bombed.

'Mummy, did God get burnt in the church?'
In the night, we ran home through burning streets, after spending hours in the bunker. 'We' were all neighbours – mainly young

women with children, and old people. In the middle of them all, I ran with my children, the youngest barely a year old, the eldest just five. The houses were blazing furiously from inside, with flames billowing through blown-out windows. The fire-storm whipped up the smoke and tossed it aloft into the night. The church was blazing fiercely from top to bottom. Incendiaries had broken through the steeple and had set light to the choir-stalls and altar.

We ran home, just hoping that our flat would still be there. Fortunately our block, with our flat on the second floor, *was* still standing. But the neighbourhood round about looked terrible: every window was shattered. As after every raid, the panes had been burst by the pressure of the bomb-blast and the splinters hurled into the rooms. Crockery was spilling out of the cupboards, and doors lifted off their hinges.

After cleaning up the broken glass and mess as best I could, I made a meal out of the few scraps left, washed the children, and tucked up the smallest in his little cot. I took the other two into my own bed and we tried to catch up on the sleep that we were all so sorely lacking.

There were draughts coming in everywhere, but I no longer had the energy to fix up the windows with wired safety-glass and nail up the door and window-frames. I slept restlessly and was awakened soon after by my five-year-old daughter's crying. She sobbed, 'The fire, Mummy, the fire . . . Did God get burnt in the church?'

How that question upset me! Hadn't I told her over and over again when we went to church that God was up there in Heaven protecting us. 'He's still there, darling,' I replied. 'Look how he's protected us again. He's left us our beds and lots of other things as well.' The answer seemed to satisfy her, and she fell asleep again.

I remember another occasion when my next door neighbour shouted, 'You'd better go and see to your little girl. She's over there playing in the bombed house.'

I ran straight down, and what I saw was certainly dangerous, there was no denying it. But it was such a scene of childhood happiness that I didn't have the heart to disturb it. The house opposite had the whole front torn away. From the street you could see right into the bedrooms. The unsupported floors were left hanging and swaying in the wind. Up on the second floor was a double bed and beneath it a chamber-pot, threatening at any moment to come sliding down. It had become the joke of the neighbourhood. The floor beneath lay at an angle on top of the rubble. 'Wheeeeeee!' My Ute shrieked in joyful chorus with the other children as, with gleaming eyes, they slid down it, just as if it were a children's chute.

All around was destruction, but the children's sheer joy showed that for them at least the world was not at an end. Gone was Ute's concern about what had happened to God, as she looked at me with sheer delight in her eyes. I was still young myself and would have loved to have joined in. I could only laugh with them, as I thought ruefully, 'Oh dear, that new coat I've just made for her!' Even 44 years later, my daughter can still vividly recall the fun they had that day. And she still remembers that I had a twinkle in my eye when I gave her a scolding for scuffing her coat.

MADGE WEAR, who now lives in Aberfeldy, Perthshire, worked in London in the thick of the blitz before marrying her husband, a widower, who had already suffered great personal loss in the war:

'We commandeered a hearse'

My husband, whom I married in 1941, was refused permission to join up because of his job in the 'front line' in London. He had already suffered a traumatic, personal, human loss and had had his home destroyed. Later he also lost a sister, killed by a flying bomb, and a brother in the Russian convoys. I also lost relatives and many friends.

We were extremely busy. All women below a certain age had to work, unless one had young children. I was recruited as a billeting officer in Bermondsey, a heavily bombed area of south-east London.

147

This was after I returned from a voyage to South Africa, in the autumn of 1940, as a government escort to children evacuated there from Britain for the duration.

There seemed to be a lot of time spent in journeys, owing to diversions because of the bombing. I can remember one morning, 10 May 1941 to be exact, when there were a thousand homeless in one night in Bermondsey. The Mayor was killed, and many more. It took me from 7 a.m. to 10 a.m. to get there – an 8–10 mile journey.

We had to empty the rest-centres as soon as possible to get ready for the next influx. I used to walk around the borough like the Pied Piper, with people trailing after me, and with keys tied to my belt, to get them into requisitioned property as soon as possible. Anything to get a roof over their heads. There were the essentials of furniture and floor covering, linen and cutlery, etc. to provide. Basic food was also provided. All the people were shocked, yet I heard few grumbles, and they were so grateful. One day the town clerk and I went round the district in a dustcart delivering furniture. Another time we commandeered a hearse. As the driver remarked cheerfully, 'Not many folk can boast of having been in one twice!'

A lovely character comes to mind. A Mrs Paddy, well over 80, and bombed out three times, and each time smiling and cheerful. I almost dreaded getting to her nearest rest-centre in the morning to hear, 'I'm back again, dear! Don't you worry about me. I'm so well looked after. I'm quite happy here.' On one occasion we were asked to find her corsets and false teeth in the rubble of her flat. A wonderful air-raid warden did just that. Alas, after the third time she was bombed out, we had to take Mrs Paddy to an old people's home in Surrey. I saw her there once, but she missed London. She died before the end of the war.

By 1944 the worst of the daylight and night raids were over. Then came the flying bombs. They were the worst. You heard the wretched things 'cut out', then dived for cover, and never knew where they were going to land. Animals heard them before we did. A little fox terrier living at the back of us used to sit on top of the air-raid shelter and when he heard it (before we could), he shot into the shelter. You knew then it was time to take cover. If he stayed on top, it went over.

By this time, my young step-daughter had come back from evacuation in the Midlands and I took a part-time job as billeting and welfare officer at Croydon Airport.

My husband got pneumonia in 1942 and was on the fifth floor of the hospital. I used to visit him every day when I could get through. The air-raids didn't stop me. One evening I was there when the sirens went. The patients couldn't be moved from the fifth floor, and it was wonderful to see the nurses encouraging their patients, with the terrific noise of the barrage outside, and the 'crunch' of the bombs. I remember we visitors all sang songs with the patients who were able.

I often wondered what mothers were feeling like in Germany and how they were coping with the air-raids.

MARTHA ZOLLINGER was born in Saalfeld, East Prussia. She married in April 1936 and settled on a smallholding near Insterburg, where her husband, Willi, had a joinery business and kept cattle, pigs and poultry. Their son, Manfred (Manni), was born in 1936. In 1939 at the outbreak of war Willi was called up, leaving Martha to run the family's affairs. By the end of August 1944 the German armies had been forced back by the Red Army almost as far as the borders of East Prussia. The evacuation of German civilians began. Martha Zollinger kept a diary of her experiences during her flight before the advancing Soviets, from which the following extracts are taken:

'Are any of us going to survive?'

Our First Flight
22 October 1944: Insterburg evacuated today. We go to stay with my in-laws in Ellerbruch.

Our Second Flight
23 January 1945: The long trek with our in-laws begins. Four days on a cart in 20° of frost! We couldn't take the cold any more, so we got lifts with army trucks as far as Büsow in Pomerania. From there we caught the train to Stolp. There we managed to get a small room. Just as cold there, with no coal for heating. Remain in Stolp from 1 February to 7 March.

Our Third Flight
7 March 1945: Set off on foot today. No one knew where we were bound. We walked to Glowitz, 30 kilometres away. The Russians caught up with us here. What a terrible sight it was when the Russians captured the village on 9 March. We only stayed one night in Glowitz. At night the Poles disturbed us several times. A lot of Russians came in, but they didn't do us any harm. On the morning of 10 March a Russian officer came with a pistol in his hand. We all had to put our hands up. Then he asked us whether we were Germans. We were searched for weapons. There were about five women, two young girls and children in the room.

Then he told me to go with him, covering me with his pistol all the way. I had to go two rooms along into an empty room. He raped me, still holding his pistol in his hand. After that we set off again. Frau Rippholz with her chidlren and a Frau Janowski with her two daughters. It had been raining. The roads were packed solid. It was the Russians bringing up reserves. We didn't get far at all, just to the other side of Glowitz, where we found an isolated farm by the roadside. There were many refugees there. We stayed just one night. The place was swarming with Russians. They left us alone during the day. In the evening they crowded us all together in one room and put the light out. Then they came round flashing torches in our faces. Any young women had to go with them into the other room. It was a terrible night. I just cried and cried. Next day we were off again to the next village. The Russians wouldn't let us go on any further. In the ditch at the roadside there were dead Germans lying, lots of them, all policemen. A gruesome sight.

We found a track across country and came to the Schojow estate. We have got a little room in the inspector's house. There are three families, eight people all told. It's all a bit cramped. The estate belonged to Countess Schwerin. The Russians shot her as soon as they got here, then looted the house and smashed everything up.

The first night here we were left in peace and got a good night's sleep. The Russians came in the second night wanting watches and rings. They just ransacked all our luggage. The third night more Russians came asking for watches. They told me to go with them. I said I was ill and they left me alone. Then we got a few peaceful nights. They kept coming by in the daytime, too, always after watches and pinching anything that caught their fancy. They stole several of my things.

29 March 1945: In Schojow. Manfred has got a headache and I put him to bed.

30 March 1945: Manfred definitely ill, running a temperature and diarrhoea.

31 March 1943: His temperature has shot up to 40.2°C. I spent the whole night making cold compresses.

1 April 1945: Today is Easter. The most miserable Easter I have ever known. Manfred really sick.

2 April 1945: Manfred has measles.

3 April 1945: Manfred has come out all over with red spots. He isn't eating anything. Diarrhoea continues. Started vomiting today. I have draped cloths round the bed, so that he doesn't get so much light. Terrible night. At two o'clock in the morning a drunken Russian staggered in and stayed till morning. He lay down right amongst us. The next morning his mate came to fetch him. It's just terrible, the way we have to just put up with them.

5 April 1945: In the afternoon the same Russian brought along two of his mates. Then things really started. The children and Frau Janowski had to leave. Frau Rippholz ran off, too. I was left alone with them. One of them went out and the officer then raped me. Then the other one came back in and wanted the same. I set up such a noise that he went out.

Manfred still no better. The Russians come every day. We have to keep ourselves hidden all the time. Otherwise everything just the same as ever. Still no sign that the war will soon be over. Today is the first Saturday after Easter. Russians from the Front are being billeted here. Everyone is being chased out of their houses on to the street, and in go the Russians. We went to the greenhouse, where the gardener is living. At least it's warm. Manfred is still very sick and I'm worried to death about him. At night we have to go through it all again. An officer came for me first thing this evening. We have to go. What choice when there's a gun sticking in your ribs. In the morning we get back into our room. What a pig-sty! They've ransacked all our luggage and stolen everything edible. We have to work for them now. We are spreading dung at the moment. It's so freezing I'm sure I've caught a chill. But I carry on working.

Today, Sunday, I have to lie down. My head is aching so much and I'm running a temperature. I really am ill, my temperature is over 40°C. How my head hurts! We are told to clear out of our room. We are sent to the castle. The room they give us is a gloomy hole. Never gets the sun. The Janowskis have got a room of their own. A lovely sunny room. Frau Janowski isn't going to cook for us any more. Sick as we are, Frau Rippholz and I have to struggle to try and cook, just so the children don't starve. Whatever we give them, they're still hungry. We have so little to eat ourselves. I don't know how I'm ever expected to get well again. I've got typhoid! I just don't think I'm going to pull through. Today is Whitsuntide. A fat lot of good it does us! Still no sign that the war's over. We would just love so much to get home again. The weather is warm now, but we have no summer clothes. We've lost everything. I could scream just thinking about it. Whatever is to become of us if the Russians are intending to stay in Germany?

6 June 1945: We all want to go home so desperately. But how, now that the Russians have ripped up all the railway lines? No trains are running at all from here. And I just don't think the Russians would

let us travel on the trains. We have so little to eat, just bread and potatoes, no meat or fat whatsoever. I'm still weak and can't go back to work.

9 June 1945: Went with Frau Rippholz to the mill today to get flour. After that we went begging again. We didn't get much. There are just too many begging, and people have stopped giving. I find it so hard to beg, but we just have to do it because there is nothing to eat. We get a quarter of a kilo of meat per week and 10 kilos of flour for the whole month. Life is getting more and more difficult. Everyone is talking about going home, but the Russians won't let us go yet. The Poles are still in Germany and plundering everything. The Russians just can't organize anything. We now have lice and it's awful. There are 125 people here in the house.

21 June 1945: The Russians are supposed to be withdrawing. A young woman from this house has died of typhoid.

24 June 1945: We have to work from six in the morning till eight o'clock at night – orders of the Russians. Anyone not working gets punished. Nothing to eat. We live by begging. The farmers have stopped giving us anything. The Russians have robbed them of everything. They're stripping our land of simply everything.

28 June 1945: Today 500 German prisoners came through Schwiringshöhe. It makes you weep to see how pitiful our men look.

8 July 1945: More and more people are going down sick, all of them typhoid cases. Are any of us going to survive? Frau Rippholz's daughter Ursel is ill, too. People speak about nothing else but going home. If only we could. Life here is simply awful, nothing to eat but potatoes and a measly bit of bread. No vegetables at all. The Russians have taken them all. The bastards know just how to finish us all off. There's only one hospital here and they've closed that. I've got terrible toothache.

13 July 1945: Headaches every day. Nerves just in shreds. I look ten

years older. My hair is starting to fall out after that illness. Only have part of my hair left now.

14 July 1945: Begging again in Stohentin today. Jubilation! They're letting us go home soon. If only it was today!

The transport to the West that Martha Zollinger had been counting on never materialized. In April 1946 she attempted to cross to the West on her own, but was turned back at the border. Attempting to smuggle herself across on foot, she and her eight-year-old son found it impossible to keep pace with the party and had to return to the farm at Kobande. On 22 May 1946 she succeeded in crossing to the British Zone at Helmstedt by hiding in the guard's van of a hospital train.

Although things were better there, food was short and documentation long in arriving. After spending May and June in a variety of camps and makeshift billets, she finally received a pass to travel to Bielefeld on 23 June and early in August was given a room there with the Killschautzki family, who treated her well.

At the end of August 1946 she at last received news from her husband, who was a prisoner of war in France. But it was not until 1948 that he returned to her. Using the time left at the end of the working day, he rebuilt a ruined house, part of which was to be a flat for his own family. Sadly, the family reunion was not to last long. On 16 April 1952 Martha Zollinger died of cancer. Her diary, from which these extracts are taken, was found amongst her effects. It was passed on to us through the great kindness of her daughter-in-law Renate Zollinger.

MRS H. B. WOOLLAMS, from Wolverhampton, West Midlands, relates an incident that occurred one teatime, when a shell came a little too close for comfort:

'The heavy rain didn't improve the sausages'

I was working six days a week at Woolworth's, near Birmingham, when the war broke out and I travelled by bus, always remembering my gas mask. At work it was decided that about six of us should learn first aid and I volunteered. Not that I thought I would be much use in an emergency, but it would be a chance to leave work two hours early once a week, to make our way to the St John's Headquarters in Birmingham. After our tuition we used to grope our way to a blacked-out fish and chip shop to have an unrationed meal, before heading for home. But I never had need to put my training to good use. Our store was hit, but during the night, when nobody was at work. The only thing left standing was the hand-operated lift which I had pulled up and down for years.

I didn't work any more because soon after that I had my first baby, so I was exempt from work. I stayed at home making ends meet. Perhaps I should say, making 2½ ration books 'stretch'. I can't imagine now how we got two or three meals out of two shillings' worth of meat, but we had a good butcher, with a sharp knife. By using sausage, offal, and fish, we had a good dinner every day. If we had meat and potato pie, I put most of the meat in one place, which I marked, so that my husband got it.

We had a gent's hairdressing shop, 'Tommie's Barber's Shop', and sometimes a customer would give him some cooking fat which was very useful. Having some fruit trees in our garden, we were very popular for fruit pies. We used golden syrup for sweetening. Once our small son fell and his teeth went through his lip, which had to be stitched. This proved to be a blessing in disguise, as at several fruit shops I was told to 'go round the back' for some bananas for him. We were allowed 1lb on a child's book, but usually you arrived to hear

'Sold Out', so the extra ones were very useful. I exchanged any we didn't need for something else.

Early one very rainy evening we heard a shell explode. We thought it was in the middle of the road outside our house. We were just going down to the Anderson shelter when our neighbour rushed out with a pan of sausages shouting, 'It's in my front room!' The heavy rain didn't improve the sausages.

GRETE WESTEBBE, of Düsseldorf, North Rhine-Westphalia, came originally from that city, but while her husband was in the German army she moved to Vienna, where she worked in freelance technical design. When the war ended, and the Russians reached Vienna, she joined the mass evacuation out of the city, hoping eventually to make it back to Düsseldorf. She set off with her daughter Kinni and her grandson Dieter. They left Vienna on 5 April 1945, little realizing the chaos and destruction they would meet on their 1000 kilometre journey. For the first part of their trek they travelled under the protection of the élite Waffen SS regiment Das Reich, *now in retreat from the Austrian capital. The danger of such a military escort soon became apparent, and they parted company from the regiment in Leitmeritz, hoping to continue their journey by train. This excerpt, from a much longer account of Grete Westebbe's experiences, begins as they take their leave of their Waffen SS travelling companions, and describes their efforts to cross the Erzgebirge Mountains and reach Chemnitz:*

'Kinni and I smeared our faces with mud'

On 6 May 1945 the company commander and his driver came to our quarters at five o'clock in the morning. He brought with him an army pass issued by the regimental commandant. They then gave us the addresses of their families and asked if we would pass on their love and best wishes when we got to the West. We shook hands. No one spoke. We were all too choked with emotion. We knew quite well the uncertain fate that awaited these men, and that they were resolutely prepared to go to their deaths. They had done more for us than we had had any right to expect.

Thanks to our army pass, we got tickets for the train from Leitmeritz to Karlsbad. And, wonder of wonders, there was actually a train running! We climbed aboard at seven o'clock, our hearts full of hope. The train stopped in Aussig not very far down the line. All out! We waited to continue our journey from nine in the morning till nine in the evening, with hundreds of other refugees, all the time under attack from low-flyers. Then we were all told to return to the station. There were no more trains running. On another line we had noticed there was a hospital train waiting. It was full to overflowing. Kinni was clever enough to manage to steal over towards the train. Dieter and I followed, and we hid behind some railway wagons. We then mingled with an incoming group of wounded soldiers, and used the few provisions we had left to share out food and medicine to the wounded. Two hours were spent emptying out a goods wagon to make room for the sick and injured. Once they had been accommodated, we were allowed up.

In the meantime hundreds of other refugees had gathered around the wagon. Pushing and fighting broke out amongst them. Everyone wanted to get on board. Within minutes there were 30 people in the truck, together with seven small children and a great mass of luggage. The children were crying and the wounded were moaning. The stink and the heat were unbearable. Finally, we set off. What relief there was in all those faces! Anyone with food left shared it out with his neighbour.

After several stops, at about two o'clock in the morning, there was a jolt. We had stopped again. This time several hours went by, and an ominous feeling began to grow in us all. We remained there until morning. Then, from close by, came the terrifying sound of gunfire. Women started screaming, the children began to whimper, and an expectant mother who hadn't long to go leaned against me. I pushed some bundles underneath her for support. One of the medical orderlies tried to comfort us, saying that our soldiers were just blowing up an arms-dump. In fact it was fighting between our rearguard and the Russians.

When it became light, we cautiously pushed open one of the wagon doors. We were on the long open stretch of line outside Karpitz. There was no house within sight, just a tiny station building. The condition of the wounded and the children was unbearable. We fetched some water from the little station and shared out what little food there was left. They tried to keep us happy by telling us that the engine would be back to take us on further. But no one could say when.

We spent the rest of that day making fires and cooking in the open air, and discussing what we could do to get away from there. I found a bed for the expectant mother in the station building, and I stayed there with her, telling Kinni to let us know immediately there was any sign of a train. Towards afternoon a brown figure appeared, heading for our wagon. The first Russian. He searched our clothing, looking for jewellery. He found Kinni's old gold watch and took it. He never discovered her good one; it was sewn into the hem of her dress. He then rummaged through our cases and disappeared as quickly as he had come. So that was what was in store for us. Nighttime would be worse. Kinni went off to see what was happening, while I waited with Dieter.

The time passed slowly, but eventually she returned and whispered to me that we should get our luggage together and steal away without the others knowing. She had spoken to three soldiers who had become detached from their unit and had managed to get hold of a hay-cart. At first they were reluctant to take us, for fear that the others would see and all want to come. That just couldn't be done. The cart was far too small. We even had to abandon some of our luggage. In the meantime other soldiers joined us, together with one of the train staff, a man called Rudi Lang from Erdmannsdorf near Chemnitz. We crept along, keeping out of sight, on the other side of the train, then had to lift the hay-cart over five sets of lines. The Red Army was moving on the main road. We had to remain hidden for ages until things were quiet. Then we crossed the road and headed off along a farm lane.

We walked until late evening, covering 35 kilometres. Little

Dieter slept soundly on the cart. Then we came to another road and suddenly there was a tide of Russians bearing down on us. There were cars, horse-drawn carts, covered wagons and mounted officers. They were all heading towards us at breakneck speed.

We paused for a moment, then decided to risk it and carry straight on. The road narrowed and became completely congested with the hurrying troops and crowds of refugees. We had slowed to a snail's pace. The Russian horses would often stumble to their knees, then spring up again and carry on, sometimes dragging carts with only one wheel behind them.

Kinni and I had smeared our faces with mud and messed up our hair, then draped old blankets around our shoulders. We kept bent low behind our cart, and no one took any notice of us. Farmers gave us bacon and eggs and often offered to let us stay in their homes. But you just weren't safe inside, and we preferred to stick close to the road. As darkness fell, we were still on the move, amongst vehicles and carts of every description: and our own soldiers marching in small units; countless hundreds of people in flight, and we moving along with them.

Then, suddenly, our column came to a complete standstill, as the Russian army appeared on the road, three columns abreast. As we made way for them, we thought at first we would only be stopped for a short time, but we had to remain there for the whole night. I squeezed in between a trap and our hay-cart and lay down on the road with Kinni beside me, while Dieter slept on cases in the cart. I tried to snatch some sleep, but the grinding of trucks on the road, the wild shouts of the Russians, the flashing headlamps, and the dust which settled on us in clouds, prevented us from getting even a wink.

All of a sudden a group of Russians jumped down from their truck and came among us, shining torches and seizing young women at random. We crouched down, pulling the blankets over our heads. A young girl nearly succeeded in drawing their attention to us, when she tried to escape them by running over to hide in our cart. We were lucky. They never found us. But all night you could hear women screaming pitifully from the thick pine-woods along the roadside. Finally, hours later, it grew quieter. We were all in a cold sweat with fear and shaking from head to foot. It was all too much.

We saw that our soldiers had put themselves between us and the Russians, so that we wouldn't be seen. A middle-aged woman went by, her arms outstretched, crying, 'Where is my child, my only child?' Czechs were suddenly in our midst, ransacking through our belongings. Another woman was crying, 'Two sons dead and now where is my daughter?'

The night seemed endless. Above the pine-trees shone Orion's stars in all their splendour. We longed for morning. My gaze wandered to the far horizon where the road stretched on through a deep ravine. At last a glimmer of light shimmered over the pine-forest. It was morning. We breathed again. I hoped that in the face of the sun, the terrible experiences of the night could not repeat themselves. It was the ninth of May. The war was lost, Germany on its knees, countless dead and wounded on all sides, and for what?

We had to get off this military thoroughfare as soon as possible. We looked upon a pitiful scene; horses and carts stood all around, their owners vanished. Food was tumbling out of sacks. Czechs were still busy looting the refugees' possessions. One of them tried to make off with my blue jacket – my only jacket. I tore it back out of his hands, and Rudi Lang, a giant of a man, put himself between the two of us.

Soon afterwards, we were forced into the woods, where we were halted by a high wall. We would have to climb over it. There was a young girl lying on our hay-cart. She had broken her foot. We now had to leave her behind. We took the cart to pieces and lifted the bits over the wall, one by one, together with what was left of our luggage. We noticed afterwards that our soldiers had gone. Our little company was now reduced to the three of us and four others. We got hold of one of the horses that were roaming about, put the cart together again and, after stowing all the luggage, off we set along a trail through the forest. The way got steeper and steeper, and the road became so rough and stony that we feared the cart-wheels were going to break off. There were more people now: cripples hobbling along on crutches and old women sitting helplessly at the edge of the track. Little children, with puzzled eyes, stumbled over tree-roots. There was misery everywhere.

We hauled and tugged at our cart to get it up the hillside. Then there was a tank barrier ahead of us. Pine-trees had been felled over the whole mountain-side for a distance of about a kilometre. What could we do now? Once again the cart was dismantled and time after time we went to and fro carrying the separate pieces round the obstacles, till we had collected everything.

After three hours' work, we had at last put everything together again. The sun was beating down unmercifully on us by now. In among the trees lay a woman with a newly-born child. The Czechs had ransacked her case, and all the baby's powdered milk and nappies were gone. I couldn't pass her by, and gave her some semolina and sugar. But I couldn't stay long with her; the others, exhausted though they were, had already moved on. We were tortured by thirst, but there was no water to be had anywhere. The stream was now way down in the valley below us. We had climbed hundreds of feet. Through the trees we saw an unending stream of Russian troops. Their equipment looked new and there were a surprising number of women in uniform among them. We had been told that the Red Army had been smashed, yet for two days and a night we had seen them march by in undiminished strength.

After the first tank-barricades, we came upon another, and then another. Each time meant unloading, dismantling and then reassembling our carts. We passed the body of a dead horse, and the bodies of two people who had taken their own lives. How peacefully they slumbered in their eternal sleep, in the soft grass, in the shade of the pine-trees.

German soldiers, now detached from their units, were abandoning their kitbags. Many were wounded and could scarcely drag themselves along. The forest was littered with people's belongings: clothes, uniforms, shoes, fur coats and suits, whole trousseaux, medals, letters and photographs.

At the next tank-barrier we discovered a little plywood cart that had fallen into a hollow. We pulled it up on a rope. It would do perfectly for Dieter. It's a miracle how our little boy stood up to the dreadful strain for weeks on end. Now at least he was able to sleep in his own little carriage, and sit up for some of the way, if he wished. He had Kinni's coat underneath him and our blankets on top. Thirsty and dead with fatigue, we plodded on. We came to a place where a puddle had formed, now almost dried out. We took our turn in the queue and got a beaker full. It was filthy, muddy water, but it tasted like heaven to us!

Now hunger was our problem. One of our soldiers had taken the bag with provisions at one of the tank-barriers, and then lost contact with us in the general mêlée. That evening, when we finally crossed the Czech frontier near Zinngraf, there he was, faithfully waiting for us to arrive. He had been waiting for hours. We made a short stop to have something to eat. There was a stray black horse roaming around, and I managed to catch hold of it by the reins. The poor beast had been made so nervous with all the commotion going on around it that it sprang right off the path and ended up with a hind-leg down the slope. I managed to pull him up again, but then he wanted to set off at a gallop. A man came to my rescue, but then tried to take the horse for himself. I protested and yelled that the horse was now mine. Luckily one of our soldiers came to my rescue.

This little incident meant that Kinni and I got separated from the others. Two Russians suddenly sprang out of the bushes. We ran as fast as we could, but they managed to catch hold of a woman who had been standing beside us. Her little boy, pale with fright, just stood there crying for his mother. We caught up with the others and on top of a small rise we stopped for breath. You were safe nowhere.

A young mother, with four children, struggled on in despair, dragging a bundle behind her. An old lady tipped out the contents of her case. But her children wouldn't be parted from its contents and were crying and fighting over them. We also had to leave heavy things behind like thick suits and ski-boots. The refugees were giving their belongings as presents to each other. But no one could accept them. They were just a burden and so were hung from the trees or thrown down on the trail. There was one young woman we had seen three times before. She was being led along by a soldier. She had left all her belongings behind and was now walking along in a trance, as if stepping forwards into paradise.

We thought we had already crossed the frontier, but we were wrong. It still lay a little way ahead. The track became steep again for a few kilometres. Our black steed, harnessed up with ropes, was now pulling the three little carts. In one of them sat Dieter, quite happy with the world.

At last we found a spring and were able to quench our thirst properly and take supplies of fresh water with us. Beyond the frontier there were houses and we begged for help at every door. But the occupants all said we would be better off out in the open, because searches were made for women every night in the houses. Many houses were burnt out. The swollen corpses of horses and human beings lay by the roadside, their stench filling the air. No one had time to bury them. We were too exhausted to go further. We headed for some nearby woods. Our soldiers took turns at keeping guard. Dieter slept in his cart. We rolled ourselves up in our blankets and lay down. In the dark we had not noticed that we were lying on ant-hills. Kinni and I were soon swollen with bites and went down to the stream to find relief. On our way, we came across an abandoned German army truck. There was still food and drink in it. We helped ourselves, and also took some socks, since our own were now in holes. When we got back the soldiers were cutting up a slaughtered pig. We took as much as we could with us in the morning.

All three did finally reach their destination of Düsseldorf. The harrowing journey took them two and a half months, much of it on foot, with Grete Westebbe in increasing pain from a bullet wound to the ankle. They arrived to find their native town destroyed almost beyond recognition by the constant bombing. But at least their own house was still standing. It was full of homeless people, so they took up lodgings in the cellar. Grete Westebbe's husband was released from a prisoner-of-war camp a year later. Now in her eighties, she still lives in that same house in Düsseldorf that was her goal and refuge in 1945.

MARY WATTS, of Wolverhampton, West Midlands, found they could still occasionally raise a smile, even during an air-raid:

'Why don't they drop tea and sugar instead?'

When war broke out, I had a baby girl and a boy of seven. My husband worked shifts at the local steel works. He told us not to go out if the sirens went when he was on night shift, but I'll never forget the first time it happened. I wrapped the baby in a bedspread and off I went with the two children into next door but one, the home of a dear friend. Another family below us went as well and after that it became a ritual – one of us would take some coal as it was the only heating we had, the other took tea or milk, and we had a rare old time. The laughter helped deaden the sound of the ack-ack. As the night wore on, a bed was made under the table for the children, five in all. If a bomb had dropped near us, the whole row would have come down, and yet we felt safe being in the middle of a row of six houses.

One night my neighbour's sister came in, in the pitch dark, in such a sweat. She said a German parachutist had landed! We discovered 'the parachutist' was, in fact, a rather bent old lady, wearing a shawl around her shoulders, who was hurrying to an air-raid shelter when she was spotted and taken for one of the enemy!

I remember another time a family in our row was scuttling down the garden into their Anderson shelter (only a few had one) and, casting an eye to the heavens and the falling bombs, the man shouted, 'Why don't they drop some tea or sugar instead!'

I remember the night of the big Coventry raid. It was a clear moonlit night and, as we stood on the back doorstep watching the planes go over, we thought that someone was moving down the garden. It turned out to be a blackout curtain that I had washed and left on the line to dry!

A black aircraft went over the day before the Coventry raids. We heard afterwards it was spying out the land. How they ever missed the steel works I'll never know, as the stacks were in a line, clear as daylight. A bomb did drop close by, killing two boys and causing a lot of damage and injuries. There was a truce around Christmas and it was lovely to go to bed knowing that the sirens wouldn't go.

We still have the Anderson shelter as a coal-house. But another equally clear reminder of those days is the memory of the day my friend came round to tell us it had come over the wireless that Germany had invaded France. I was feeding my baby daughter at the time. To comfort me, my friend told me of the sermon their Methodist minister had delivered the previous Sunday. He said, 'If you get a bundle of sticks and try to break them you can't. But separate them and one by one you'll break them. That is what we must do – keep together, then no nation will separate us. We must stick together!' It really bucked me up. I've never forgotten it.

MRS M. DUCE, of Linthorpe, Cleveland, found that a whole generation later the war could still spring a surprise:

'I am that baby'

In the war sirens would sound every night for the approach of enemy planes. Being young, with two young boys, I would take them to the air-raid shelter at the bottom of the garden. (My husband was a railway driver, working all hours.) Well, this particular night the sirens sounded and I had just got into the shelter with the boys when a bomb dropped close by us. There was a huge flash and the whole shelter lifted. I was terrified. My husband was at work and wouldn't be home till midnight. I heard later that the explosion had killed another young mother who was coming downstairs, carrying her baby. Although she died the baby was saved. Two years ago, in 1984, I had a man round to do a job of work in the house. The conversation got round to that episode in the war. I remarked how sad it was that the young mother was killed. To my amazement, he said, 'I am that baby.' Life is strange.

ANNA GRÜTERING, born in 1915 in Dormagen, North Rhine Westphalia, West Germany:

'I saw his sad eyes but could do nothing to help him'

I got married in 1941 and we lived with my mother in Dormagen. The family consisted of two sons, a daughter-in-law, and two grand-children. I worked in the sales department of a large factory until February 1945.

A little story about our wedding: After the ceremony in the register office was over, we were officially handed a copy of Hitler's *Mein Kampf* [literally 'My Fight']. It was raining, and, as we came out of the office, the book slipped out of my husband's hand and fell into the mud. My uncle, who had been one of the witnesses at the wedding, laughed and said, 'I can see you two are going to have a splendid "fight" ahead of you!' But our 'fights' were only ever little ones and I never did manage to read *Mein Kampf*. It was just a lot of hate and mixed-up stuff. In fact, we burned it. But, unfortunately, later on, our sons needed a copy for school.

When you compare the number of bombs that were dropped on Dormagen with the damage that was actually caused, we must have had a guardian angel. At the start of the war we were all terribly worried in Dormagen because of where we were situated. There were a number of industries, amongst them I.G. Farben and Bayer Leverkusen. The main B9 road went straight through Dormagen. Then there was the station, and railway lines, and the Rhine, and all the big cities like Cologne, Düsseldorf, and Neuss right close by us.

166

I remember one day at the end of July 1942, there were air-attacks on Düsseldorf and Neuss and finally they came over Dormagen. A big blast bomb and several hundred incendiaries were dropped over the Bayer factory. But the worst damage was done to a sugar factory, a brewery, and a housing area close by Bayer's. There were 13 dead, many injured, and the survivors were left standing in front of the wreckage of their homes.

There were often bombing raids, but mostly the bombs fell in the wooded areas and on a mock airfield that had been constructed on heathland and farmland. But the mock airfield didn't work for long. The Allies soon got wise to it. We felt most afraid when the big towns around were getting it, especially at night when the 'Christmas trees' (marker flares) hung in the sky and Dormagen itself was lit up by them. When we were sitting down in the cellar we could feel the earth trembling through our feet.

Our house was not completely spared by the bombs. We lived in a neighbouring street to the B9. There were just gardens to the front and back of us, and only a very few houses. It was 25 November 1944, and my mother and I were busy doing the Saturday cleaning. Suddenly two doors flew at us, together with broken glass, dust and rubble. Without thinking what I was doing, I dashed for the hall, climbed over the front door and found myself outside. A great yellow cloud of dust was hanging in the air. When I calmed down I noticed that both my hands were bleeding. My brother, who was home from the army at the time because of a head wound, made a joke of it, saying that now I, too, was entitled to the medal for the wounded.

The odd thing about the damage – something I don't understand to this day – was that all the cupboard doors were shut, but, when we opened them, dust and splinters of glass poured out. Then I went up to the attic. My husband was away in Norway at that time and I had hung up his suits there to air. You could see the whole sky through the rafters, but the suits were all there hanging in perfect order.

The damage did have its good side. My husband, my younger brother, and another relative all got compassionate leave from the Front. My younger brother returned to the fighting at the beginning of January 1945, and he was killed in action on 23 February. He was only 18½ years old.

In my mind's eye, I can still see clearly my route to work. I had to travel 10 kilometres every day by bike. In the last years of the war it was 'bomb alley'. For most of the way it was fields and heathland. They had dug ditches on either side as protection against bombs and shrapnel. Often we were strafed without warning by single aircraft or by groups of them. The drill then was always to jump off your bike and down into the ditch. I didn't need gym lessons in those days, I was as thin as a lath and could fit into the smallest hole. But woe betide you when it was night and raining. Once you had been jumping in and out of ditches, you could forget about being neat and tidy. But that was neither here nor there to us in those days.

I remember an incident that happened at work. Often I had to go across the factory yard. One day one of the works' foremen was there with a Soviet prisoner of war. He said jokingly that I should get the prisoner to give me a 'blessing'. I was so indignant about his tactlessness that I didn't say a word. The prisoner, probably a Muslim, had already raised his arms and was uttering words I couldn't understand. The foreman was laughing and sneering so nastily that it quite frightened me. I looked at the prisoner and saw his drawn face and sad eyes but could do nothing to help him. As I walked away I felt as if Christ had looked at me from the cross. A short time after that the same foreman was found drowned in the Rhine. I can still see that scene before me to this day.

There was also another event that upset me. My boss, Herr Wegelin, had a brother who was an army officer. He had once been in a heated discussion with fellow officers about an article by Joseph Goebbels. Herr Wegelin's brother had disagreed with the article, which was all about the inferiority of the Russian people, and had said that Germans and Russians were all the same. One of his comrades had reported him for the remark. He was stripped of his uniform, was sent back home and had to report daily to the army command post in Cologne. That was early in 1944. On 20 July 1944, my boss's brother was standing by me when the phone went. He took the call himself, then just said thanks to the caller and replaced the receiver. Then he said to me, 'Someone's tried to assassinate Hitler.' I was shocked when I saw his face, because he had gone as white as a sheet. He left the factory immediately and a few days later my boss told me that his brother was in Moabit Prison in Berlin. His trial came up in August 1944 and he was sentenced to five years. There was an appeal and this time he was sentenced to death by hanging. His mother put in a plea for clemency and he was sent to a suicide company on the Eastern Front. That was his good fortune. In all the chaos and confusion he managed to escape alive.

I once heard Cardinal von Galen, the so-called Lion of Münster, preach. In May 1943 we made a pilgrimage to Kevelaer and we had the good fortune to hear one of his sermons on 'The Killing of the Mentally Ill in our Mental Hospitals'. There was a lot of commotion in the church during his sermon, with boos and whistling. He stood like a giant in the pulpit and raised his hands in peace, and they all fell quiet again. A few weeks later, we got this sermon in printed form. Some of us girls took copies and handed them around. We were certainly a bit frightened. People had been speaking about these events for some time, but never openly. We were appalled at what the sermon disclosed, but at the same time full of admiration for this priest's courage and frankness.

The war finished for us in Dormagen on 6 March 1945. We were all sleeping peacefully in our beds when Dad came rushing in in his night-shirt, at six o'clock in the morning, shouting, 'For God's sake, the Amis [Yanks] are here! Get down to the cellar!'

I first took a quick look out of the window to see what was happening. What I saw was a shabby young German soldier beneath, armed only with a spade. He asked me about the ferry, saying he had to get across the Rhine. Mum had made a white flag and hung it up outside. My brother took it down again. Being seriously wounded had made him very depressed and he was worried that it might get him into trouble. Outside there was an ominous silence.

From the next day on we were allowed to leave our houses only between nine and eleven o'clock in the morning. Then there were people milling about on the streets. Outside a burnt-out German tank, two dead German soldiers lay on the pavement. We weren't allowed to move them. A bazooka leant against the wall of a house. Gum-chewing American soldiers were everywhere. They looked a bit slovenly to our eyes, with their helmets askew and their guns stuck under their arms. Once or twice they made as if to kick us. But in general they were decent people. A few months later the English troops took over. You would hardly have noticed the British soldiers in Dormagen.

But the war had not quite finished for us, after all. On 6 March 1945 we came in for shelling again from the other side of the Rhine. This time it was our own German troops shooting at us! In the towns and villages close by the Rhine, like Dormagen, many people were killed and there was a lot of damage. The shelling did most damage to St Michael's Church. The church tower was badly damaged and several good stained-glass windows were destroyed. My brother and I were nearly caught in the shellfire. We were standing outside our house when one flew over our heads and landed in the garden. A lovely plum tree took the brunt of it.

Now we were free to listen to the English radio broadcasts. Up till then it had been a crime carrying the death penalty. My boss, who spoke good English and had studied in England, used to listen to the BBC. As a result we were always kept well informed. His favourite phrase was, 'Churchill knows how to lead a people – Hitler can only lead a war.'

ROSALIND SMITH, of Barnard Castle, County Durham, discovered that evacuation to the countryside was not always the rural idyll that parents hoped for their children. Her story begins as she sees her husband off at Sunderland station, the day before war was declared. He had had less than a day's notice to leave:

'Their lovely clothes were in rags'

When that long train disappeared into that tunnel I felt the end of the world had come. Going up the steps to get to ground level, I fainted and was taken into the ticket collector's office. I can't remember getting home. The children were still asleep and my neighbour, who had been looking after them, made me a cup of tea. I went to bed, but not to sleep. The following morning war was declared, and, two minutes after the announcement on the wireless, the sirens went. We lived in a semi-basement flat and the tenants of the three flats above us came rushing downstairs for shelter. There we were, myself, three boys, four women, and three men, all standing in my passage when there was a loud wail outside. We all thought it was the all-clear, so the men told me to go outside to investigate. I went out to see, but there wasn't a soul in sight, except an air-raid warden who swore at me and said, 'Do you want to get killed?'

On the Monday morning I was sent for with other mothers and was informed that the children were being evacuated to the country for their safety and I could go as well. I said that my two eldest boys could go, but I was staying at home with my three-year-old. I packed all their best clothes in bags to be slung round their shoulders and, when they were ready to leave at six o'clock in the morning, my eldest son, who was twelve, said to me, 'I promised Dad I'd take care of you. How can I, when you're sending me away?' I ran back into the house and burst into tears.

Very soon after that I had word that I, too, with my little boy, had to be evacuated. We were told to take one suitcase with us and to lock up anything of value as the authorities might need to requisition the flats we were living in for billets. The lady who lived in the top flat, and had a little boy of three and a baby of three months, was stone deaf, but she could lip-read me, so I promised her husband I would take care of her during the evacuation. We were to be evacuated at five o'clock in the morning. The station, just outside Sunderland, was crowded with mothers and children. My heart sank as I stood there. All I knew of the rest of my family was that my husband was somewhere down south and my two boys were somewhere on the Yorkshire wolds. We didn't arrive at our destination until late that night. We were all tired and by that time all the children were crying – grown-ups too.

We were taken into a village hall, where we were seated around the walls. There was a parson, four women, and the schoolmaster from our children's school at Roker, in Sunderland. At the end of the room were a few villagers. I asked if Mrs Nelson, my neighbour, and her children, could come with me, wherever I was sent, as I'd promised her husband to take care of her because she was so deaf.

The parson then said, 'They can go down to the Castle.'

I informed Mrs Nelson that we were either going to a castle, or to a hotel, or a pub called that.

Before we got into an estate car, I gave the chauffeur a card to post to my husband, as it was our 14th wedding anniversary. (He got it too, although a bit late.) After a long drive we came to a real castle. I learned from the driver it was Sledmere Castle. We went through a courtyard and into a long kitchen, where sitting around a massive table were several farm workers and a woman. Everyone just gaped at us. We were sat on forms along the wall and were eventually taken through an iron-studded door and up a spiral staircase and through another iron-studded door into a round room with arrow slits for windows, and wire netting over them. I realized we were in a turret room. There was no plaster on the walls, just bare stone. There was one three-quarter sized iron bedstead, with a straw mattress on it and two coarse dark blankets, a bare wooden floor, and one kitchen chair. I'll remember it for the rest of my days.

Mrs Nelson sat on the chair, breastfed and changed her baby, then burst out crying. I was too furious to cry. So I arranged that she and her baby and the two little boys would lie on the bed crossways, and I would sit on the chair. They went to sleep right away as they were all exhausted. Then, all of a sudden, a man burst in. I asked what he wanted and he said, 'Don't you go shining any lights up here as the aerodrome is close by and the Germans will come.'

In a few choice words I told him where to go and I put the chair, with me on it, up against the door after he left.

When it got light I made my way downstairs. In the kitchen was the woman, and the men from the previous night, having breakfast. I asked for hot water for the children and they charged me sixpence for it.

When Mrs Nelson came down I told her to wash the children and stay put, as I was going to the village to find out if we could go home.

LEFT: 'Waiting for Daddy to come home.' Dorothy Griffiths and her son Stephen in 1945.

RIGHT: 'Home on leave'. Dorothy Griffiths, her husband Griff, and Stephen, in 1943.

BELOW: Dorothy Griffiths (with hands clasped in centre of picture) receiving condolences from the King and Queen during the Remembrance Ceremony in London on 23 February 1940, for those killed in the Battle of the River Plate.

ABOVE: *Elizabeth Smith (formerly Craig) taken at the end of the war which destroyed her home, killed her husband and sister-in-law, and badly injured her young son and herself.*

ABOVE LEFT: *Elizabeth Smith's husband James Craig, who was killed when their home was destroyed by a bomb during an air-raid on Sunderland on 16 May 1943.*

LEFT: *Elizabeth and her son Jim in 1945.*

RIGHT AND INSET: *Elsie Lee and her husband during the war.*

BELOW: *Marjorie and John Townsend at the outbreak of war.*

BELOW RIGHT: *The photograph of Marjorie Townsend's baby son Colin sent by the Red Cross to her husband John in Changi prisoner of war camp, Singapore.*

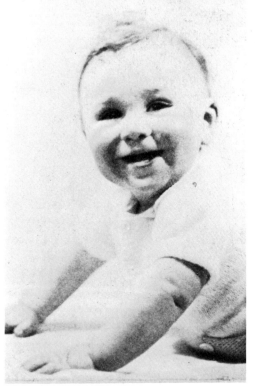

FAR LEFT: *Rosalind Smith.*

LEFT: *Harry Smith.*

RIGHT: *Mary Clayton and her son Bobby, 'waiting for news', January 1940.*

ABOVE: *Sammy Clayton, taken before leaving for France.*

LEFT: *Bobby Clayton, taken when his father was missing, believed dead.*

BELOW: *'The wives who waited.' Photograph taken in 1941, with Mary and Bobby Clayton third from right at bottom of picture.*

LEFT AND INSET: *Molly Smith and her husband, in uniform.*

BELOW LEFT: *Edna Hughes and a family friend.*

BELOW: *Margaret Holland and her husband George, on the steps of their Farnborough home, just before the war.*

LEFT: *Elizabeth Buxton and her late husband Wilson Boyce, taken at the Tower Ballroom, Birmingham, at the beginning of the war. They won the waltz competition that night. He was killed shortly afterwards and posthumously decorated for his bravery.*

BELOW: *Kay Crockett, in 1941, in her National Fire Service uniform.*

ABOVE: *Rene Smith and her family at the end of the war.*

RIGHT: *Eve Poore and her baby David in 1941.*

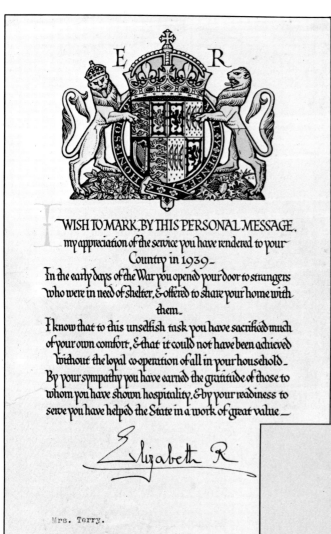

I WISH TO MARK, BY THIS PERSONAL MESSAGE, my appreciation of the service you have rendered to your Country in 1939.

In the early days of the War you opened your door to strangers who were in need of shelter, & offered to share your home with them.

I know that to this unselfish task you have sacrificed much of your own comfort, & that it could not have been achieved without the loyal co-operation of all in your household.

By your sympathy you have earned the gratitude of those to whom you have shown hospitality, & by your readiness to serve you have helped the State in a work of great value.

Elizabeth R

Mrs. Terry.

LEFT: *The certificate presented to Mabel Terry and the thousands of other women who opened their doors to evacuees during the war.*

BELOW: *The telegram of condolence received by Mabel Terry from the King and Queen on the death of her husband.*

BELOW LEFT: *Mabel Terry pictured in June 1943 with her husband Bob and sons Colin and Malcolm. This was to prove Bob's last leave with his family for he was killed a few weeks later.*

BUCKINGHAM PALACE

The Queen and I offer you our heartfelt sympathy in your great sorrow.

We pray that your country's gratitude for a life so nobly given in its service may bring you some measure of consolation.

George R.I

Mrs. R. Terry.

It was pouring with rain and I hadn't a clue where I was. Outside the courtyard was a high wall with a door in it. I opened the door and fell straight into a pile of cow manure. I had on a brand new, stone-coloured trenchcoat – my pride and joy – and I had it laid out on the grass trying to clean it, when a postman came up to me. He said, 'Are you new here?'

I told him where we had come from and he told me that people from Hull had been evacuated there but had only stayed for two days. I asked him the way to the village and who was the big noise over there. He told me to go to Sledmere Hall and ask for Sir Richard Sykes, and told me how to get there. He told me to go through the fields. It was heavy going. I was so hungry, and tired too, for I'd had no sleep. I got to the village of Sledmere and found my way to the back entrance of the Hall. I was passing the gardeners' cottages when I fainted. When I regained consciousness I was lying on a sofa in front of a fire. After I had showed the couple who lived there my identity card and told them everything, the lady cooked me some breakfast of bacon and eggs and made me a lovely cup of tea. Her husband was the head gardener. They succeeded in getting us out of the Castle and no one was ever sent there again. They allowed us to have an empty gardener's cottage instead.

I still hadn't found out where my other two boys were and no one seemed to know anything at all about them. I was so worried. I managed to get some work, helping out in the local post office. The son of the postmistress was a master at Pocklington Grammar School and eventually managed to discover where my sons were. They were in a small village several miles away and he arranged to take me there to see them. We were directed to a small general store. Yes, they were there, we were told, but they were doing their chores. When they eventually came in, I was horrified. Their lovely clothes were in rags – no buttons on their shirts, holes in their socks, and a lot of horrible scabs on their faces and knees. It was impetigo.

When we were alone, they told me they had to get up at six o'clock in the morning to deliver milk before going to school and after school had to clean out the pigs. I was broken-hearted when I came away and wrote and told my husband. He managed to get a 48-hour pass and succeeded in making his way up to Sledmere. Carl, the schoolmaster, met him and brought him to the cottage. What a joy to see him again!

We managed to rescue our boys from the family they were living with and eventually, along with Mrs Nelson and her family and four other Sunderland women and their children, we made arrangements to return home. We had to wait for hours at York station as every train that came in heading for Sunderland was full of troops. As the overcrowded trains pulled out, each one leaving us behind, they played Vera Lynn singing 'We'll meet again' over the loud-speakers. It was the same song they had played when I saw my hus-band off after his short leave. I was at my lowest ebb, especially with the children crying beside me.

We did not get back to Roker till late evening and arrived in the middle of a heavy air-raid. We were absolutely terrified as we dodged from doorway to doorway for shelter. At last we reached the sea front where our flat was. When I opened the door, the carpet was six inches deep in a mould that waved in the draught. Everything was damp. The boys and I put a waterproof sheet across the double bed and, all together, fell into an exhausted sleep.

Once back in Roker, it seemed that every day and night we were being bombed. We had lino and boards up at our windows as they were all broken. The front door was boarded up as it was made of glass and was also broken. The ceiling was down in our boys' bed-room and the water was dripping from a burst pipe in the flat above. We had to put the boys' bed in the living-room and the youngest one's bed in our bedroom.

One night, in the middle of winter, two sea mines were washed up on the rocks in front of our house. There wasn't a whole window on the sea front. It was windy and snowing and my husband, who was home on sick leave, had once again to nail linoleum over the broken windows, but no sooner had he got one lot up before it was blown off again. The soot came down all the chimneys and went everywhere, even spoiling all our rations.

I had to have a tonsil operation in the middle of it all and my nerves were getting so bad that my husband suggested we moved to the country, to the small town of Barnard Castle. We did – and it was so peaceful after all the bombing in Sunderland.

There were German and Italian prisoners of war in Barnard Castle and we invited some German officers home for Christmas. We also got to know a young Polish soldier, from Lodz, whose family had all perished in Ravensbrück concentration camp. When he knew I was going to have another baby, he asked, if it was a boy, would I call him Maurice after him as he hadn't any family left of his own. So I have a younger son called Maurice who is in Australia now. The Polish boy went to Germany to be an interpreter at the Nuremberg war trials. He sent his namesake some clothes and shoes, but, sadly, we eventually lost touch. The German prisoners of war we entertained have been back to see us, but we are all getting older now. My husband and I are both in our eighties now and have been married for over 60 years, but the war years still remain as vivid in our memories as if they were only yesterday.

MARIANNE SCHMUTZ, from Mannheim, Baden-Württemberg, was a qualified draughtswoman working in Mannheim at the start of the war. She married in 1940. Her husband was called up in 1942 and attached to a panzer unit as a non-commissioned officer in the Medical Corps. She served as a flak auxiliary after 1943 and later did technical drawing for the army, living in barracks and only managing visits home in her free time. Between March and June 1945 Marianne Schmutz kept a diary. She was aware that Germany's defeat was not far away and wanted to leave something behind for her husband, just in case anything happened to her. His name was never mentioned in the diary because of the problems that it might cause him with the political authorities:

'I finished burning all your letters today'

10 March 1945
Today, Saturday, I begin to keep a diary, so that perhaps at a later date we will see how things were and how they ended. Yesterday,

9 March, they told us for the first time that we might soon have to reckon with leaving our homes. American tanks have reached Koblenz . . . How much longer have we got? That's the question in everybody's minds. We're worried about where to go. There's the same suffering and misery everywhere, so why not stay here? But the air-raids are so bad now that we can't stick it out for much longer. Perhaps I'll go up to Mum's on my bike. But isn't that just out of the frying pan into the fire? The place is getting smaller and more and more crowded all the time.

Many have seen the light by now – but there are others who never will. Perhaps they just don't want to recognize the truth because they're just too frightened to! There are so many questions to be answered. But the people you can really discuss things with are getting fewer all the time. So you just have to come to terms with things on your own, which is pretty hard sometimes, when you don't want to just follow the herd.

It takes a war to show you how people can be fooled. People do whatever they are told: one day it's 'Hosanna', the next 'Crucify him'! Will there ever be a day when sensible people are giving the orders? There must surely come a time, though you'd hardly believe it at the moment.

Sunday, 11 March 1945
Rainy and miserable all day. Went over to see my in-laws at lunchtime. Old people are finding it pretty hard to cope. We talked about what to do if it comes to evacuation. They're definitely staying here. I offered them my flat. At least it's nearer to a bunker than where they are now, right in the middle of the gun positions.

I shall bury the cutlery, if I get the chance. I have packed my rucksack. Every item I packed has special memories and the most beloved items I must take with me. It's so hard saying goodbye to things. I'd like to take everything with me. So the first preparations have been made. The situation looks as though it's getting pretty grave.

15 March 1945
Spring has arrived! Over all the garden snowdrops and crocuses are

blooming, the shrubs beginning to grow green and come into bud. Clear blue sky again today. It is as if nature with all her beauty is trying to tell mankind something . . . Inge arrived here on Monday morning. We cooked and baked. The potato cakes are probably the last we'll manage to make because fat is getting more and more scarce.

In the afternoon we went for a walk in the spring sunshine. We found our first spring flowers. Now and again there were fighter bombers flying overhead. Have dismantled everything in our bedroom. How sad I felt. Just as though I was moving out for good. The whole flat is topsy-turvy.

We are going to bury the cutlery. But where? Have handed in my new address. Are they really going to let us go? Most of the girls who are coming with us will work on farms. They'll be living in a camp. It's not far from here, where we're going. If things get bad and the Front moves closer, we'll have to move on again. The cinemas are all closing. A lot of shops, too. The staff are being sent to work on the defences. Many mothers and children set off on the last special train yesterday bound for Allgäu in the south. They all left here with heavy hearts.

Yesterday I got your letter from Grafenwöhr, posted on 27 February. I am always so happy to read that you are still there. You know how worried I get when you are about to go into action. Also news from my little brother in Prenzlau. He's ended up with the flak, working in signals. He was a wireless officer on planes before. He writes to say that that's all finished now. Most flyers are being transferred to the infantry.

16 March 1945

The American offensive has started the whole length of the Western Front. That means the Front is getting closer and closer to us in Mannheim. Fighter bombers are increasing their activity. Precautionary measures are still in force. Worked all day in the garden yesterday sowing yellow turnips. Will we ever harvest them ourselves?

Full alert this evening. They're imposing a curfew. I dashed home, got out your letters – and started to burn them. There are so many, I can't manage them all at once. I was so upset, having to destroy them. I couldn't bear to read them, or I would have just wanted to save them. In spite of all the hardships, one feels more and more that the end is not far away.

17 March 1945
Got your letters of 23 February and 3 March yesterday. And a photo of you. You in full battle dress! What a long time the post takes! And today I got a love letter from you. You're so worried about me and think I'm no longer here. I'll explain the mix-up in my next letter.

We were packing all day today. What a mess everything is in here at home. I'm clearing things up in the house and carrying everything down to the cellar. It lets you see just how much we have in the house and how things accumulate. The hardest things to leave are my books. So I packed a couple of the Insel books and the pretty one with the children playing that you gave me one birthday. Unfortunately I just had to leave all the rest. Will we find anything left, if ever we manage to return?

Things are really getting tense here. When will we be leaving? The British advance tank units have already reached Münster and Alzey.

I would just as soon stay here, if only for the sake of the flat. Also, you did write that I should just stay where I am. But if you were in my place, you'd do the same as I'm doing.

I finished burning all your letters today. I was so upset. I put a few lovely cards away on one side. Perhaps I can still manage to save them . . .

22 March 1945
I am now in Hochhausen! That says it all. It all started on Sunday [18 March 1945]. From midday no one was allowed to leave the school. We had to pack. All night long there were lorries and people on the streets. No one could sleep. Alerts as ever. Planes flying over-head the whole night. On Sunday evening they let those of our colleagues living on the left bank of the Rhine go home. The tension is growing from hour to hour.

On Monday [19 March 1945] there were alerts all day long. In the evening they let some of the girls leave. I was a bag of nerves. I just couldn't take another air-raid.

In-laws have also decided to leave, but they're not going far, so that they can come back again after the first attack. They have taken their radio and hair-dryer with them, together with an iron, cooker and clothes. I have also packed some of your clothes, including suits and shoes. I do hope Dad arrives all right.

On Monday I went to our captain and asked permission to leave that evening. He said the time hadn't come yet. He couldn't send everyone away, so I should just be patient. More of the girls left in the evening with their luggage. We're all getting more and more anxious. When there was an air-raid warning in the evening, I went with one of my female colleagues to sleep in the cellar. It was full of refugees and other people who had come to seek protection in our shelter. They were kicking up such a din and the benches were so hard and narrow that I just went back upstairs to my own bed.

On the night of the 20th, at three o'clock, one of the girls came up with news. The first tanks had arrived at Grünstadt. It can only be a matter of hours before they reach us here. Between half past five and six o'clock in the morning, there was an almighty explosion. We thought our building was about to collapse. Then we heard they had blown up the bridge over the Rhine at Worms.

Just then our captain arrived and told us to get ready immediately, we were to leave at once. It didn't take long, as I had gone to bed fully clothed. A quick gulp of coffee and a roll was all there was time for.

We were issued with provisions for three days' march, but I never got the chance to eat any of it, as it all got left behind in the confusion.

We girls were taken by truck to Heidelberg. Saw the first fighter bombers at Ladenburg. Things were hotting up. The first attack came at the station in Heidelberg. I loaded up my luggage on to a bike and was off. The station area was too dangerous. I didn't dare ride, because the bags were too heavy. There was no cover at all between Heidelberg and Neckargemünd and I got really scared. There's nothing for it but to keep on going, I told myself.

Once at Neckargemünd I tried riding. It wasn't too bad. But the dynamo kept rubbing on the wheel. A shipworker tied it back with a piece of wire. What a relief!

I kept having to dive for cover. The rucksack was hurting my back so much, I thought I'd have to abandon it. I took it off, whenever I had to push.

I reached Neckarhausen, seeing signs of attacks all along the road. Railway engines lying on their sides, burnt out goods wagons, shoes lying all singed and holed, pieces of bloodstained clothing. It was terrible to see. All along the road there were whole processions of people. Old and young, with little children, some pushing prams, others with all their possessions loaded on to carts and bikes. Soldiers looking for their unit, and the wounded who had been released from the hospitals. These are scenes that I shall never forget.

Marianne Schmutz eventually reached her destination of Hochhausen and remained there until the middle of April 1945. During this time she witnessed, and recorded, the occupation of the area by the American army and air force. On 15 April she left with her bike and bags and set off into the unknown. She found refuge working on a farm for a while, before finally undertaking the trek back to her home in Mannheim. Though broken into and ransacked, her flat was habitable and she set about turning it back into a home for herself and her husband, of whom she had in the meantime heard nothing. He did return, unexpectedly, in mid-June 1945, having been released from prison camp by the Americans. Marianne Schmutz still lives in Mannheim, as does her son, who was born just after the war. Her husband died in 1982.

MRS H. CAMPBELL, of Liverpool, Merseyside, recalls a tragic story of the Liverpool blitz told by her father-in-law:

'They were both still under 21'

My father-in-law was a verger of a Liverpool church and in 1941 a young couple, in their teens, came to the church to see if they could put the wedding banns up for them. My father-in-law told them that they would have to get permission from their respective parents before they could be married, as they were both still under 21.

The young girl, Anne, was pregnant and her parents gave their permission, but Peter's parents refused. My mother-in-law grew quite attached to the young couple and went along to Peter's parents to try to persuade them to change their minds. They were quite abusive to her and were adamant about the whole thing – they would not give in.

One Sunday evening a few weeks later, Anne and Peter arranged to meet in an ice-cream parlour to have a chat over a cup of tea. He kept telling her that night how much he loved her. They then parted and Anne went home. Next morning she got a terrible shock. She found out that Peter had thrown himself under a train just after he left her.

Eventually the time came for the baby to be born. Anne knew she would have a part of Peter in the baby and if it was a boy had decided to call it after his Dad. She went into Mill Road Hospital to have her baby and she got her wish – it was a little boy. A couple of days later the hospital was bombed. Both Anne and her baby were killed. Whenever I think of the war I remember that poor, tragic, young couple.

MRS G. RUSSELL, of Fleet, Hampshire, worked at M.K. Electric in Edmonton, north London, throughout the war years doing vital work on Air Ministry contracts. The office staff, of which she was one, worked from a hut with the windows constantly boarded up, from which they had to evacuate almost daily to race to the shelter in the face of yet another air-raid. Her husband having been called up, she lived in a flat just round the corner from her parents:

'It's left to women to pick up the pieces'

I can remember going along with my mother to the local butcher because we had been told he was going to have some sausages in that afternoon. We were half way there when suddenly old Moaning Minnie, the siren, went and we could see the doodle-bugs going over our heads. We dived into the nearest garden and hid ourselves under a thick hedge – and we weren't alone! One minute the street had been crowded with folk, the next there wasn't a soul to be seen. We had all learnt to become very agile. That bomb demolished our very popular local cinema. After about 10 minutes the street was full of people once more, going about their business, but looking a bit grey, and not quite so cheerful.

One night we were down in my mother's shelter when the four houses opposite us were demolished by a bomb, and quite a few others badly damaged. We lost a lot of dear friends and neighbours of long standing during that incident. It was a really terrible experience, but we all went off to work the next day. I think we were all a bit like zombies. It really doesn't hit you till later.

My sister lost her dear husband in the Anzio beach-head onslaught. It was certainly a grim time to live through.

One weekend Mum put on a small 'do' and we had quite a houseful. All the services were represented. She put a mattress down on the floor for the lads to sleep on. It was all a few hours' good fun. The sad thing was that the sergeant air gunner who was there was killed the following Saturday, and a sister of the navy fellow was killed by a bomb a week or so later.

Most folks went down to the big shelters in the local parks. You could see them every night, complete with their hot-water bottles and blankets. It was quite a ritual. I never did, neither did any of my family. We just didn't fancy it.

My dear father worked very long hours at the J.A.P. Motor Works in Tottenham, north London, and all my family did their bit under very difficult conditions, but my most fragrant bouquet must go to my darling mother, and those like her, who put their shoulder to the wheel, just when they thought they had come to a time of life when they could begin to take things a bit easier. What would we have done without them? Men make wars, men fight wars, but it's left to women, all over the world, to pick up the pieces.

ILSE HERRGUTH, of Solingen, North Rhine-Westphalia, was only 18 years old when in November 1944 she was transferred by the German Labour Service to work in a maternity hospital in Friedeberg, East Prussia. When the Red Army broke through in January 1945 she escaped by the skin of her teeth. A troop-train heading west saw the column of girls crossing the snow-covered fields and made an unscheduled stop to take them aboard. Her next posting was to Naumburg an der Saale, where she worked in the army munitions depot. The futility of the war now became more than ever apparent to her: the Allied forces were closing in from east and west, and she was issuing arms to old men and young boys. Well aware of the dire penalty for deserting her post, she decided to escape back to Berlin, where her parents were now enduring the heaviest bombardments of the war:

'All alone in the world except for my suitcase'

No one knew for sure *how* the war would end. But one thing was certain: it *was* coming to an end, and Germany was losing. Only one thing mattered at a time like that, and that was to be with your family. I was homesick. I was just turned 18 years old. I began to make preparations. There were three other girls who thought the same way as I did and wanted to go back to their families in north Germany. (I was the only Berliner.) The 1st of April 1945 was Easter Sunday and we met to decide on an escape plan. On Easter Monday we went out for a stroll and fell into conversation with two soldiers who, in their broken-down old truck, were on a company commission delivering barrels and leather goods to Stendal, north of Magdeburg. We asked them to take us with them. We had to use all our charms before they finally agreed. We knew perfectly well the risk we were running, but our minds were made up.

It was no easy matter packing up our things in front of all the other girls. We couldn't afford to let them know anything about our plans. Sneaking past the guards was difficult, too, but we made it and in the pouring rain reached the pick-up point, well away from the depot. We crouched down behind a cemetery wall and waited for the truck to arrive. We heard the alarm bell ringing at the depot and knew that someone must have noticed we were missing and given the game away. But then the truck drew up, and we were off.

We drove on till late at night in the direction of Magdeburg, in constant fear of roadside checkpoints. On the outskirts of the city we stopped at a village inn, where straw and blankets had been put down for refugees and soldiers. But we didn't get much sleep that night. Soon the dark night sky was lit up with flashes and we heard the dull rumble of bombs and guns. We knew what it was well enough: a night-raid on the city. The whole sky over Magdeburg was on fire, the city a blazing inferno. Afterwards we found out that it was the last and worst raid that Magdeburg ever experienced. Our horror was mixed with a sense of relief; if our soldier friends hadn't insisted on stopping off at the inn, we might have ended up in that storm of fire.

The next morning we set off again, skirting round the town, as we couldn't enter it, and were diverted in a westerly direction. At the north and eastern intersections of the autobahn, we had to make a decision which way we wanted to go. I was determined to go east, to get back home to Berlin. My three comrades wanted to carry on northwards with the truck. There was no time for goodbyes, the truck was off again immediately. As it left, a Jeep drew up, and an officer asked me if I wanted a lift. He was only going as far as Burg, but I got in and thought at least that was a step nearer Berlin.

On reaching Burg I had to get out of the Jeep and stood there by the edge of the autobahn, all alone in the world except for my suitcase. I was still miles from Berlin. To the right and left stretched the huge fields of the Magdeburg Plain. Several times I waved to passing cars, but none of them stopped. I started walking, feeling pretty low in spirits. Another car passed. I carried on. Suddenly the car that had passed came hurtling backwards and screeched to a halt beside me. I was pulled in, and it set off again at breakneck speed. When I had time to collect myself, I found myself sitting on squeaky tan-leather upholstery in a Mercedes Four-Seater. A Waffen SS soldier was at the wheel. In the passenger seat was another SS man who held a machine-pistol at the ready and kept glancing to either side and skywards. Beside me was seated an SS general!

He poured me hot coffee (real coffee!), gave me a ham sandwich, and formally introduced himself. Then he asked me to tell him exactly where I was from and where I was going. What was I to do? I decided to make a full confession. He listened and then said he thought I had done the right thing. He told me he was from the Western Front and was heading for Berlin Halensee. I couldn't have been more lucky.

We passed through Potsdam and then reached the Berlin city boundary. Since our family home was on the Potsdam Chaussee, the general had the car stop right outside our front door. I might have been a society lady, the way he took his leave of me. His last words were, 'If ever you are in need of help, please come to me.' I thought to myself, there may soon come a time when you're the one in need of help!

Ilse Herrguth may have reached home, but she was far from safe. In late April the Soviet pincers closed and the siege of Berlin began. The Herrguth's house, on the outskirts of the city, was in the front line of the fighting. She survived that terrible time, however, as did her mother and father, though not without undergoing terrible experiences at the hands of the victorious troops. Ilse Herrguth now lives in Solingen.

MARGARET WADE, of Ashford, Kent, found that bringing up three children alone in the countryside wasn't quite the rural idyll she had imagined it might be when she left bomb-stricken London:

'Never come between a Home Guard and a well-earned pint'

I arrived in Smeeth, near Ashford in Kent, from South Ealing, London, with my two small sons, on 22 May 1940. I didn't want to go to Wales with the other evacuees from South Ealing. I found it lovely countryside here, but very backward; no gas, no electricity, no running water in the cottages. So different from East Lothian, in Scotland, where I came from originally. There every farm cottage had electricity, running water and a bath.

Except for 'dog fights' over the Channel, we were quiet until September, then planes seemed to fill the sky. It made it not very pleasant to go out walking.

One Sunday I noticed three men slinking through the orchard in front of my cottage and pondered over the clothes they were wearing. Word had it later that three Jerries went into the pub at Sellindge and tried to give themselves up to the Home Guard who were in there quenching their thirst after the church parade. However, these worthies would have none of it and sent them on to the next pub at Newingreen, to give themselves up there. (Never come between a Home Guard and a well-earned pint!)

Although soldiers were billeted in all the big houses round about (Lord Brabourne's estates), the war seemed to pass me by until I was having an operation in Ashford Hospital in November 1942, when over came the bombers and bombed the railway yards. Sister ran up the ward shouting, 'Get down, and put your pillow over your heads!'

They also bombed the railway works and the women who were injured in the raid were brought into our ward. They'd been caught in the blast. The young woman who was laid out next to me died within minutes. Yes, I was very sorry for her, but more worried about my two small sons left with a good neighbour.

Peculiar thing war. Sometimes it seems to go on and on, then you get a respite and quiet, like childbirth. You seem to put it out of your mind and just get on with living. Then suddenly you get a jolt. My little boys, Grahame and Donald, and I went to Ashford one day to visit the dentist. The siren went as we walked up the High Street, followed almost immediately by the overhead warning. We rushed into the nearest shelter and sat there till the all-clear went. Well, out we came to confusion, dust and ARP men. Down Harding Street we went, with rubble all over the place. 'Hurrah,' shouted Grahame, 'the dentist's been bombed!' Yes, the place was flattened. Funny how children don't seem to be impressed with destruction or loss of life – not at five and three years of age.

Once, too, when the Jerries were machine-gunning all around, I yelled at the boys to come indoors. 'Can't come in yet, our tatties aren't quite cooked in the campfire,' was the reply.

I never was really afraid of the bombs for myself, just worried when the boys were out of sight.

We didn't really find too many shortages in food. I had a very large garden which I cultivated. I kept rabbits and hens and I went out to work, cherry- and apple-picking in the orchards round about. I also went out doing housework. The boys came with me everywhere. They were good lads. They didn't like their Daddy. 'That man', they called him when he came home, hobbling on crutches.

One night our peace was shattered by a different sound: the flying bombs came to Kent. We watched these peculiar machines, never wavering off course, fire coming from their tails, making straight for London. Then the awful thought came to me – they were unmanned. The next day we had some news about these new bombs on our wireless set, and in a couple of days we were all given a Morrison shelter. The three old couples in our row just left them lying inside, but I managed to put mine together in the middle of our front room. The boys loved it. They played cowboys and Indians in it during the daytime, but at night they wouldn't sleep in it, so the peke and I slept in the shelter by ourselves.

By now our air force and the ack-ack were getting the better of the doodle-bugs and were shooting down many before they reached London. They landed all round Kent. Apple and cherry orchards made a good resting place for them and saved lives and destruction of property.

Our turn had to come and it did. One Sunday afternoon, while we were feeding the hens and rabbits and the ack-ack and fighters were screaming across the sky, a big-looking doodle-bug filled the air with noise. Then suddenly it cut out and there was silence – a deafening silence. 'Down!' I yelled at the boys and they did so – instantly. After the silence, there was the noise of houses crumbling. Looking down at our cottage, what looked like smoke was mounting skywards. We rushed down the garden, thankful to see no fire, just dustclouds. There was no back door, the windows had gone, and in fact, the whole backs of the four cottages in our row were a mass of rubble. When I managed to get inside, the place was a shambles. But what upset the boys most was to see our lovely peke lying in his basket covered with bits of linoleum off the floor. But he wasn't hurt and after dusting him off we went to help out our old neighbours.

After some time help arrived and in a few days the boys, the peke, and myself were safe at home in Haddington, in Scotland. We were greeted like heroes. One day in the Co-op, I was presented with a tin of Lyle's Golden Syrup by the manager and staff, and the boys were given oranges.

When the cottage was made habitable again we returned to Lily Vale.

Not much of a war experience – but there it is. Anyway, I was glad when it was all over. Mind, I don't remember being as frightened as I was in the First World War, when we lived on the Bridges in Edinburgh. I remember a 'Zep' coming up the Forth, heading for the Bridge. People round about were screaming and crying, so I cried, too. But I never cried in my own bit of the war, a generation later. I just got angry and very sad at the terrible waste of it all. I was sorry for the people who were killed and hurt, but, nastily, I was always pleased the bombs had not fallen on us. I suppose I'm a coward. Ah well . . .

CHARLOTTE RECK, of Jüterbog in the German Democratic Republic, met Edgar Lipmann in 1940 when she was on holiday in Hohndorf. She was then 24. He was a soldier in the German army and staying in the same village whilst on leave from France. They became engaged in 1942. Then came the news in January 1943 that Edgar's unit was being sent to the Eastern Front:

'I waited and waited'

While Edgar was an army interpreter in France, his letters were full of the beautiful countryside and all the historical and cultural places of interest he had been visiting. Not now. On the Eastern Front it was a question of sheer survival. Leave was being stopped, and weeks went by without news. Then, on 15 July 1943, he came back, completely unexpectedly. He had got three weeks leave. On 23 July 1943 the church-bells rang for our wedding. Mother was sad because it was a bit of a drab wedding, but we weren't bothered. We were happy! We put all thoughts of the war and the dangers of the Front behind us.

Reality returned all too quickly. At the end of November Edgar's unit was encircled at Kharkov. I lived in fear for weeks. How can you describe your feelings? We all knew so many women who had received those dreaded letters with the words 'For Führer, Volk and Fatherland . . .' But my Edgar was going to live. He didn't need to be a hero for my sake. All I wanted was for him to survive and come back to me. The official army reports on the radio spoke of 'straightening the Front' and 'successful strategic withdrawals'. But most people knew better and made sarcastic remarks, even though it was dangerous to do so. For me 'withdrawal' meant only one thing: he was on his way back! It's astonishing how you can still manage to hope and dream, even when the situation is really hopeless.

In May 1944 hopes began to rise again. The army situation seemed calmer, the withdrawals more orderly. The men were getting leave again. Edgar wrote: 'Try to understand if it's another two weeks before I can come back again. One of my comrades begged so hard to take my turn, because his wife's having her first baby. Just remember, only another two weeks to wait!'

I waited. I slept very lightly, thinking every noise could be him. If I went anywhere I would always leave a note to say when I would be back. I was determined to be there for that moment when, at long last, he would come back. He did not come. He would never come back.

The army reports spoke of heavy fighting on the Eastern Front. All leave was cancelled again. Letters from him arrived only intermittently, one of them telling me how he had gone down with jaundice. At home, meanwhile, all the talk was about evacuating the civilians.

My husband's last letter to me arrived in August 1944. His unit was withdrawing towards Kiev. By the end of September my letters to him started coming back, marked 'Await new address'. Rumours were beginning to circulate. Many people were now listening to Radio London and Radio Moscow and getting very different situation reports from the ones Greater German Radio was putting out. No one dared to speak openly about what was happening, but news was filtering through nevertheless. And that's how I heard that Edgar's unit had been encircled at Kiev and almost totally wiped out. Any survivors had been sent to the prison camps. There were dreadful reports about the Russian treatment of prisoners, but I just clung to the hope that he was a prisoner all the same. Just as long as he was alive. He was such a good, kind man. He hadn't wanted to be in the army. He'd never had any choice. Surely they wouldn't take it out on him? None of it was his fault! Just to stop myself going mad with anxiety I started to make my own enquiries. I wrote to his company HQ in Rudolstadt, only to get the reply, 'Personal files have become mislaid due to enemy action.'

On 20 January 1945 came the order to evacuate. I had to set out on the road. There followed 10 terrible days of travelling – but that's another story . . . I made my way to Saxony, to be with Edgar's parents. It seemed the only way he would ever find me again, if he came back. On 8 May 1945 Germany admitted defeat. But I wasn't going to admit defeat. I went on searching and hoping. I even wrote to

Colonel Marenko, who was in charge of the men Russia had taken prisoner. No answer.

But prisoners of war *were* coming home again, even those who had been given up for dead. Wasn't it natural to cling on to hope? Then something happened that made a very deep impression on me. A girl I knew, whose husband had been missing for years, like mine, decided to have him officially declared dead so that she could remarry. After all, she had waited five years for news. Three years later, her 'dead' husband turned up at the door and found her in a family that was no longer his. He committed suicide.

So I waited and waited until 1956. I never had any children of my own, although I was a teacher for many years. Now I am a widow for the second time.

MRS A. BOTTRILL, of Balham, London, knew the trauma, twice over, of giving birth during an air-raid, and here tells us of her abortive search for peace in the countryside, as the bombs continued to rain down on London, and how her husband was to discover that fire-watching could often prove as hazardous as life at the Front:

'My face came out in a rash'

In 1939 I was expecting my daughter and had just gone out shopping when an air-raid warning sounded. A woman asked me to come into her shelter in the garden, but I was only a few days away from my baby's birth and couldn't bend down, so I stayed above ground, all by myself in the house. When the all-clear went, the people came in from the shelter and said how brave I was.

When my other daughter was born, 14 months after that, I had to travel to Kingston Hospital and, just as we got there, there was another bomb scare. My daughter was born the next day. My hus-

191

band came to see us, but he could not be let in as a bomb had been dropped on the hospital and we were being moved around.

I had been home a couple of weeks when a land mine was found hanging on a wire nearby. We had to get out of our flat. My husband said we would go to my mother's house. I took a couple of blankets, the clock, put the children in the pram, and we stayed there until it was safe for us to return. That same week, the docks were on fire. My husband was a docker and he was on watch that night. Of course I worried about him. My face came out in a rash and I used to cry about it.

The government said that mothers with children could be evacuated, so my husband said, 'I'd go, if I were you.' He got the day off to see us off to Staffordshire. When we left, he went to the pictures and when he came out and got back to our house, our road had been bombed and our house was in a mess. If he had gone straight home after he left us, he would have been killed.

When we got to Staffordshire we were put in a hall, to find people who would let us stay in their home, for the time being. We had some food and drink, but, sad to say, my daughters and I were the only ones that no one seemed to want. A couple with a young daughter were told to take us and we went to their house. The room we were put in, the rain came in, and a couple of pails were left in the room to collect the rainwater.

After we were there a while, my elder daughter was put in a school. I had to take my younger daughter out of the house during the day because the woman's little daughter used to pinch and claw my little girl whenever she saw her. After a few weeks in Stafford, I asked my husband if it would be all right to come back. He said, 'Yes, we'll be all together.' So we came back and we all slept together on the floor, and if we had an explosion, or if my husband was fire-watching, we slept in the shelter at the top of the road.

One night my husband was fire-watching on a small wharf. As a light was showing, he had to climb up to cover it up, and he fell. He was knocked unconscious and the fall caused an abscess on his thigh. He waited about a week, then he called in at Bart's Hospital and the surgeon lanced it, but, sad to say, a piece of gauze was left in the wound. He was still limping so badly a year later that the doctor

192

examined him and found that the gauze had rotted in the wound and had rotted to the bone. My husband was on crutches for the rest of his life – until he passed away at the age of 77. He didn't go to war because, on the docks, he was safeguarding our food supplies, but he suffered from it to the end of his life.

***

MRS J. MARWOOD, of Thirsk, North Yorkshire, was in the unenviable position of living in close vicinity to three aerodromes, being only two miles from Topcliffe, which itself lay between Dishforth and Leeming air-fields. Her husband worked at Topcliffe Aerodrome, but was transferred away when war broke out, leaving her alone with the children. This little episode is typical of the ad hoc measures mothers were often forced to adopt to save their children from the bombs:

'I put the children in a cupboard'

One night, in particular, the siren went and I put the children in a cupboard near the fireplace, then I put a square table in front of it, and got under it myself. A bomb screamed overhead and I thought it was going to hit our house, but in fact it demolished a bungalow just at the back of us. They had dropped one close by us, in Thirsk, just previously, killing one woman. After dropping the one at the foot of our garden, they turned and dropped another which dropped on Thirsk racecourse, but luckily no one was killed, although quite a lot of damage was done.

Mrs Marwood, a mother of six, is now a widow and still lives in the vicinity of Thirsk.

MARIA JÄGER, of Hamburg, was a schoolteacher working and living in Hamburg in 1943. Her first baby was due in September of that year. In the July her eye caught a small newspaper insert which to her seemed very ominous. Luckily she acted on it just in time. On 24 July 1943 the terrible series of air-raids on Hamburg began with the arrival of nearly 800 British bombers over the city. Why did she react to the warning, when so many others didn't? Why was the article not given maximum prominence? Maria Jäger's story suggests that the German military and civic authorities were certainly well aware of the impending raids:

'You only dreamed it'

We always read the *Hamburg Anzeiger* at home and on 13 July 1943 a strange little notice caught my eye. It was on page three, in the middle of some unimportant article or other. It was only the fact it was in heavier print that drew my attention to it. There was one sentence which seemed to be speaking directly to me: 'All those not involved in the war effort, and in particular women and children, should arrange to be evacuated to relatives outside the city.'

I immediately explained to my in-laws, with whom I was then living, that I wanted to leave Hamburg. They did their best to persuade me to stay, arguing that the provision of air-raid shelters in Hamburg was much safer than anything in the country. I would not be dissuaded. I packed a few things and the following day I travelled to my own parents' house which was about 50 kilometres south of Hamburg.

My sudden arrival took them by surprise, particularly as I could give them no rational explanation for being there. The week following my arrival from Hamburg was very quiet and on Sunday 23 July 1943, I decided to return to Hamburg. During the night of the 23rd, I was woken by my father. From our house we could see Hamburg burning. The whole sky over the city was red with fire. Overhead we could hear the continuous drone of countless bomber squadrons. I thought to myself, so that's what the newspaper article was trying to say.

The sky was still so dark with smoke at ten o'clock the next morning that you could only guess where the sun was. A few days later my parents-in-law arrived at our door. They had been wandering around completely dazed ever since the raid. Their eyebrows were singed from the heat of the fire-storm and they were clutching a little packet of paper-hankies. It was all they had managed to rescue. It was obvious that as a mother-to-be in the late stages of pregnancy I would never have survived.

For a long time afterwards I wondered what it was that had made me react to the newspaper notice the way I did. I spoke to others who had escaped the bombs and tried to find other people who had been warned as I was. But they only shook their heads in disbelief. The usual answer I got was, 'You were expecting. In that state you're more prone to dreams and hallucinations. There wasn't any newspaper article. You only dreamed it.'

Maria Jäger had not been imagining things. She was so convinced that, after the war, she set about searching for the article, and found it. The text of the disputed article read:

What is 'Family Aid'?

This scheme enables people in high-risk bombing areas to go and stay with relatives in safer areas.

All Hamburg civilians not involved in the war effort, and in particular women and children, should arrange to be evacuated to relatives outside Hamburg. Relatives accepting evacuees must sign a certificate of acceptance in their own area. With this certificate you are free to leave Hamburg. Further details obtainable from National Socialist Welfare Offices.

To this day Maria Jäger finds it difficult to understand why she should have heeded this warning when, tragically, over 50,000 people did not, and met with a terrible death during the bombing raids on Hamburg between 24 July and 3 August 1943. In those few fateful days, countless thousands more suffered severe injury and almost one million lost their homes and all their possessions.

MRS A. BAGGELEY, of Stoke-on-Trent, Staffordshire, suffered a fate that all young brides dreaded:

'My husband then had to leave me at the church'

I was 16 years of age when war broke out and I was working in a grocer's shop. In 1943 my fiancé was called up into the army. In 1944 he joined the First Airborne Division and everything about it was very hush-hush. We made several dates to get married but each time it had to be cancelled due to the army.

On 11 August I was 21 years old, and on 15 August 1944 I was working as usual in the shop when in walked my fiancé dressed up in all his camouflage – rifle over his shoulder and bandoliers of bullets around his neck. They were going into action and were on their way to Brize Norton aerodrome. But the padre had asked permission for my husband to come and see me and to explain why our wedding had to be cancelled once again.

The padre suggested that we could get married straight away as the banns had already been read out three times in the church. So the padre, his driver, my husband and I got into the Jeep and went straight to the church and we got married. My husband then had to leave me at the church. He went back to his army unit and I went back to the shop to work.

I carried on working and on 17 September 1944 my husband was dropped on Arnhem in Holland. I had word from the War Office that my husband had been severely wounded and was reported missing in action.

On 1 January 1945, to my great relief, I received the first letter from my husband. He had survived, but he was a prisoner of war in Holland, and had had a leg amputated.

Every night I listened to Lord Haw Haw on the radio to hear if he gave out my husband's name. I had to notify the War Office to tell them my husband was still alive. On 26 April 1945 I received a telegram informing me that he had arrived back in England.

My husband weighed 12 stones when he joined the army. When he came back he was six stones.

FREDA SYKES, of Poole, Dorset, had two young babies so could not enlist for war work. However, when her husband was invalided out of the army, she obtained a job in the radio and record department of Beales department store, in Bournemouth:

'You've gone very white'

It was a job that I loved, because of the variety of customers, and the fact that I was interested in music. It was there that I met what I called 'my morning ghost', at five minutes to nine, while rushing to clock-in to work.

In the alley-way leading to the store I passed our Dispatch Manager and thought no more about it until I was greeted by my department boss. 'Isn't it terrible about Mr Mills?' he said.

I opened my mouth to say, 'I don't know, he looked all right a few minutes ago in the alley-way,' but the words wouldn't come out, and my boss continued, 'He was killed last night on Home Guard manoeuvres.'

I can remember just looking at him and opening my mouth, but no words would come out.

'Are you all right?' he asked. 'You've gone very white.'

I muttered something and escaped to an audition room with a duster, on the pretext of doing some cleaning. I tried to tell myself that the person I had just passed *and spoken to* in the alley-way must have been a twin brother. But Mr Mills didn't have a twin brother, as the first edition of the *Echo* revealed, when we read it all together in the shop. Mr Mills, who had worked at Beales since he left school at the age of 14, who had worked his way up to become Dispatch Manager, and had then joined the Home Guard at the declaration of war, was now dead. But I had just seen him. I had spoken to him, even if he didn't answer, but just looked at me, as he passed by up that alley-way.

When the enemy did strike our town he was particularly vicious. One Sunday, in particular, we were just sitting down to our meagre ration of a Sunday roast when we were startled to hear the sound of 12 planes zig-zagging over our house, before dropping their deadly load. A church was destroyed, a large store and an hotel, in which a lot of airmen were killed. Even our beloved Beales was hit, and a very rare clock-tower – the highest building in Bournemouth. Next day we went down to see the resulting damage, and all of us from my department stood looking at the blackened, smoking ruin, unashamedly weeping. So were the angels, for it started to pour with rain.

AUGUSTE LÜHR, of Bremerhaven, Germany, was a mother of four during the war. Her husband was working with an aircraft firm in Berlin, so, like many mothers, she faced the air-raids alone:

'I'm not ashamed to say I had to steal'

I was living on the fourth floor of a block of flats. I couldn't go down to the air-raid shelter any more when the alarm went. My place had been taken by others. I wasn't in the Nazi women's organization, so there wasn't any point in trying to make a fuss about it. One day there was a very bad raid. Our block remained standing, but in my flat the furniture was all smashed to pieces and all the windows broken. My father came to the rescue. My parents lived just outside Bremerhaven and he was always worried about me and the children. He had already seen women and children buried alive or burnt to death in the street where I was living.

He managed to get me into a home for bomb-victims outside the town. I moved in in February 1942. It was bitterly cold, with a metre of snow lying in the fields and just a little path leading to the house. But the worst thing was that there was no electricity or running water, except for one little pump serving the whole building, and a smelly paraffin-lamp. No matter what you did, it still used to smoke. I felt absolutely desperate. But what was the point in complaining? At least out here you were safer than in the town. I had to hand over all my electrical appliances, my radio, and the lamps that I had rescued. And the rent was exorbitant. But I just had to put up with it or do without a home.

Meanwhile my husband had had to leave his job in Berlin. He was called up into the army and sent off to France. He took part in the capture of Cherbourg. Then he went missing. I wrote off to the International Red Cross, but no one knew what had happened to his unit.

Food supplies got really short. There were no clothes or shoes to be had for the children. So I went out working. I decorated people's flats in exchange for cast-off clothes, bread, or sugar. I made up things for the chidren out of old clothes. I did sewing for other people, too, and would occasionally get a few coupons, or a bar of fish-soap. It smelt terrible, but at least it got things clean, which was important. It was made by fishermen from fish-oil. Sometimes I got a little bottle of fish-oil for cooking, which was fine for frying the potatoes in. It all sounds primitive today, but in those days our hunger was just awful.

Sometimes I would go out gathering wild plants to make a sort of cabbage-soup. I ended up nearly poisoning the lot of us. The plant I had picked tasted fine, but God help you if you ate it after flowering. It was poisonous then. I didn't know that, of course, and my eldest boy was so ill he nearly died. I stopped using wild plants after that.

That meant really racking my brains to see how I was going to get the children something to eat. I'm not ashamed to say I had to steal. The farmers refused to give you any food. I had already bartered just about everything I had, just to get a few potatoes. They had taken everything off me, carpets, net-curtains, clothes and sugar. How was I supposed to manage with four children? So I went out at night and used to help myself to some potatoes from the fields. Whenever one of the children had a birthday I would steal a few potatoes to make a potato-cake. Otherwise there would have been nothing for the little ones.

I remember that on one occasion, before he went missing, my husband sent a little packet from France for the children. There were a few bars of chocolate inside. When it came to sharing them out, the two eldest could still remember what it was. But the two youngest were puzzled by it. When I asked them why they weren't eating it, they said, 'Mum, it's just wood.'

What a problem it was finding enough to stave off their hunger. Often they would cry in the middle of the night and say, 'Mum, we're so hungry.' That just breaks a mother's heart.

Then supplies of coal ran out. If you were lucky enough to get any, it was only a few kilos. So we had to go out gathering sticks, so that we could have a little bit of warmth in the flat and maybe put some soup on. Once again I just had to swallow my pride and go out stealing coal. One freezing night when I was out, it was bright moonlight and the ground was hard with frost. I was carrying two heavy bags of coal and stopped for a breather. (None of us were very strong in those days.) A young girl had come along with me. I said to her, 'Look, there's a lovely bit of firewood lying there.' I picked it up. Dear God, it was a *whole loaf of bread*! I just wept for joy.

'You see,' I told her. 'God is always at hand when you really need him most. The minute I get back home, I'm going to cut a thick slice for each of the kids.' And that's just what I did. The children couldn't believe it. Their eyes just popped out of their heads. They still talk about that loaf to this day.

Twenty years later I found out that a fat old farmer's wife had dropped it. She wasn't short of anything in the war, but she was hopping mad when she heard I had taken it. But then she had never known what hunger was.

The bombing was getting worse. The planes were coming in swarms. It was awful just listening to them droning overhead with their heavy bomb-loads. We were on the approach run for all the big towns: Berlin, Hamburg, Bremen. Often they would off-load their bombs on us on their return flights. I remember it was on the afternoon of 4 February; the sky was overcast and low, and the bombers were approaching. They were dropping whole strings of bombs. I could actually see them being released – one lot right over our house. I was petrified and pulled the children to the ground, throwing myself on top of them. One landed behind us and the other 50 metres further on. But our house wasn't hit. I told the children the pilot must have just been lighting up a cigarette and that's how he came to miss us.

Some people I knew had a radio and used to listen-in to foreign stations. They told me that the Americans were threatening to reduce Bremerhaven to rubble and ashes in 20 minutes. You can imagine how our fears grew after that. Then came the big raid in 1944. The Americans did what they had said. In 20 minutes Bremerhaven was flattened. Those poor people. So many dead and injured. It was terrible. From my attic window I could see my parents' house ablaze. Where was my poor crippled mother? Where were my little brothers and sisters? And what about my father, who was an air-raid warden?

Then I heard someone calling out my name. I went to see what they wanted and was told that my mother and my brothers and sisters were in the bunker and that I should come immediately. I rushed off and took them all back to my little room. All six of them! My mother had been dragged out of the blazing house in her wheelchair. My little brothers and sisters were almost naked, with the clothes just burnt off them. The attack had come so quickly. My father was critically ill. He had inhaled too much smoke and it had poisoned him. He was trying to rescue some things for the family, but the house was burning too fiercely. It was a real fire-storm.

The next day the Red Cross set up stalls in the town and were giving out buttered rolls. I went to get something for our family. I had nothing at all to eat in the house, and now there were six more mouths to feed. Afterwards I ran back across the town, through all the rubble, to look for my husband's parents, because their house had gone, too. I was told they had survived and were in a camp for bomb-victims. But where? Eventually they were evacuated and I got word from Westphalia that they were living with their eldest son.

Neighbours told us one day that we could send messages to our husbands and sons on Radio Hamburg, just to let them know how things were back home. It took weeks before I got a radio message back from my husband. But he was alive, and he knew that we were all still alive. In spite of all the hardship we felt so happy that so far all of us had survived. But when would we be reunited? That day was still a long way off.

Then came the news that the children were to be compulsorily evacuated. I didn't let them take mine! They threatened me with the police but that didn't frighten me. I kept them close by me. Our family had been torn apart enough during the last few years. But many mothers did let their children go and they were often evacuated out east, even nearer to the Front. It was absolute madness. But they didn't realize it till it was too late.

My nerves were just about in shreds. The sirens were going night and day. You just never got any rest. The Front was getting closer all the time. You could hear the guns and see the flashes at night. Then you just wondered what the morning would bring. At night we used to pack up the little bit of food and clothing we had left into a wash-tub and bury it in the garden. The next morning we had to dig it up again so that the things didn't spoil. Our only thought in those days was, if only it would all end. By now we knew that the war was lost. Berlin had been taken by the Russians, and we heard the news that Adolf Hitler had committed suicide. We all breathed a sigh of relief. Perhaps that would bring release for us all. But the war went on and the Front got closer.

The food allocations got smaller and smaller. The only people who got enough to eat in those days were the people who were at the start of the supply line. I kept on with the sewing work to try and keep us fed, but it got harder. I made ski-hats for the soldiers and they would sometimes have a loaf to spare for the children. In the daytime I would go out searching the ruins for bits of wood to burn. It meant a lot of leg-work, but what else could I do? There had been no fuel supplies for some time and the washing just had to be boiled once in a while. There was no soap at all now. We used to fill little linen bags with ashes and then add a dash of sal-ammoniac to get a lather.

Sometimes the low-flyers would drop leaflets. They said that

Bremerhaven should surrender. We were very frightened. What would the enemy soldiers be like? Like the Russians? The refugees from the east had told frightening tales about what they had done to the women. The following day there came an announcement: Bremerhaven was surrendering without further fighting. That was our good fortune.

We saw the victors march in, but we had no need to fear them. Many were even good to us, although there were the ones who took away what little we had left. So the war ended for us on 6 May 1945. Thanks be to God.

Because I was a soldier's wife I had no money coming in now, but I had managed to save a little, because you just couldn't spend money during the war, as there was nothing in the shops to buy. So I tried to get food by buying on the black market. A piece of meat cost you 300 Reichs-mark. A single egg was 10 RM. In desperation I started doing washing and ironing for the occupying troops. That was the only way I could get food for the children, or soap.

My husband ended up as a POW in France. He was put to work in the potash mines. He was so determined to get back to the family that he made three escape attempts. We had not seen each other for almost seven years. On the third attempt, he managed to escape and got back to Germany on foot, with a price on his head. On 22 November 1946 Dad came home again. The boys who were born during the war only knew him from pictures.

Please God, let there never be another war. Even today, when I see pictures on television of how things were, I feel ill. Writing about it has made me relive it all again.

RACHEL MCDONALD, of Liverpool, Merseyside, took her young family to Dumfries, in Scotland, to escape the bombs, but, after a few weeks, she decided to brave the blitz and return home:

'It just took their breath away'

In Liverpool we lived on the banks of the river Mersey which was flanked by golf links, later used for anti-aircraft guns. Any flat roofs nearby were used for sham anti-aircraft guns to give an impression that we were ready to deal with the enemy.

It was at this time that I had my sixth child, who was born at home, as was usual at that time. We had to collect gas masks for the whole family. For the two babies there were things like large card-board boxes, each with a pumping device. In the event of a gas attack the babies would have been placed in these containers and the gas pumped out manually. I worried about how I could possibly operate the pumps on two containers simultaneously if my husband was on fire-watch duty, which he was regularly.

We were given a choice of air-raid shelter. We could have one to be dug down in the garden, known as an Anderson shelter, or one for the house, like a big metal table, known as a Morrison shelter. We chose the one for the garden and my husband dug it well down in the earth so we had to step down a small ladder to get into it. We put wooden benches down each side, then cross planks half way down so that we could allow the younger children to sleep. We took all the children's beds and cots down to the dining room where there was a door to the garden. Every time we had to take pillows, eiderdowns and blankets into the shelter and also the wicker cot for the baby. All this had to be taken back into the house the next morning and the condensation was such that everything was wet and had to be dried by the kitchen fire all the next day.

When the siren sounded, we would have to take the children from their beds, put on their warm clothing, and take them out to the shelter. My husband had to go on fire-watch duty at night with the

LEFT: *Winifred Watkins pictured with her son Ronald on their first peacetime picnic.*

ABOVE: *Winifred Watkins' husband Harry.*

BELOW: *The bride and groom whose wedding Cicely Bower organized, and the village hall, Langton Matravers, where the reception was held.*

The Village Hall, Langton Matravers.

LEFT: *Erna Arntz and her children, Easter 1941.*

ABOVE: *Julia Kraut and her children pictured during their evacuation to Lauenthal in 1944.*

RIGHT: *Erica Hildebrandt, before her flight from East Prussia.*

RIGHT: *Lisa Helmerking, aged 24.*

BELOW: *Heidi Prüfer in 1943.*

BELOW RIGHT: *Heidi Prüfer's two sons, Günther, aged 6, and Wilfried, aged 7, taken during evacuation in August 1944.*

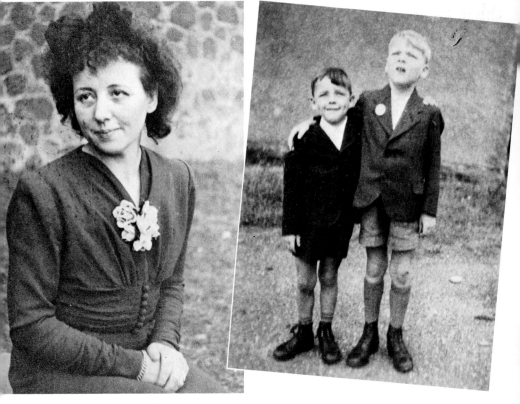

RIGHT: *Maria Schuster and her children.*

LEFT: *Martha Zollinger and her husband just before the war.*

BELOW: *Auguste Lühr.*

ABOVE: *Margarethe Onken and her children during the war, braving the bombers bound for Wilhelmshaven and Bremen.*

LEFT: *'F.H.' and her children, pictured in 1944, in Breslau.*

BELOW: *Marianne Schmutz and her husband during the war.*

LEFT: *Sigrid Wendt, in 1942, dressed in the uniform of the compulsory 'German Labour Service'.*

BELOW LEFT: *Irmgard Müller and her husband on their winter wedding day.*

BELOW: *A Sunday morning walk. Anna Grütering and her husband.*

OPPOSITE ABOVE: *Ria Bröring 'down on the farm' during evacuation.*

OPPOSITE BELOW: *Document of expulsion from the Hitler Youth issued to Ria Bröring for anti-Nazi activities.*

Begründung

Maria S c h i r p gehört dem Bund Deutscher Mädel angeblich
eines Fussleidens erst seit April 1940 an.

Ihre Äusserungen über den Dienst u d die Zugehörigkeit zum
Bund Deutscher Mädel aber zeigen eindeutig, dass sie sich in
keiner Weise dem Bund Deutscher Mädel gegenüber verpflichtet
fühlt. Ihr Dienstbesuch war so unregelmässig, dass sie in der
zuständigen Einheit kaum bekannt ist. In ihrer ganzen Art, die
anmassend und herausfordernd ist, bringt sie zum Ausdruck, dass
ihr all die Eigenschaften, die bei einem echten BDM-Mädel
selbstverständlich sind, abgehen.

Selbst der höheren Dienststelle gegenüber gab sie sich in einer
Weise, die nur als disziplinlos angesehen werden kann.

Anlass zu diesen Feststellungen gab die Störung einer Theater-
vorstellung, des Schauspiels Heinrich IV., an welcher sie sich
beteiligte. Sie trug eine Trillerpfeife bei sich, die sie zur
Erhöhung des Tumultes benutzte.

Wenn M.Sch. auch angibt, ohne den Vorsatz die Vorstellung zu
stören, ins Theater gegangen zu sein, so muss dies als unwahr-
scheinlich zurückgewiesen werden, da sich in der gleichen Auf-
führung ihre ältere Schwester und ihr Bruder befand n, die
ebenfalls mit anderen bekannten Jugendlichen die Störung verur-
sacht haben. Dieser Vorfall gibt eindeutigen Beweis dafür, dass
M.Sch. sich der Pflichten dem Bund Deutscher Mädel und sich selbst
gegenüber nicht bewusst ist.

Durch ihr Verhalten schadete sie nur dem Ansehen der Hitler-
Jugend, was zur Folge hat, dass das HJ-Gericht auf sofortiges
Ausscheiden aus dem Bund Deutscher Mädel erkennt.

M.Sch. hat sich in keiner Weise bemüht, sich in die Gemeinschaft
einzuordnen.

Die k. Mädelführerin des Gebietes Düsseldorf (34)

(Klebe)
Bannmädelführerin

zuzustellen an:

Maria Schirp	1
gesetzl. Vertreter	1
HJ-Gericht RJF.	1
Gebiet 34	1
Bann 39	1
Einheitsführerin	1
	6

Einspruchsbelehrung anliegend.

RIGHT: *Helga Baumhäckel and her baby son, in 1944, on a farm outside Berlin.*

BELOW: *Inge Willmanns and her children, in the garden of their Kiel home.*

other men, and my eldest son, at the age of 10 and wearing a tin hat, took on the responsibilities of the man of the house. He helped me prepare the shelter and take the younger children out. He was marvellous. I found it very exhausting putting in all the necessary bedding and then settling the younger children to sleep in such a small area, and lit only by one small oil lamp.

Inside the shelter there was no room for the elder two children to lie down to sleep, so they would just lean on me and fall asleep. I warned them not to lean on the walls of the shelter because if a bomb dropped nearby one could be killed by the blast.

Sometimes, if the weather was intensely cold or foggy, we wouldn't take the children out and would put them under the kitchen table instead until the all-clear sounded. They were all very good and didn't seem to be scared when the guns in the field opposite were firing and shaking the ground. I suppose that was because I didn't show how terrified I was.

For a couple of weeks the raiders came promptly every night at about 1.30 a.m., which was really dreadful. We had a few incendiary bombs fall in our garden and that, plus the noise of the enemy aircraft going over, was very frightening. If it was a starry night we would not be so worried because we knew that the enemy would rather avoid being spotted by the anti-aircraft guns.

My husband was obliged to do fire-watch duty with the other men, but he would come round to the shelter at night to see how we were. I always took a potty into the shelter for the younger children. Although the door to the outside toilet was just opposite the shelter entrance, it was very dangerous to go out.

One night a landmine, which seemed to be a vast container of explosives, fell a short distance from us and many people were killed. Fortunately for us the blast went in the opposite direction, otherwise we would certainly all have been killed or very seriously injured. The terrific noise when it landed was so frightening and many of my friends within a short distance of us had their roofs blown off.

Another night an ammunition train was hit and the blast from the explosion was so enormous that it moved our very heavy wardrobe a few feet along the floor. The sound of the aircraft became so familiar that very soon we could tell the difference between our own and the enemy aircraft.

At this time I remember so well press photographs of children being evacuated, with name labels and bags of clothing. That upset me – we could not even think of parting with our children, although I know many people had let them go for their safety.

In March 1943 our seventh child was born, a lovely wee baby, Christina. By this time the raids were not so frequent and certainly not every night. In the summer months the raids were less frequent because of the longer daylight hours and this gave us more peace of mind.

There were many sad stories of families whom we knew personally. One family had put their four children in one bed, that night the landmine came and they were killed by the blast. It just took their breath away and they didn't breathe again. There were no injury marks on any of them. That night the weather was so bad we were under the kitchen table, and my husband, who was at the back door, saw the same landmine swinging in the air and shouted at me. I was just getting under the table with the baby. I bashed my head badly, but the baby was all right.

My own war experience was, I'm sure, very comfortable in comparison with the dreadful experiences of so many others. We were so very fortunate to be in a place where deaths and gunfire were all around us, and yet we survived. On every road there were marks of destruction of some sort, but we somehow managed to escape the dreadful things that happened to other people.

ERNA ARNTZ, from Hildesheim, Lower Saxony, had a husband serving in the army, who was stationed close to their home. A mother of six children, she was in a better position than many in Hitler's Germany, since 'productive mothers' enjoyed special status in the Third Reich and got extra food allowances. Hildesheim, the medieval town of her birth, with its fine half-timbered houses, was spared the full brunt of the air-raids during the early years of the war. But the Allied bomber squadrons that droned overhead almost nightly on their way to Berlin and other big towns served as a solemn warning of what was in store later for Hildesheim. Erna Arntz here describes the first major raid on her home-town:

'We stared for hours at that scene of desolation'

The first air-raid in Hildesheim came on 15 February 1945. As I dashed down the cellar steps, with little Ursula in my arms and Waltraud hanging on to my hand, broken glass came showering down about us. The whole household, father, mother, sister and the other children were already down there, shivering with fright beside the other residents from the block. My mother and my sister took it particularly badly, because they had already been through the experience of bombing in the Ruhr district.

When everything was quiet again we went upstairs and found that the dining-room window had been completely blown out, frame and all. It was lying out in the road. A big bomb had fallen in the quarry, about 500 metres away, and the full force of the blast seemed to have hit our house, because the rest of the street was undamaged. My mother and my sister went straight round to the Winter Relief Office to demand to be evacuated somewhere safe in the country. They moved out to an address in Dingelbe, about 20 kilometres away.

We stayed where we were, and a few days later there was another air-raid. There was a dreadful explosion and our whole house started shaking. We were in the cellar and the cellar door was blown off its hinges. My son Bruno, just eight years old, was saying his prayers out loud. 'God have mercy on us.' In all probability a lone flyer had dropped his last bomb as he went over. It had hit the house opposite and it was demolished right down to the ground floor. The whole area was full of dark-grey dust. But the people were in the cellar and had survived. In our house all the keys from the doors and cupboards were missing. We never found them. Probably they had been blown out and were then cleared away when helpers came in and lifted the carpet to get the piles of broken glass out of the house.

It was that raid that made me face up to my responsibilities towards the children. I knew I could not run the risk of exposing them to another raid. I went to the Winter Relief Office, and there I was told to get in touch with the mayor of Bavenstedt, just a short distance away, to see if I could get evacuated there. I borrowed a bike to get there as soon as possible. I was given a few addresses to try, but as soon as they found out I had six children, it was the same story: 'Sorry, the rooms are needed for relations.' I went back to the Mayor and told him I hadn't a chance of getting anywhere like this. He told me to come back tomorrow, when there would be a meeting of the councillors. This time my husband came with us in uniform, and we were promptly told that a farmer's family, named Garbs, had two rooms all ready for us!

We packed up all the necessary in the form of bedding, pots and pans, and Farmer Garbs sent over one of his Polish farmhands called Siegfried with a horse and cart to pick us up. The farmer had no children of his own, but it was a friendly enough household, even if space was a bit tight. My youngest children enjoyed more freedom than they had ever known before. They were most taken with the cows, of which there must have been at least 80. For me the main problem at first was the lack of heating. I had been promised a simple stove to cook on, but that took time in arriving. So I just had to make a nourishing one-pot meal in a big pan and put it on the Garbs' stove first thing in the morning. By midday it was ready to eat.

The oldest boys had a long walk back to school in Hildesheim, and often they were sent home early because of air-raid warnings. My wireless set didn't work here. It must have been something to do with the wrong wavelength. There were no newspapers, either. So we knew nothing of what was going on. I spent the evenings reading. Storm's *Schimmelreiter* was my favourite. The turbulence of the story seemed to match what we were going through at the time.

Bruno, now eight, was the happiest of all of us. The cowshed and the stables were his whole world. Whenever Farmer Garbs was on the farm he would carry Ursula around in his arms. He was often away with the fire brigade, where he was the fire chief of one of the crews. He certainly had his work cut out, attending fires after the air-raids on the railway lines, the station and the factory buildings.

Of the Polish workers, Siegfried was the nicest, always friendly and ready to give a hand. Another of them was a lad of 17 and he gave the farmer a lot of trouble. He got called a 'damned Polish pig' which didn't sound good to the children's ears, coming from someone who was a regular church-goer. The Polish workers had separate sleeping quarters. The women used to knit white, chunky pullovers for their youngsters out of unravelled sugar-sacks. They looked good in them when they wore them on Sundays. In general their clothing was very shabby indeed. They got enough to eat, but were not allowed to sit at the farmer's table. There was a Ukrainian girl among them. What she had experienced at home had left her with a deep hatred of Germans.

So the weeks of February and early March passed. They were ominous weeks when you could actually sense the threat from both east and west getting closer. Things were not good, but could they get even worse? The answer was not long in coming.

The 22nd March was a beautiful sunny spring day. I decided to walk to the bank in Hildesheim with the children, to get enough money to see me over the Easter period. I remember I drew 400 Reichs-mark. I was on the way back when the sirens went: full alert! We set off running for home, sticking close to the ditches. Then we heard the all-clear, so we stopped and gave the rest of the children a chance to catch up. Then the full alert sounded for the second time. We reached the farmhouse and bounded down the cellar steps. The cellar had been propped for extra strength, but it had never been put to the test till now.

The bombing started and the farmhouse shook, even at this distance from Hildesheim. It seemed to go on for hours on end. In fact

209

the attack only lasted about 20 minutes. It left us absolutely para-
lysed, and it took us a while to realize it had stopped.

We went out. Dense clouds of smoke were drifting across from
Hildesheim. With the children in my arms I dashed over to the edge
of the village to see better. A wall of smoke was completely obliterat-
ing the town. Mushrooms of smoke kept billowing up, some light in
colour, some dark grey. The defenceless town of Hildesheim, with
all its one thousand years of history and traditions, was rising
to Heaven in one gigantic pall of smoke. We stayed there for hours,
just staring at the scene of desolation. Finally, at around four
o'clock, the sun, now in the west, peered dimly through the curtain
of smoke. The tall group of trees at the central cemetery became
visible in silhouette. To the south you could make out the outline
of the Galgenberg Hill. Then the spires of the Church of St
Elisabeth emerged out of the smoke. That was a small ray of hope for
me. Could it be that our house, right by the church, had been
spared?

Now we could see people flocking out of the town, their faces
black with smoke, looking for refuge. Without my noticing, my two
eldest boys had made off into the town. When they got back that
evening they reported that our area in the east of the town was still
standing. But the whole of the town centre had been destroyed. Our
farmer told us his experiences with the fire unit. None of the fire
services had been able to get into the town because incendiaries were
still burning. The hydrants were all dry and so were the storage
ponds. Our two boys had been helping friends fight roof-fires, to try
to stop them from spreading to the rest of the house. I later found
out that a fire had started in our building, but one of the residents
had managed to put it out.

The worst scenes were described to me by two young sisters who
had survived after being caught in a shop cellar in the middle of
town. They said that the only people to get out alive were young
people on their own. The only way was to bind a cloth over your
mouth and make a dash for the trees near the Cathedral Square,
where there was some shelter. There were many who didn't make it.
They suffocated in the smoke and were found later on the street corners, shrivelled by the heat to the size of the shoes they were wear-

ing. More than 1,000 people met their deaths. According to later reports at least 500 were incinerated.

Our house that evening was full of desperate people. I put down bedding for some in the hallway. One woman left me her two children to look after whilst she went off to look for somewhere for herself. That evening my husband managed to get back home. He had had to make a wide detour and only managed to get through because he was wearing a Red Cross armband. In our bedroom there were 10 of us in five single beds. 'Let's have a song,' my husband said and struck up with 'Happy is the Gypsy's Life'. He was just overjoyed that we were all safe and sound and together again. Really he should still have been at his post.

The full scale of the destruction only gradually became apparent to us. You didn't dare go back into the town. Those who did came straight back out to the villages, even though their house might still be standing. All the churches, except for three, had been destroyed. The only school left was the Moltke School, which one of our eldest attended. The Cathedral had been hit by 11 bombs and was just a shell. The wonderful Church of St Michael, completed in 1048, was in the same state. The first time I ventured through the rubble I went along by the ruined theatre right on the edge of the old town centre. I could see right across to the other side. It was just one big gap in the middle. All the half-timbered houses from the sixteenth and seventeenth centuries had burnt away to nothing. There had once been 800 of them.

Those were sad, dreary days we lived through. But at least my little world was safe amongst those dour, but good-hearted country folk. There were so many less fortunate than us, especially those on the road coming from the east and seeking refuge in the unfamiliar west. We often thought to ourselves in those days that perhaps we were now reaping the reward for all the destruction that Germany had caused amongst the countries of Europe.

MOLLY SMITH, of Farnborough, Hampshire, found herself acting as a wife, mother, and air-raid warden:

'I always had the leg of a chair handy'

Sometime before war was declared, volunteers were called for to join in Home Defence. There were several branches, including Air-Raid Precautions. My husband, my father, and I enrolled and took courses in gas detection, bomb drill, and fire drill (the latter requiring one to crawl through a smoke-filled shed on hands and knees). We also had to pass the St John's first aid certificate.

When war was declared, we were allocated to various air raid posts. I was employed part-time at the local headquarters, from 6–10 p.m. My duties, all on my own in this large house, included receiving the air-raid alert, going down to the basement and pulling the alarm switch to activate the siren, then standing by to sound the all-clear signal. Looking back, it seems a bit 'Heath Robinson', but we were all very conscientious and dedicated to the cause.

I gave up the part-time work when my daughter was due to be born in March, 1940. However, I resumed my duties a few months later, patrolling the streets with my father during an alert. (My mother took my baby down into the air-raid shelter.) It was so uncanny, no traffic about, no people, just Dad and me in this unreal world. I remember discussing with him about my daughter's future should anything happen to my husband and me. In retrospect, it all seems so strange, but the reality of the time, and the possibility of what might happen to us, subjected people to problems and emotions that can easily be smiled at by those of later generations.

The first serious raid in our area was in the August. I wasn't on duty and had taken my small daughter down into our Anderson shelter. A string of bombs fell in an adjacent street, demolishing the houses in direct line with ours. The noise was terrific, the ground shook, but I consoled myself with the knowledge that the noise was coming from our own defences (as we had been informed by the media). It was rather alarming to discover afterwards that our area defences consisted of one Hurricane and one old Gladiator fighter plane!

The house that received the direct hit was occupied by an air-raid warden. Luckily, his family were in their shelter and were unharmed. The following day, my father and husband were with others helping the family salvage what they could from the ruins. I was in my house with my baby, knowing that there was an unexploded bomb in the vicinity of the wrecked house. (Although it had been sandbagged, its size wasn't determined.) Suddenly there was a terrific explosion. My doors and windows blew open. My one thought was for my husband and father. I grabbed up my baby and rushed into the street. A neighbour had come to his front gate. Fearing heaven knows what, I thrust my baby into his arms and ran round to where the lads were. There they all were, carrying on as if nothing had happened! One held up a pyjama top riddled with machine-gun bullet holes.

The most hair-raising experience was when the church bells rang one night – the signal for a German invasion. Again we were asleep and roused by my father knocking on the door saying, 'Come on, the beggars are dropping!' We were expecting an invasion and knew we were a prime target.

My husband grabbed his rifle and I always had the leg of a chair handy! As it happened, it was a false alarm, but all the emotions it triggered off were for real. We were fighting for survival and hated the thought of foreigners taking over.

Strangely though, after hostilities ceased and my husband was demobbed, we were asked to invite German prisoners of war into our homes for Christmas dinner. We had three: one very young lad who was having difficulty in finishing his meal; another with the 'Hitler touch' – obviously ordering him to eat all before him! The third had just a little English. I rescued the young lad and took him into the garden for a walk. Apart from the tough one, they were just nice lads. What on earth were we doing at war with each other? Things were very bad in Germany and, having got their home addresses, I collected a few extra rations together and sent food parcels to their parents.

To me, the most agonizing part of the war was being separated from my husband. He was called up in 1942, having been in a reserved occupation he wasn't allowed to enlist. Whilst he was stationed in Britain, he would find accommodation for my small daughter and me so we could be near him. The first trip was to Aberdeen for his initial training. I had the most wonderful landlady – Ma Milne – we became part of her family, and friends for life. She usually charged £1 per week for the room, but, as I was a 'sojer's wifie', it was only to be 12s 6d. She just refused to take more.

She noticed that I was off my food and came in with a beautiful kipper, to make sure I was eating. Rations didn't seem so strict in Scotland and we had friends on a farm at Ellon, just outside Aberdeen, which helped. But, as always, the stay came to an end when my husband was posted to Donnington.

I returned to Farnborough until my husband once again found us somewhere to live. This time it was the most horrendous place and only being together made it possible to tolerate it. We were there for about a year and then he was posted to Nottingham. It was our turn for a lovely landlady again who insisted that my next baby be born in her house to save me going home.

Eventually my husband was posted to West Africa and I returned home with my two daughters.

All these moves were fraught with memories – good and bad, funny and sad. But the sheer joy when my husband was demobbed and returned to work, and life gradually became our own again, with dreams and plans for the future. Sadly, they were not to be fulfilled. He died suddenly, and I was left to face the coming years without him. But that's another story . . .

ERNA WIEGAND, of Düsseldorf, North Rhine-Westphalia, lived with her parents in a big family house, in the small Westphalian town of Hagen. One day, in September 1943, as they huddled in the cellar for protection, they knew that this time it was to be their turn:

'My big strong father was weeping'

The pressure from the blast was so violent that all the cellar windows were pressed in and you had to fight to get breath. There were sudden shouts: 'The house is on fire!' Incendiaries had come in through the roof. Everyone ran upstairs. There were buckets of water on every landing and the men went up to the attic where there were two full bathtubs.

I dashed into our flat and threw the feather beds down into the yard. Down below was my mother, who carried them off into the garden, away from the flames. I was just emptying out the cutlery-drawer into a bucket when I felt my back burning. Fortunately my father noticed and emptied a bucket of water over me. We didn't manage to save much from the house. The fire took hold too quickly. To my eternal shame I have to admit that I left the cutlery upstairs. I mixed up the buckets and came down with a bucket containing an iron and three pans without lids. But even those were to prove useful!

The house was completely burnt out. Only the cellar was intact, protected by the rubble falling down above it. The next day we went down and retrieved our suitcases with some clothing and a few small things.

We spent that first night in a bunker nearby. My big strong father was weeping! I can still hear the sound today. My mother lay on her bed and recited those famous lines from Schiller:

> The town is burnt and empty,
> And in the gaping windows
> Horror dwells.

215

There was another memorable thing that night. We lived on a hill that overlooked the town of Hagen. The centre of the town was blazing fiercely. In the midst of the fire-storm, the bells of Hagen's five churches began to ring, one after the other. It was weird and yet there was something splendid about it. The people standing around me reacted in different ways. Some broke down and wept openly. Others were transfixed. A few ran back into the inferno of blazing houses. I just stopped and stared in fascination, determined to absorb the whole scene. I was gripped by it. Soon the fire burnt through the beams that supported the bells. One after the other the bells crashed down into the church below. The silence that followed was ghostly.

The fine little valley town was destroyed.

MRS K. A. CROCKETT, of Wallasey, Merseyside, was married to a sergeant in the Queen's Own Cameron Highlanders, who was posted to the Middle East. She spent most of the war years beneath the bombs in Liverpool, but, by an ironic quirk of fate, it was when she managed to escape to the sanctuary of the countryside that tragedy struck:

'She looked like a pretty wax doll'

My father was a civil servant and he worked in the Dome Room of Liverpool Customs House. I remember him saying that a hit in the Dome would be disastrous and he was proved right. In late August 1940, whilst fire-watching, he sustained serious injuries during a bombing raid and died from them on 3 September. My mother was asked to permit a post mortem so that the doctors could find out the effects of bomb blast and the type of injuries it caused.

In late December 1940 Arthur, my husband, was home on leave. Our house was on a main road, opposite a railway goods yard – an obvious target. The siren sounded and, when the raid became heavier, we had to shelter under the stairs. I remember hearing the whistle of a bomb, then a tremendous crash. We were huddled over the baby who began to cry. We were covered in dust and plaster, but we managed to clamber out to find broken windows, torn curtains, and débris everywhere. The bomb had fallen in the next door garden and a high stone wall had taken most of the blast. Thankfully, our neighbours were away.

It was very dangerous outside, with enemy planes overhead and the ack-ack guns retaliating. Arthur put me into an Anderson shelter while he went off to investigate. There I was, quite alone, with the baby in my arms, in pitch blackness, during a terrifying air-raid. Suddenly I heard a rustling in the darkness. Then a disembodied voice started, 'Hail Mary . . .' and it went on praying – on and on in the darkness. It was really eerie. Arthur came back and, in a lull in the bombing, we dashed to his mother's, so I never did find out who it was. It certainly couldn't have been my neighbour.

The next day, with the aid of a pony and cart, we salvaged as much of our goods and chattels as we could from the front rooms of the house. The back of the house was too badly damaged to save anything. The house was totally unfit to live in, so we ended up moving in with my mother-in-law. However, Arthur insisted that I should pack and go back to Banbury, in Oxfordshire, with him. He was stationed there for winter training. Although we found very good digs, the baby was not very well. She had contracted pneumonia. A poor little mite, whose short life had been spent in an air-raid shelter and who had also been bombed, stood little chance. She was just six months old when she died after a couple of days, in early February. She looked like a pretty wax doll. I was shattered. My father's death as a result of fire-watching during an air-raid I could understand; but not this – not when we had come away from the Liverpool area to be safe.

I returned home to Liverpool via the Mersey Underground and was saddened to see people already bedding down for the night on the platform. It made our Anderson shelter seem like a veritable palace.

In March 1941 Wallasey, where I now live, was badly bombed –

the target being the River Mersey and the docks. I arrived to visit an aunt and uncle, both in their seventies. Although their house was still standing, there were bomb craters everywhere, broken windows, rubble, and no gas or water. But, somehow, Uncle had got hold of a kipper and Auntie was furious because he insisted on cooking it on the element of the electric fire.

In May 1941, we endured the eight-night 'May blitz'. Night after night the heavy bombing raids seemed to go on for ever. It caused terrible devastation and at the end of it everyone was totally exhausted.

It must have been in 1942 that Mrs Crockett, Senior, decided we ought to keep hens. Thus I became part owner of two Rhode Island Red cockerels and ten pullets, aged one day. An incubator was constructed for them and they were fed on fine oatmeal and chopped egg. (Someone must have sacrificed their egg ration for the time being.) Mrs C. had a hen-run in the back yard and soon our investment began to pay off. There was just one snag – Rufus, the boss cockerel! He was a fine big bird and he certainly ruled the roost. He also took a dislike to Nell, my sister-in-law. If she went out to get the coal, or to go to the loo, he would go for her. Poor Nell would be penned up on the loo steps until someone went to her rescue. She was scared stiff of that bird!

The year ended with a problem over the killing of one of the cockerels – Rufus – for Christmas dinner. Mrs Crockett, Senior, didn't feel equal to the task, nor did any one else. But fortunately a neighbour obliged. We must have overcome our scruples about killing it, or maybe it was because Rufus had been a bird of character, but we all thoroughly enjoyed that meal!

My sister-in-law, Nell, died very suddenly in December 1944, which was a great shock to us all. As Arthur's father had died in 1939, our two families had had bereavements each year of the war, except for 1942. To complete the list, my mother died in April 1945. So there I was, a 28-year-old orphan (I was an only child) waiting for the end of the war.

In the early hours of 28 November 1945 I was awakened by loud knocking on the front door. Half asleep, I went to answer it and there, laden with kit-bag, a box containing his demob suit, and various other bags and parcels, stood Arthur. It was my 29th birthday and what a present!

So ended the war for us. At long last we were able to pick up the threads and very soon I was pregnant once more. The coming year looked like being a very happy one and lived up to its promise, for our daughter Elaine was born in August 1946.

Mrs Crockett had one more daughter and a son after Elaine was born. She is now a widow, and a grandmother, and still lives in Wallasey, in happy and active retirement.

MARIA HERBRAND, from Niederkrüchten, North Rhine-Westphalia, met her husband-to-be in 1936, the year of the Berlin Olympics. But the outbreak of war meant that wedding-plans had to be postponed until Christmas 1942. The war continued to interfere with their lives. Her husband, Ludwig, was posted to Bremen, later called up into the army, and ended the war as a prisoner of war. For safety's sake Maria remained behind in Wegberg, close to her parents. In November 1943 the first of three sons was born. Anxious for his safety as Allied bombing increased in intensity, she decided to seek sanctuary with relatives in the countryside, north of Rostock. That sanctuary turned into a nightmare when the victorious Red Army swept through north-east Germany and engulfed them. She found herself trapped in the Soviet Occupation Zone. Now with a second son, she was determined to get back home to the West and succeeded in escaping into the British Zone, and worked her way back across Germany again. She reached home again on 8 September 1945. She was persuaded by her family to write a full account of all her experiences. We present here a few scenes which capture the spirit of those uncertain, turbulent, occasionally humorous, and frequently sad years:

'A cross and a steel helmet'

On 10 March 1943 I was at home when I got a phone call from my sister-in-law Annemarie's next door neighbour. She said, 'You'd better come quick. Your sister-in-law has just had bad news.' All I said to Mum was 'I'm just popping over to Viersener Strasse', and I slipped out.

I sensed the worst. Later Mum told me she had had the same sense of foreboding. But you know how it is. You push thoughts like that to the back of your mind, because you don't want them to be true. As soon as I arrived at my sister-in-law's she showed me a card she had just got from a Captain Herpertz, a fellow-soldier and close friend of her husband, Hans. On it was a drawing in black ink of a cross and a steel helmet. Beneath was the name of her husband, my brother Hans. It read:

Hans Heinen. Shisdra Front, 22.2.43

Annemarie always came over to us for her lunch, but this particular day she had waited for the postman, hoping to get a card from Hans on her birthday. Instead of that she had received this shock. You have to have gone through something like that to know what it does to you inside. We went back home, to where Mother was waiting in a terrible state of agitation. She was still clinging to the hope that maybe the news would not be the worst. The grief of my father and mother was indescribable, unimaginable to anyone who has not lost a son.

Later Captain Herpertz visited Annemarie. He said he had wanted to let her know the news as soon as possible. He thought the little card he had drawn was nicer than the cold official notification of death.

The little white loaf

We didn't have a wireless-set of our own, but old Grandma Oellers did. She lived, with her three daughters, in the same block as my parents. They were the proud owners of a little Philips that they nicknamed their 'white loaf', because it really did look like one.

Listening-in to foreign radio stations was a very serious offence. So at the times when we knew that the British were broadcasting, one of them would set off upstairs to the bedroom with the 'white loaf' under her arm. Up there on the second floor you were at least safe from unexpected visitors. Also, you needed absolute peace and quiet, because reception was very bad with continuous interference.

It was due to these broadcasts that we came to learn that it really wasn't 'victories all the way' for Germany, as we were told by the weekly newsreels. We learned that the enemy was getting closer all the time.

A pig on the cheap

Grandma Oellers had friends from Wassenberg called the Fleckens. One day Herr Flecken came to say that he could get us a pig on the cheap, providing the slaughtering and butchering could be done at our place. Young Käthe Oellers said if my husband Ludwig did the killing, they, the Oellers, would attend to the 'surgical work'. It was no sooner said than done. A few days later along came Herr Flecken with the pig. The problem was how to get it into the wash-house without the neighbours seeing.

The pig was unloaded from the car at the Hermanns, two doors further down, then bundled into a paper sack. The plan was to bring it in through the back gardens. I stood watching from the kitchen window, worried to death that someone would see what was going on and report us to the police. The pig, presumably guessing what was in store for him, broke out of the bag and set up a hideous squealing. My husband Ludwig snatched up his gun and took a shot at the creature. But the bullet just bounced off its skull, and the pig just stared at him as if nothing had happened. An axe was fetched and after more commotion the beast was stunned. It was a tragedy, but it had to be killed. My sharp meat-knife was brought, but it made no impression at all on the thick hide. However, it finally did its work, and the pig was dead. Käthe collected the blood in a bowl.

In the meantime, Maria had been busy stoking the fire under the copper so that there would be lots of hot water for softening the bristles. Ludwig had made a scraper out of a sardine-tin lid. But the work of getting off the bristles was not the easy job we had imagined. I don't know where we went wrong; maybe the water wasn't hot enough, the scraper not rigid enough, or the bristles too thick. Anyhow, we amateurs made a proper hash of it. In spite of that, after several hours hard work, the pig was ready for cutting open, and was then hung on a ladder to cool. Next day things went much better and the pig was cut up. The biggest pieces were put into a barrel for salt-pickling. We also made brawn and sausages. Soon after, I was evacuated. By the time I returned all the salt-pork had been stolen from the cellar. The hard work and excitement had all been in vain.

An old camel-hair jacket
It was late in 1944 that the order came to evacuate all the women and children out of Wegberg. We talked it over and decided that the best thing was for me to go with Wolfgang, my small son, and join my sister, on Olga's farm out east, in Mecklenburg. We sent off a telegram saying when we would be arriving. Then we imme-

diately started packing all the essentials into wicker baskets. In went clothing and bedding, then everything was sewn up in canvas, cords tied around it, and each basket carefully addressed to Olga's farm. They weren't accepting freight at the station in Wegberg, so Ludwig and his sister drove through to Paderborn to dispatch them from there. They got back the next day, and we got on with the rest of the packing.

I had to remember that another baby was on the way and take things for him. So we also packed a cot and a play-pen. Then we had to fill the pram. First we put in a side of bacon, then preserving jars of beans, some more food, and some Nestlé's baby food. On top of this went baby-clothes. To solve the problem of carrying the eider-downs, I made a rucksack out of a linen table-cloth.

All the dirty bed and table linen that we were leaving behind was put in a zinc bath down in the cellar. Ludwig heated up some salt and put it into a jar. He said it would absorb any damp, and sure enough, when we took them out again when we got back, there was no mildew. In our little part of the cellar – we called it 'the wine-cellar' because there was a rack for wine bottles – there was a big chest-of-drawers, and into that we packed books, papers, photos, and even a precious old musical clock we had inherited from Aunt Bina. We brought down another cupboard and crammed it full of under-clothing. There was an old camel-hair jacket that I was going to cut down for a little coat for Wolfgang, but hadn't got round to it. That was also put down in the cellar. It was to be our undoing. When we got back everything had been taken. The Oellers told us that the jacket had been mistaken for a Nazi uniform and that had been the excuse for ransacking the whole house.

We just had to catch that train
At seven o'clock on 6 November 1944 we set off for the station. We had a pram, a push-chair, and 13 pieces of luggage. It was a misty evening, and as we were leaving, the air-raid siren started up. We had to ignore it, because we just had to catch that train. As we drove through Rheydt, I took a last look at my parents' house. The white inside walls of my father's burnt-out factory could just be seen, despite the blackout.

We sat in the waiting-room at Gladbach, and, after a short time, the Düsseldorf train arrived. We soon arrived in Düsseldorf and headed for the waiting-room. Each time a Berlin train was announced, we got up and stood at the ready on the platform. But every train that stopped was so full that it was impossible to get on. So we stayed on the platform and pinned all our hopes on the next train to arrive. Still no luck!

I'll never forget the scene: hundreds of people milling around with cases, crates and baskets, all pushing and shoving, while fruit, vegetables, and all sorts of other things rolled around the platform. People were just desperate to get aboard, even if it meant abandoning half their possessions. We knew we would just have to fight our way on to the next one. Ludwig's leave was nearly up.

The next time a train stopped we were in luck, because the compartment for women and children was right by us. A soldier let down the window and shouted, 'Climb in here. I'll help you.' Ludwig lifted, the soldier pulled, and I was in. Wolfgang and the cases were then passed up after me. Now Ludwig had to rush with the push-chair to the other end of the train, where the luggage-van was situated. Luckily he had moved our heavily laden pram up to that end of the platform beforehand. As he arrived, the guard shut the door in his face, with the prams still on the platform. Pleading and shouting did no good. The guard steadfastly refused to open the heavy doors again. Luckily a young man on the train came to our rescue. Ludwig managed to prise the doors open and hold them back, while the other man pushed in the two prams. I don't know what I would have done otherwise. The compartment was packed to overflowing. The corridors were blocked with luggage, cases, and people. Even the toilets were full with people sitting on the seats. I was feeling sick, but glad at least that there was now some chance of getting to my sister's in the country.

MRS L. BARRY, of Liverpool, Merseyside, was one of the first mothers to be evacuated – and one of the first to return home:

'Come on, love, you must be hungry'

When war broke out I had no thoughts of being evacuated, until a nurse came on the Saturday and said that as I had a baby of 18 months it was my duty to go. I gathered a few clothes together for my baby Joan, and hardly anything for myself, and off I went to Edge Hill station. The train was very slow but eventually we arrived at Crewe. I got off the train to go for two cups of tea while my friend minded the baby. I got the tea just in time to see the train moving up the line. I dropped the two cups and, seeing one of the train doors open, I jumped in, falling and bruising my knees. It had been only moving a few yards up the line to bring the other coaches up to the platform, but, of course, I wasn't to know that at the time.

We eventually arrived at Kington Hereford at one o'clock in the morning. You can imagine how we felt. We had to go to a church hall. Most of the other evacuees were placed before me, but a Mr Jones, a farmer, said, 'Come on, love, you must be hungry,' and drove me and the baby back to his house. But as soon as his wife saw me she said, 'I asked for two boys, not a mother and baby.' You can imagine how I felt.

While I was there, I did what I could in the way of washing up, but I had to look after my baby. I was told I should be thankful to be there at all. Well, my husband sent on my warm suit and in the pocket were two pound notes to come home. In the meantime, my brother-in-law had arrived in the village to visit the little boy from next door to him. When he saw me, he said, 'You're coming back with us.' I gathered my things together and gave Mrs Jones the two pound notes for my keep. Little did I know at the time that she was getting paid by the government.

I am now a widow, in my eighties, with two lovely daughters, and four grandchildren, but I still remember my first and last taste of evacuation.

JENNY GRAUBAUM was born in Berlin and still lives in East Berlin. Like so many other wives, the war forced her to spend years on her own acting as both mother and father to her young children. When her husband was finally demobbed, they found the years of separation had taken their toll:

'Things weren't the same between us'

Just after getting married we lived in the Wiener Strasse. Just a living room and kitchen, but really nice and not too dear at that. Five stairs up, we were. I lived there with my two young boys, one born 1935, the other 1936. I had to bring them up pretty much on my own. Their dad was called up in 1935. That happened, you know. He was on active service from 1935 to 1937. Stationed at Wünsdorf. He was a car mechanic by trade. Then in 1939, right at the start of things, they called him up again. He was away till 1948. Nine whole years, he was away from me! By the time he got back, our eldest lad had already been confirmed. Later he took over his dad's garage business. 'Graubaum's Car Services' it's called, on the Kölnische Strasse in Niederschönweide. We bought it in 1949. Still going as a family business today. Except that the family is not the same. The damned war has seen to that.

Well, let me tell you how it all happened. Things didn't look so bad at first. My husband was sent to France. Working with a tank-repair unit. He'll soon be back, I used to tell myself. We'll survive. I'm not the sort to worry, you see. Typical Berliner: ever the optimist.

At first things didn't go too badly. I couldn't complain. As a service man's wife I got 270 Reichs-mark a month. Sometimes a free ticket to an operetta at the Metropol or to a revue at the Friedrich Strasse Palace. There were all sorts of stories coming back from France. You never heard of those letters with black borders. I fixed things up nicely at home for the two boys. We often went to visit my parents on Kiefholz Strasse – that's actually where we went when we got bombed out of the Wiener Strasse. We went out on trips with the boys, to Neuruppin. I had relatives there.

Later my husband was sent to Russia. And here in Berlin the bombs started dropping on our heads. I was lucky, though. We were evacuated out to Mecklenburg; Rühlow the village was called. That was 1943. I'm really not the worrying type, and although my husband was out on the battlefields, there just wasn't time to get worked up, not once the bombs started dropping. You were just left to fend for yourself. The main things were to keep the kids close to you and look after your parents, so that nobody got lost.

The worst thing was the air-raids. I remember once, we were all down in the cellar, then the all-clear sounded, so we went back up to the living room, five flights up. Then it started up again. The Amis and the Tommies – that's what we called the Americans and the British – started dropping their bombs on us all over again. Back down the stairs to the cellar, kids and all. I always wrapped up their heads in thick towels whenever there was an air-raid and I put lint bandages over their mouths. Suddenly the cellar light went out. That's it, we're finished, we all thought. It was such a shock for me that my brow came out in a cold sweat. I grabbed the children – we're getting out of here was my only thought. I simply pushed the air-raid warden out of the way, I was in such a rush. It's a terrible thought, being buried alive. I just sat down in the entrance lobby with the children. Then I prayed. I'm not really all that churchy. But I really prayed that night. 'Dear God, we will thank you for the rest of our lives, if you just let us survive. Dry bread every day would be better than this. Just let this war be over!'

Well, after that, our luck changed. Evacuation to Mecklenburg. It was just wonderful to be out of Berlin and away from the everlasting air-raids. I did all sorts of jobs in the country: milked cows, planted beet. You got paid in produce, so I was able to send my ration coupons to my parents in Berlin. Some of us were Berlin women, others were from the Rhineland, but we settled in very comfortably in the village. We were just young people then and liked a bit of fun. In the evenings we used to put out tables and chairs under the linden tree to have our meal together. Then we would pool all our food so that we had enough to make cakes for the children. We played the accordion and sang songs.

But then the news from my husband stopped coming. That would be in 1944. So I sat down and wrote to his commanding officer.

'Dear First Lieutenant,' I wrote, 'I would very much like to have news of my husband, Staff-sergeant Graubaum, who is now serving with your regiment. I have had no news for a long time and I am sure you understand how terrible it is to be living with all the uncertainty. Please write and tell me whether my husband is missing or whether he has been killed or what has happened to him.' Back came the answer: his company had gone south of the Berenisa and had got as far as Minsk. But my husband wasn't with them. He had got stopped at Bobruisk. That's where he was. A prisoner of war. He didn't get released till 1948.

When the war was coming to an end, in spring 1945, we all started returning home. In the end all the evacuees had to leave the village. We wanted to get back home anyway. Before he had gone off to Russia, my husband had said to me, 'If we lose this war, don't just run off. Stay put. Wait at home.' So I set off for Berlin with my children. We had to take the long way round, though. And even then we nearly copped it. That was in Güstrow. We had found a place to sleep in a pretty derelict hotel, when a messenger or courier, or whatever you call them, came round saying that they were blocking up all the roads with tank traps. How pointless! What did they think they were trying to defend? It was just a smashed-up town full of women, children and old folk. So I woke up the boys. 'Come on, come on! We've got to get out of here right away!' We met the first Russians at Sternberg. That was the moment we knew the war was over.

But our house on the Wiener Strasse wasn't there any more. Bombed flat! Two weeks before the war ended. It was so senseless! The whole area had been flattened on 27 April 1945. Wiener Strasse, Görtlizer Ufer, Reichenberger Strasse. All gone. I can never forget that. Why did they bomb women and children?

When my husband came home again in 1948, I had been out working for a long time. What's a young woman supposed to do? Sit at home, waiting and moping? Not me! I still had my strength. I went out looking for a hard manual job. You got a special allowance for that. I worked for the Russians, helped put up the Treptow War Memorial. Take on anything, me. Digging foundations, then plastering and mortaring up on the granite slabs at the entrance that represents the lowered flags. Just to get my manual worker's card and my meals at the 'Kotikow Canteen'. They called it that because Kotikow was the Russian commandant and he was the one who allowed German women and children to get food from the Russian army supplies.

No, I never whined and complained that if only my husband would come home, things would get better for us. I looked after the boys all on my own. No, women are not such weaklings. They can get things done, too, just as long as they don't start whining. It might even have been the best time of my life.

When my husband came home, we had to start getting used to each other all over again. The kids were used to only listening to their mother, and that's just what they did. My husband and me, we worked together to get the garage business going. That was in 1949. But things weren't the same between us. I had been nine years on my own, having to take my own decisions. That changes you. My husband wasn't the same man either, when he came home. We separated. That damned war had finally even broken up our marriage and family.

NORMA TROY, of Little Plumstead, Norfolk. Norma, whose husband was in the army, lived in London throughout the war, working full-time with a firm of solicitors in the City, and part-time in the ARP. Despite the dangers, being young and full of life, she could still appreciate the lighter moments in the dark days of the blitz:

'So many large bottoms'

My husband was in London all through the blitz, but I saw him only occasionally when he was able to get a pass home. My family spent every night in the air-raid shelter and, during the lulls in the gunfire, we would come out to the kitchen to make cocoa. My sister and I maintain that we were the original Frank Sinatra 'swooners', as we had a record of Tommy Dorsey's band, with a vocal by 'Ol' Blue Eyes', which we would play on a portable gramophone and drool over his voice whilst we were waiting for the kettle to boil.

Then came the V1s – hideous-sounding contraptions which, when the engine cut out, dived to the ground. That moment the noise ceased was always terrifying whilst you waited for the inevitable crash. I remember one occasion when I was in a bus going along Gracechurch Street, in the City, at nine o'clock in the morning. It had just stopped to take on a number of rather plump cleaning ladies who were going home after their stint cleaning City offices. They all piled into the bus and took their seats, when we all became aware of the drone of a V1 very close by. Suddenly it cut out and, without exception, all the ladies dived beneath the seats and I don't think I've ever seen so many large bottoms at one time. I was so helpless with laughter that I completely forgot the danger. Luckily, when the crash came it was beyond us, on the other side of the river.

MARY CLAYTON, of Willenhall, West Midlands. Throughout the war years Mary's life was one long struggle to find a comfortable, secure home in which to bring up her small son until the return of her husband from prisoner-of-war camp. This proved easier said than done:

'My feet never seemed to find the ground'

Diary extract: 30 July 1942:

By the light of a small candle, at 3 a.m., I write this through a very bad air-raid. All this week air-raids have been bad. Tonight is worse than ever. I would feel better if I had someone to sit with me. I am sorry to say this, but the people around here think I am stuck up. Perhaps I am, but I couldn't join in the get-togethers over beer and laughter when so much terror went on. Bombs drop around us.

That night my cousin Bill knocked at the door at 4.30 a.m. His face looked white. 'Our Mary,' he blurted out, 'they've had it up the New Road!'

On went my coat; my little son and I were already dressed. I hurried down our dark street carrying Robert in my arms. As I got near the town centre I could see the glow of fires in the sky. A policeman stopped me before I could get near the inferno. 'You can't go down that road, love.'

'But my mother-in-law and family live that way!'

'Sorry, love.'

'Please, officer. I promise not to hinder nurses, doctors, or anybody.'

'It's more than my life's worth, but go on if you must.'

I passed through the crowd of onlookers; my mouth was dry. Everywhere seemed light. I reached my mother-in-law's house. There it stood, intact. 'Thank God!' I cried out loud. I rang the bell and Mum came to the door.

'I can forgive 'em for us having no food and light, but no water for a cup of tea – that I can't forgive!' she said.

I burst into tears. My little four-year-old son began to cry because I was crying and the lights were out all over the area. My brother-in-law had dashed off to see if he could help, as he was in the AFS.

In January 1940, I gave up our home to be a lady's companion and help to a vicar's wife, about 50 miles from my home town in the Midlands. Companion-help? I was expected to rise at 5.45 a.m., wash in cold water, dress quickly, and be downstairs to light fires with paper (no wood). I learned how to twist and turn newspapers to act as sticks of wood. The tables I'd laid the night before. I'd to make breakfast for eight people. All this was done on such meagre rations, it just wasn't worth taking it to the table. Lots of hot water that passed for tea was handed around and table napkins placed back in their rings. Then I would hurry and wash up, feed my baby son, and put him in his playpen. The day's washing, dusting and cleaning all had to be finished before 1 p.m. After a lunch that once again seemed to be all silver service, straight lace and grace, I'd be expected to be washed, and dressed in afternoon wear, to be able to answer the door to callers before 3 p.m.

Now why did you do this, you may ask? Well, £1 10s army pay didn't seem to buy very much. My logic in 1940 worked out that my situation would be better if I could bring up my son in a good Christian household where there were things to do and no coal, electricity, or rent bills to pay. I should be able to save for when the war was over. After all, I'd been promised five shillings a week for my services. But there was a problem with getting paid. First I would ask, in a mild way, 'Is it possible to have my £1 per month, please?' I needed to get back to the Midlands to find out why I wasn't getting any mail from my husband. 'Sorry,' I was told, when £16 was due. 'Give me a little more time, please.' I found out later that the vicar's wife had had more than her share of trouble, but that was their business. My own mother helped out financially in the end.

Six months went by. My husband was presumed dead. I absolutely refused to believe all the reports.

No longer could I work in a place where my Christian beliefs had been shattered. My little son and weary me had no place to lay our heads. My mother had lost her husband in the 1914–18 war. Later, she married a man 16 years younger than herself. Drinks, rowdy parties and singing were all commonplace in their home. I found myself living with my mother and stepfather. It was more than diabolical.

Soon I found myself doing service again; this time for two priests. I was able to get most of my furniture back to the Midlands, where I put it in store, then I got it all moved to where I now had a full-time job, in the home of the two young clergymen. Now I could at least keep an eye on it.

I went to work for the clergymen, but there was no good news for me on the personal front until September 1940. 'I live again,' I wrote in my diary. My husband wasn't dead – he was a prisoner of war!

One of the priests I was working for fell in love with me; but after being rebuffed and finding out my husband was still alive, he joined the army. So it was back to Mother for Bobby and me. She let me have the boxroom. My child was being shuttled from place to place. One time it was church life and prayers, the next it was beer, cards, rows, and fun-loving people getting together to forget the horrors of war. Coping with rations, shortages, washing baby's things with shaving soap, listening to an unhappy uncle whose marriage had broken up, as so many did during the war, I felt I would go mad.

Mother gave my uncle a room in her home. He only added to the stress. The poor man was weak and so afraid of life in general, he let himself be blackmailed for years, until my mother, who could stand things no longer, demanded to know where his money was going.

I had sleepless nights with a baby who didn't seem to know anything about peace. I had to work very hard – shopping, washing for six of us (my brother making up the six). Night after night there were the air-raids. Always the supper-beer had to be fetched and I was the drudge who had to go for it. I remember the fog, snow, rain and thunderstorms, and raids, raids, raids . . .

At long last a nurse friend said to me, 'If you don't get away from home soon you'll have a nervous breakdown. Let me help you.' She did. I was told, 'There's a tiny house in a very poor locality, a rough area, but it'll be a place to put your furniture in.'

I went to see it. In my wildest dreams of degradation this was the worst. Holes in the walls, gas-tar borders top and bottom, nails in their hundreds to keep up blackouts, and bags at some of the windows. My mother went with me to look at this hellhole. 'Over my dead body do you come here!' she almost screamed. 'Come on, take the key back.'

'No,' I said quickly. 'I'll keep it. I'll come back again and see if there's any way I can possibly make the place ship-shape.'

Mother took care of my little son. Armed with disinfectant (soda), bits of soap, brushes and buckets, I worked on the place for three weeks. I covered the walls with brown parcel-paper and covered the holes with cardboard. Cheap paint, dark green, went on the bottom walls, cream for the top halves and the ceiling. Lino was difficult to lay because my baby who couldn't walk yet kept sliding over it.

The day the furniture was delivered was one to remember. Everything was dumped in the house and I was left alone. I could see no reason to live as another raid began and I had no idea where to put anything in such a tiny place. There was no help from a soul. The front door was so close to the road that every time a car went by, or I heard footsteps go past the door, I felt so distraught I just sat there holding the baby and shaking. After I had put my son Bobby to bed, I cried.

Next morning I looked out on the backyard. Six tiny houses, all in a row, had to share just two toilets, far from the houses themselves. There were two broken-down wash-houses, but no place for me, as I was a newcomer and had to wait to see if there was a spot when I could use the boiler. My neighbours were hostile. 'Lady Muck' was their name for me. But my mother needed assistance with her washing, so did my husband's mother, so I used to ask if I could use the wash-house at four o'clock in the morning, then leave the place clean and ready for the regulars . . . Washing on the line in front of my little patch; fire in a very small corner of the grate; one armchair and an oh-so-small table filling my kitchen. It wasn't much, but, nevertheless, I had my own key to my own 'little box'.

Lots of nights, during the air-raids, Bobby and I slept under the stairs, with plaster from the old beams falling on our faces. German planes came so near the road, dropping their incendiary bombs, there would be no sleep for hours at night. It all seemed too much to bear at times. Letters from Poland, where my husband was a prisoner of war, were the only comfort, apart from my darling little son.

Soon I had to do my bit for the war effort. I volunteered to cook for 90 children, and 12 staff, while their mothers did war work. At the nursery, Bobby would get his breakfast, lunch, tea, milk and cake, medical care, and kindergarten education. I would be there as cook-housekeeper, to see he was well looked after along with the rest of the children. It was a well-staffed, council-run place here in my own locality. Pity the matron had to spoil it all. She fell out of favour for pilfering the food allotted to us. A kind judge let her off because of the circumstances of her home life. I never did get my wages from her.

My health began to give way under the stress. I had to give up the very long hours of service, plus voluntary this and that, although I still did washing for both Mums. My feet never seemed to find the ground. I was always flying here, there and everywhere. Strangely enough, our home became so nice after all the DIY effort I had put in now that I had more time to spare. Soon everybody got to know I was at home these days and the teapot was rarely cold.

Bobby used to ask me, 'Why haven't I got a daddy?' He had noticed other men playing with their own children. Of course, they were men doing long hours of war work, etc. After I'd told him 'Your daddy is a soldier, darling', he once went up to a soldier and asked, 'Are you my daddy?'

'Not bloody likely!' was the blunt reply.

My son began to cry. 'Mummy, I haven't got a daddy, have I? He's only a fairy like those you read about to me!'

After a particularly nasty air-raid, as we came out of the shelter, Bobby said, 'Mummy, I will protect you from those germs (he meant Germans and had mixed his words up) and I will be your husband-daddy, so don't cry any more, will you?' He took his hands from my face, where he had placed them to comfort me . . . A very tender moment to remember over 40 years later.

My little son and I had been tossed about a lot and life was hard in those years. Then suddenly there was repatriation news. My beloved was coming home!

Once the people in the area heard about it everything changed. What a welcome they gave him! There were flags everywhere, presents, flowers, toys for Bobby, coal, food, fruit, free tickets to the cinema, and parties laid on. 'The war's over!' they cried. 'Somebody's coming home!'

After the flags had been taken down, we tried very hard to recover from the excitement of the repatriation. The Press and their photographers were there. Everybody, it seemed, wanted to call at the tiny house my husband had come back to. 'We want Sam! We want Sam!' the crowd had chanted on that day, 28 October 1943, and it

235

had been very hard to get through the door as people pushed forward to see an ex-POW.

I suggested that Sam went upstairs and pushed up the sash window so that the people at the back of the crowd could see him, because they had waited so long outside. He did and there was an almighty roar as the whole world, it seemed to me, shouted, 'Welcome home, Sam! Good luck! Well done!' Women were crying and babies in arms were crying too because of all the noise.

When we came down the twisting old stairs, it began to dawn on my husband that this was where he had got to live. He had left, in 1939, a beautiful twelve-roomed house, with a Regency front door, and now, looking at the tiny room, which I had made as comfortable as possible, the ex-POW stretched out his arms and said, 'I feel as if I could almost touch these walls!'

My heart sank as I saw the disapproval on his face. Surely it's better than a prison camp, I thought. But there was no time to discuss anything in private because up till midnight friends and relations flowed in like spring water.

Bobby was staying so close to his daddy that he almost cried when I insisted that he went to bed. He was five and a half years old now. How did he know this was his daddy? Because every night before he went to bed he used to kiss his daddy's photograph and salute it. Then he would say, 'Goodnight, Daddy. God bless you.' The last time Sam had seen him, he hadn't even begun to walk.

It was a shock to my beloved man to find that he had to share a toilet with other families and wait his turn before he could go to bed that night.

I was 15 years old when we first fell in love and Sam was 17. I told him then, 'I shall marry you one day!' And I did, on 25 July 1936. Ever since we first met, I had placed him on a pedestal. Up to that night he was still there, but he was now a man with secrets to confess before he reclaimed his wife for the first time in three and a half years. In the darkness Sam talked about his little disloyalties before he was taken prisoner in a village near the Belgian border in May 1940.

Before Sam came back, the YMCA, where I cooked snacks for 'the boys', had become something of a nightmare, fending off advances from lonely soldiers. After supper in the church hall there was occasionally dancing and singing of the old favourites such as 'We'll Meet Again' and 'Run Rabbit Run', etc. A group of young soldiers decided to 'capture' and make fun of me one evening because I always refused to flirt with them.

'Got yer!' I was surrounded by a lot of handsome men. One took the tray of dirty dishes from me; the others carried me, struggling, to a high church window and pushed me on to the sill. I felt so silly looking down on all the laughing soldiers. 'Let me down or I'll jump!' I said angrily.

'No, we won't,' one said. 'You are now Saint Mary!' Then they chanted mockingly: 'I'm married. Why don't you stop flirting? You're a married man. No, you can't see me home . . .' and lots more quips.

With the help of a supervisor, 'Old Goody Gumdrops' managed to get down out of the window. The lads cheered. 'What a waste!' somebody called, as I picked up the tray again and fled to the back room to wash up.

Yes, I was a prude. And now, in the darkness, my blood ran cold as Sammy whispered into my ear, 'I'm sorry, Sweet . . .' I was brave enough to ask why he had chosen to tell me these little stories on such a night as this. 'I needed to confess,' he said, 'before we resumed our lives together. After all, it was wartime . . .'

'Saint Mary' flashed before my closed eyes . . . all my chances of dates, affairs, companionship . . . What good times I could have had. Nevertheless, I hadn't, and here I was, with all the longing of a love-starved woman, lying beside my own 'god'. In my mind was a burning jealousy, yet at the same time the needs of the body. Why punish my husband any more?

Months passed and there was much adjusting to be done. I mothered and smothered Sammy. First thing in the morning I would get up and blacklead the grate, light the fire, cook what little rations there were, take Bobby to school, then I would come home and take a tray up to my husband in bed, still suffering the after effects of malnutrition. Eventually he had to go back into hospital; he wasn't accepting the outside world too well.

After a rest, and being seen by a psychiatrist, my husband came back home, irritable, and needing to keep the door closed to all the people who used to be regular callers. Flowers were left next door, fruit and coal left outside in bags. More and more Sammy would say, 'Don't answer it! Lock it.' That ever open door became a prison gate. People soon got the message.

Bobby, too, was beginning to suffer. Daddy didn't like him being left-handed, but he had to adjust to more than that habit. Like so many families we all had a lot of adjusting to do when the war was over.

Looking back over all those years, I now realize just how much hope and faith I'd put into prayer and how I'd trusted that God would take care of my dear ones for me. Bobby, my son, and Sammy, my husband, are still as precious to me as ever, after all these years.

W.J., of Dormagen, North Rhine-Westphalia, tells of a particular incident during a bombing raid when she was sure their time had come:

'We were just waiting for the bomb to explode'

It was a day like any other. But it is a day that has remained in my memory over the years, perhaps because it was the day that we first came to realize just how senseless this war was.

The 22nd March 1945 began like any other, with attacks by fighter bombers as soon as it became light. They were Lightnings, very fast and highly manoeuvrable twin-bodied aircraft, which dropped bombs and rattled off their machine guns at every swoop. All we could do was retreat to our 'cellar'. It wasn't really a cellar at all, just a lobby with our rooms on one side overlooking the street, and with a boiler-room and storeroom on the garden side. That was all we had, and it offered no shelter at all. We kept all our valuables, documents and baby-things ready to hand at the top of the stairs. My father had set out for the neighbouring village before dawn. You didn't dare go out on the streets during the daytime for fear of getting caught in the airmen's gun-sights. On this particular day it was especially bad, with four attacks before lunch. But we survived.

Cooking meals was an adventure in itself. If we had to go and shelter downstairs, the cooking had to be taken off the fire. Food was too precious to let it get burnt. The afternoon started quietly, almost uncannily so. They were obviously having their lunch-break. But then . . .

They had stopped bothering to sound the air-raid sirens ages ago. We had to trust our own ears, and they had become pretty sharp! Things started to get uncomfortable at about five o'clock. Bombs were falling thick and fast, and in between you could hear bursts of machine-gun fire. The three of us – my mother, my sister and I – were standing huddled together in the lobby with my baby boy wrapped in a thick bedspread between us. Suddenly there was an almighty crash followed by the sound of breaking glass on the cellar stairs. It seemed to go on and on. A bomb had blown out the whole lobby window from second floor to cellar. The door to the boiler-room was blown off its hinges into the lobby, missing us by inches. The mortar and plaster dust was so thick you could hardly breathe. We had wrapped a cloth round my baby's little face. We were all crying – an odd sort of crying, with the tears just cascading of their own accord down my face. We felt a mixture of sheer helplessness and rage. But we had to stick it out.

Bang! Another hit. At the station this time, followed by a horrible whining and whizzing. Then a dull thud. Silence . . . We waited and waited – nothing happened. Probably the airmen had run out of ammunition and were turning away again. We just stood rooted to the spot where we had been standing at the start of the attack, weeping and praying, our nerves in tatters, just waiting for the bomb to explode. Finally I could stand it no longer and left the others. If the thing went up we were all done for anyway; if it didn't, then at least I could see what was to be done. I climbed out through the boiler-room into the garden, over mounds of rubble and scattered coke. That's where the thud had come from, we had felt it in the soles of our feet.

239

Then I saw it. There in the garden, close to the house – just about 20 paces away – was a piece of railway line, twisted up like a corkscrew. It must have been blown from the station right over the house by the bomb. There it lay, all buckled – but harmless!

I stood staring at it in disbelief. Then, shouting for the others to come, I started to laugh hysterically and cry all at the same time. They all thought I'd finally cracked, until they saw what I could see. Then we fell into each other's arms, laughing and crying for joy. What a relief! My little boy didn't understand the adult world any more: first they squeeze him between them, then they put a cloth over his face and now they are cavorting around like idiots. He finally cried himself to sleep, once I had gathered up all the weeds, strawberry plants, snails and other forms of life that were filling his room and thrown them all back into the garden again.

Soon after that, Dad came home. He had seen the attack from some way off and was worried to death about us. On the way he had had to throw himself into the ditch four times. But as soon as he saw us, he spread his arms and said from the bottom of his heart, 'Thank Heavens! You must have had a guardian angel watching over you!' He was right. We had!

MRS M. PRICE, from Bilston, West Midlands, was a young bride when war came to Birmingham and strange things began to happen:

'Fur coats were being swilled down the street'

The day war was declared my husband and I had our marriage banns called for the first time. We were married on 30 September 1939. I worked at GEC in Birmingham making torch batteries. I travelled by train for ninepence return each day. My husband worked at GKN at Darlaston making nuts and bolts. He also had to take his turn on fire duty. One night when he was on fire duty at GKN a landmine dropped on the church which they had just left. When the dust settled, they went back with the ARP warden to inspect the damage. Imagine their surprise when they found the church had completely disappeared. Not a thing was found of the church or its contents. It was blown up and completely buried. The church was All Saints and situated in Walsall Road in Darlaston. There is now a new 'All Saints' built on the exact spot of the old.

My firm decided we should begin work at 7.30 a.m. instead of 8 a.m. The first morning I went in there was a bomb in the workshop. Another morning, on arriving in the centre of Birmingham to catch the tram, there were 18 fires blazing around us at the same time. Water from the fire-hoses was flooding everywhere and fur coats were being swilled down the street. It was wicked to see.

I was the first woman in Bilston to have a shopkeeper for overcharging for food. This was done through the food officer, Mr Fred Barnett. Then there was the time I was in the doctor's with my two children with whooping cough and my ration books were stolen. It was about a fortnight before Christmas when we had double rations for the children. I reported it to the local police station and asked for a form to get new books, but they refused. When I asked why, they said they did not know me and so I told them I didn't want the likes of them to know me. They then said they would put me down the hole and I replied they would have to feed and keep me. I didn't get the forms and had to go to the local vicarage where I got satisfaction. The vicar was quite mad about it.

I had to work until 8 p.m. and didn't get home until 10 p.m. and had to be off again next morning at seven o'clock. I had to do my shopping during the dinner-hour. Every morning we had a free cup of tea brought round. As soon as we had the cup of tea in our hands the sirens would go and down we'd have to rush to the shelter. We can laugh about it now.

One evening, my husband and I went to fetch some fish and chips and the bombs started to drop all around us. We dropped flat on the floor and all the fish and chips went flying everywhere. When it was all over none of it was fit to eat. My husband and I still laugh about it.

ELIZABETH BUXTON, (formerly BOYCE), of Dudley, West Midlands, was married to a Scotsman from Glasgow, Wilson Boyce, and was the mother of a small son, Brian, when war broke out. Not wanting to be called up into the army, her husband volunteered for the navy, then later on volunteered for the landmine disposal squad. Disposing of landmines was not a task for the fainthearted and called for great bravery on the part of the men involved. These huge, pear-shaped, eight-feet long contraptions were originally anti-shipping mines and contained nearly a ton of explosives – enough to rip the heart from a battleship. Unlike normal bombs, they descended slowly by parachute, coming to rest on the surface of the ground, and the shock waves of one explosion were quite capable of demolishing a whole avenue of houses, and shattering windows several streets away. But most worrying of all, they were detonated by various types of fuse, the most feared of which was magnetic and could be activated by any metal object. Even a fire engine or ambulance in the vicinity could act as its trigger. The men called upon to defuse these monsters constantly diced with death, and for their wives the worry was often even more intense than that of the ordinary Forces wife:

'I still look for one face in a crowd'

While my husband was away, I was living in the family home in Dudley, with my son and mother, and took a part-time job in Birmingham to help out the naval allowance. To my surprise one afternoon my husband, in uniform, walked into my place of work saying they had been rushed up from London, as they expected Birmingham to be blitzed that night. (He had been allowed a 20-minute refreshment break, hence the chance to see me.) He told me to ask if I could finish then and catch the bus home, but, alas, the sirens went within 15 minutes and everything stopped. All the staff had to evacuate to the shelter.

The raid, which was a really bad one, lasted until eight o'clock the following morning. We were in the city centre and between the waves of planes coming over we could see the fires engulfing C.&A.'s

and Marshall & Snellgrove's, etc. Every time a new wave of bombers came over the firemen would go from standing to kneeling, then on to their stomachs, without ever moving their hosepipes from the flames.

That night they dropped 39 landmines on Birmingham, but, thank goodness, the operator allowed me to phone home to let my mother know I was safe in a shelter, and to assure myself that there was no raid on Dudley, eight miles away. During the night a landmine was dropped near us, by St Philip's Church, fracturing a gas-pipe. The people affected were brought into our shelter and one little girl could not stop shaking. I nursed her for the rest of the night and, after the all-clear went at 8 a.m., I asked her mother if I could take her home with me to get some sleep. (Dudley was considered safer.) The mother agreed, so I gave up my job and the little girl stayed with us for a month.

Of course I didn't see my husband again that night, they were so very busy. But later I was to hear that for detonating one particularly dangerous landmine that night, my husband was to be awarded the George Cross.

During a period of leave, in February 1941, we talked of when he would be summoned to Buckingham Palace to receive the medal, and I told him I had an awful feeling I wouldn't go with him. He just laughed and said, 'You'll probably have the flu and not be able to come, not looking after yourself with me away.' Little did we know . . .

When the worst of the blitz was over and things were much quieter, only a skeleton staff was needed to detonate the landmines in the major cities, so the other men were sent back to sea. My husband was put on the destroyer HMS *Jersey*. He was only at sea six weeks when they were engaged in the Battle of Crete. There were casualties and on 2 May 1941 I received a telegram saying he was missing, presumed killed. In another six weeks my allowance book was exchanged for a widow's pension book. Eighteen shillings for me and two shillings and sixpence for my son.

In October 1942, my son, in his kilt, and I, in mourning dress, went to Buckingham Palace to receive the medal from the King. My son now has the medal, which in turn will go to my grandson.

Even now, after all these years, and even though I remarried and was widowed again, when there is film from the war years on television, I still look for one face in a crowd. And I still have my memories, both wonderful and sad, of 10 years as a housewife and mother.

INGE WILMANNS, of Duisburg, North Rhine-Westphalia, lived during the early years of the war with her three young children in a large, rented house on the outskirts of Kiel. Her husband Franz had a job in industry and was seldom at home. She kept a diary throughout those years, and its contents today record the young mother's constant struggle to keep the children warm and happy. As temperatures fell, bombing became a regular occurrence and supplies dwindled:

'The doctor came and prescribed coal for us'

4 January 1940
Minus 12° centigrade today. I hear that coal is available in Kiel, but supplies are not getting out here to the country areas.

6 January 1940
Jen's little feet are dead with cold. What a bitter wartime winter! All the pipes are frozen up, but at least the pump in the yard is still working.

16 January 1940
After a few days' thaw the Siberian cold is with us again. Snow storms, too. The toothpaste in the children's room is frozen solid. Ruth finds it interesting.

21 January 1940
No fuel for the stove today. No electricity. No hot meal today. Just

managed to get the children's milk lukewarm on the dying stove. Franz now in Sweden. The coalman has taken pity on me. After dark (!) I was able to go and fetch 50 kilos on the sledge. What bliss!

14 February 1940
Gisela and Jens are sleeping in the living-room overnight (+3°C). Ruth and I stick it out in the bedroom (−3°C). Whenever I go to empty her pot the contents are already frozen, no matter how quick I am.

21 February 1940
Ruth and I have gone down sick. The doctor came and prescribed coal for us. But only because I'm expecting another baby.

24 March 1940
Franz has pruned down the fruit-trees and is busy stuffing branches into the stove. We daren't cut down anything else, because we're only renting house and garden. Spring is coming!

10 May 1940
Yesterday our little Horst was born. His 'big' sister (3 years) has her own name for him. She calls him 'Holli'. Two-year-old Gisela wants to play with him. Jens takes not the slightest notice of his new brother. In the night the air-raid sirens go and there is heavy artillery fire. Unfortunately the guns are quite close by. The windows rattle and the walls shake. I jump with fright at every bang as I lie in my bed.

19 June 1940
Ruth can't manage to sleep at night. She wakes up as soon as the sirens go and starts crying when the guns start banging.

1 July 1940
Had to take the children down to the cellar today for the first time. Gisela and Baby Holli sleep soundly in their makeshift beds. Ruth is wide awake, anxious about what's happening. Jens sings his entire repertoire of songs.

3 July 1940
Two daytime air-raid warnings today. I have to breast-feed Holli in the cellar. Every time the guns go off Jens shouts 'Ahoy!'

7 July 1940
In the cellar for three and a half hours tonight. It's especially hard for Ruth. It makes you really despair!

29 July 1940
This miserable war! Ruth and now Gisela are quite changed in character. I'm afraid they're going to bear the scars for the rest of their lives. I've changed, too. I'm no longer the happy Mum I used to be.

25 August 1940
Five hours in the cellar tonight. The bombs are just raining down.

11 September 1940
Everyone has made their cellar into a sort of second home. We now go down first thing every evening.

31 January 1941
It's so cold in the house that I'm in tears.

The above extracts cover a young mother's life during one wartime winter. The war had many such winters. Inge Wilmann and her family survived the war. The children are all in their forties, and Inge herself lives in Duisburg.

MABEL TERRY, of Copmanthorpe, York. When war was declared Mabel was a happy and contented young wife and mother, but very soon her world was to be turned upside down. Life would never be the same again:

'A beautiful place, but so sad'

In September 1939, when war was declared, my elder son Colin was three years of age and my baby Malcolm was 10 weeks old. My husband Bob, a gardener, was earning £2 10s a week. We lived in a very charming old cottage, with no mod cons, but life was peaceful and happy. Little did I think, like millions of housewives all over the world, from then on everything would change because of a madman called Hitler.

Shortly after 3 September, because we lived in a quiet village, two bus-loads of sad, bewildered children arrived to be accommodated with us as evacuees. So Cyril, a shy seven-year-old from a very poor part of Sunderland, became a member of our family. His table manners were dreadful and we thought he had lived on broken biscuits and chips. But with a lot of loving care he soon became a healthy, happy little boy.

On 14 September 1940 my husband's eldest sister was killed in the crypt of Chelsea Old Church, in London, during an air-raid. This shattered Bob and he said he would volunteer for the RAF. I agreed with him. As a result, he went off to the RAF at Blackpool on 5 January 1941 and I moved to a house in Darlington to be near my parents. Until then we had never been apart for a single night. However, we wrote to each other every night and just lived for leave time, even if it was only a 48-hour pass, and half of it spent travelling.

He passed out as a wireless operator, air gunner, with Coastal Command. On his last leave, in June 1943, he looked older, but assured me everything was OK and we had a lovely holiday with the boys. Colin was devoted to his Dad and Malcolm was now a charming three-year-old.

Six weeks after returning to Haverford, in South Wales, I received the dreaded 'priority' telegram to say he was reported missing. Something told me it was final and, six months afterwards, he was presumed killed. I can't tell you how I felt. Night after night I just wept and wondered how on earth I could bring his sons up without him.

The following amounts are what we received during the war, and afterwards, in the case of my war widow's pension: my husband's pay as a sergeant wireless operator, air gunner, was 7s 9d per seven-day week, plus 6d per day extra. My allowance as a war widow, payable from April 1944, was a weekly pension of £1 11s 3d, plus 18s allowance for the two children, which made a total of £2 9s 3d. (My weekly rent was 13s per week.)

The service estate of Sergeant Terry 1126976 was:

Balance of pay and allowance	£17 10s 2d
Service Post War Credits at 6d per day	£15 7s 6d
Cash found in effects	£ 4 0s 0d
Total	£36 17s 8d

This was sent to me on 25 April 1944.

When I got my pittance of a pension, on which we could not live, I had to get a job. But first I had to get Malcolm into a nursery school, which I did. I then got a job as assistant cook at a nearby school. The cook in charge was a lovely person and we became life-long friends. We worked a 44-hour week, including Saturday mornings, so I had to take the boys to my parents, and then go to work. Life seemed to be a constant battle against time, and the work was very hard because we had such poor, makeshift equipment. But we enjoyed it and had lots of laughs.

One Saturday after leaving work I rushed into town and did my shopping and got on an empty bus to return home. A crowd of angry women came rushing on and told me to get off. It was a workers-only bus. But I was by now a changed person and I promptly asked them what they were thinking about. I was doing two jobs and they were doing one – and so I stayed on the workers' bus.

The food rationing was a problem and I often had to shop after I left work, so any extras had been gone long before I got there. However, one day before sweets were rationed, seeing a queue at Marks and Spencers, I joined the end of it and wondered what was in the white bags people were leaving with. My turn came and it was half a pound of dolly mixtures. The boys were delighted, but I would have loved some biscuits to have with a cup of tea. We had one egg per person every fourth week and what a joy that was. But what a real tragedy if the yolk broke, as it so often did.

The food rationing made us rather dishonest. I had a wonderful friend and neighbour who had a happy way of talking to the poor old manager of the Co-op and so he often forgot to cut the little portions out of our ration books. So we happily went to another shop and got another jar of jam, or packet of cornflakes, for which we had to give 16 points.

Another very dishonest thing we did and thought nothing about it was to rob the railway. Our menfolk were issued with warrants to travel home when leave was granted for seven days or more, but for 48-hour passes they had to pay all their own fare home. So we arranged very good methods to save money. Before he was killed in action, Bob would get on the train with a platform ticket and I would send him the return half of a ticket from a station about 10 miles from home. He would then wait on the station until a train from this place came in and then he walked through the barrier with his ticket, and thus got home for a few shillings. To get back to camp he reversed the process. This happened often and he was never caught. All his pals were up to the same trick.

We had coupons for everything, even socks. My boys used mine and their own. I went to bed in nighties made out of old summer dresses. My dear mother could do wonders with her sewing machine.

In Darlington we did not experience bad air-raids, but the sirens often went and we were advised by the air-raid warden to go down into our Anderson shelters. I decided against it. All three of us stayed together in one bedroom. If it had to be so, we would all go together. However, Darlington did have a very tragic experience. A young Canadian pilot, returning to a nearby air base from a bombing raid, lost control and almost crashed on a school and houses, but he managed to crash land in a nearby field. As a result of his heroic act a road is named after him, McMullen Road.

After Bob was killed, I got in touch with the next of kin of most of the crew. The observer was an Australian, Colin Hughes, one of four brothers. His parents wrote to me and sent the most wonderful parcels, containing everything we were short of, even knitting wool. When we opened these exciting parcels, out would fall a shower of wrapped sweets. We could hardly believe our eyes. These parcels still arrived long after the war, until rationing was over and food was no longer in short supply.

We could hardly believe it when, at last, it was all over. Thankfully, my two brothers returned safely, and my sons enjoyed hearing their stories. The war brought lots of sadness for me, but I survived and worked until I was 60.

Bob's name is on the War Memorial at Runnymede, which I have visited often. It is in memory of 20,000 RAF Commonwealth personnel with no known grave. A beautiful place, but so sad. Bob was 35 when he was killed, but the average age seems to be about 20.

Mabel Terry now lives in retirement on the outskirts of York. Colin and Malcolm both married and presented her with seven much-loved grandchildren.

MARIA SCHUSTER was in Limburg, Hessen, during the war and still lives there today. She kept a diary of all her wartime experiences and its contents reveal graphically the acute problems of coping with children, parents, and relatives when bombs were falling and the American forces advancing. Despite all the strains she never despaired and was determined to defend her few remaining possessions, right down to the last eiderdown.

'Throwing caution to the wind'

15 October 1944

On Sunday the 10th our house was bombed. The back of the house took the brunt of it. There were bombs in the garden, too. What a terrible time we had! The heavy props that had been put in to strengthen the cellar might just as well have been matchsticks, the way they were jumping about. Windows that we had already repaired were blasted out. Suddenly there was a flash, and the cellar was filled with thick clouds of dust. Then darkness. I fumbled around in the dark trying to turn off the gas-tap. Then I put on a gas-mask and wrapped a damp cloth round myself and went over to the cellar door, which, stupidly, we hadn't shut. We saw that the stairwell had been brought down and that the side and back walls of the house had collapsed. That was a dreadful moment. Then a neighbour came and shouted, 'Anybody hurt?' I calmed down immediately, and was relieved when my husband Albin arrived, safe and sound, with the children. They had been in the bunker outside.

We moved into Albin's office. There are seven of us penned up in the kitchen, together with our little herd of dachshunds. It's not too bad, apart from the severe cold. Now I have to do everything. The place is always dirty, with everybody being in the one little room. There's no water, no gas, no toilet, not even a drain. What I miss is just being on my own. All this work with my aching back and not even a chance to take a lie down for a few minutes on our chaise-longue. I miss my piano, too, funny as it may seem, because I wouldn't have either the time or energy to play it at the moment.

14 December 1944
Albin, Grandad, and Uncle Josef succeeded in rebuilding the walls of the house again. What an effort that was! There was no skin left on their fingertips. There was still an awful lot left to do, but at least we had the hope of moving back into the downstairs rooms by the end of February. Then on 29 November another terrible bomb! It destroyed the street side of the house this time, and brought down the outside walls of the music room, Dad's room, and Grandad's room. Huge cracks now run right through the whole house. It stands there with a great gaping wound. The whole garden is wrecked. So too are our hopes of ever moving back in.

Now Christmas is just round the corner, and there's nothing for the children, and nothing for the adults either. Albin has managed to get us a little Christmas tree, but all our decorations have gone in the bombing. We'll just have to beg and borrow. Yes, I'm having to learn to beg now. Begging to use the wash-house, begging to hang up the washing. You'd think people would be only too glad to help, having escaped the bombing themselves. The other day the water was off, and you should have heard the complaining they set up. I've been 11 weeks without! And no gas and no toilet!

2 April 1945
The Americans have taken Limburg with very little resistance. On 25 March there was a heavy air-raid. I was outside, on my way back to the children. I saw the whole raid and watched the bombs glinting in the sunshine as they fell. Then there was such a deafening noise, you'd have thought the world was coming to an end. I kept on going, though soldiers were throwing themselves flat. Many empty houses were burnt out. They could probably have been saved if the owners had been there.

We spent the following night at home, even though we knew how close the Americans were. There were loud explosions during the night. We thought it was artillery-fire, but it was the Staffel railway bridge and the autobahn bridge being blown up. It didn't stop the Yanks! The next day our own soldiers blew up our 700-year-old bridge over the Lahn. That was a terrible shame.

On Monday 26 March there was a full alert. Everyone disappeared off the streets. Albin took the children to the bunker and I got on with my work. I made several trips to the bunker with blankets and food that I had specially cooked, knowing full well that the Americans would be here before long.

In the afternoon there was a tank-alarm and lots of people came out of the shelters on to the street. Suddenly we heard tanks firing and our own artillery firing back. Then the first tanks trundled up. Soon fires broke out in several parts of town. That afternoon, right in the middle of the exchanges of gunfire, the Americans made the men come out of the shelters and open up their houses. Albin was away a long time, and I was relieved when he reappeared. The Americans had let him lock up again but wanted to know where our white flag was.

We spent a most uncomfortable and sleepless night in the bunker, then crept home at six in the morning. The sight that met our eyes was worse than what we had imagined. All the cupboard doors had been ripped off their hinges and the contents scattered over the floor. The beds had been torn open and – worst of all – the eider-downs were missing. Someone said to me that the Americans were sleeping on them out in the road.

Taking my courage in both hands, I went out to the command post to complain. I had to go twice before I met a sergeant who understood me. He let me into one of the houses, and there were the American soldiers in a drunken sleep on the floor on my bedding! Throwing caution to the wind, I stuffed one of the eiderdowns under my arm, and then had to spend ages arguing about my other one, which was on a truck that was ready to leave. What a relief I could make myself understood in English. That impressed them.

MRS V. G. COLES, of Morden, Surrey, recalls her time in the WVS and as cook for the fire service during the bombing:

'The doodle-bug followed the bus'

As a member of the WVS my first task was to see to all the families involved, after a bombing raid. We gave them food and tea and handed out blankets and clothes to those who had lost everything. We had an underground shelter in Morden Hall Road and I was the warden. I've still got the whistle I used to get them all down to the shelter. We celebrated my neighbour's 21st birthday one night down there during a bombing raid.

We had two bombs fall on our road – a 60-pounder and a 100-pounder, which was a very nasty one. My husband was in the Home Guard and was first on the scene after that one fell. We lost two of the loveliest people you could ever meet. It was a Sunday evening and they had just come home from church, with their daughter, and their son who was home on leave, when the bomb dropped. The mother and father were killed, but, luckily, the beam from the ceiling saved the son and daughter. When an air-raid started they always used their Anderson shelter, but as their son was home on leave they decided, as it was a special occasion, they would remain in the house and have their dinner all together. But, alas, it was not to be.

I got a job as a cook with the national fire service and what a grand bunch of men they were. I remember catching the bus to work one morning at 6.30 a.m. when the siren went. It seemed as if the doodle-bug followed the bus all the way to work. As I got out it fell into a field opposite the fire station and one of the firemen, who knew I would be on the bus, rushed me into the shelter just in time. The next morning my friend, who was also a cook on Red Watch, was killed coming in to work. Very sad.

When I left the fire service, they gave me a lovely party and all signed their names on a Player's cigarette box and brought me home on the fire engine. How we laughed at that. I was really sorry to leave such a nice bunch of colleagues.

PATIENCE KOHLMORGEN, of Aldershot, Hampshire, experienced more of the bombing than most during the war – first in the Channel port of Folkestone, then later on in London during the worst of the blitz. Like so many others, she had to go through the trauma of giving birth during an air-raid:

'The wall of our building started to move'

In 1943 my daughter was born in the local maternity hospital. It was a frosty, foggy, February morning and at night we lay in bed in the ward listening to the noise of the bombs dropping around us. Soon after I got home with the baby the doodle-bugs arrived. We had a clear view over allotments at the back of our flat and used to watch them. You felt quite safe as long as there was flame coming out of the back, but when the flame went out it was time to get worried, for then it would drop. As well as the doodle-bugs we had the Molotov cocktails. These were fire bombs which started off in one piece, but, before they landed, they spread out into lots of smaller parts to spread the fire as far as possible.

One morning I was picking up my milk from the front door when there was a great explosion and the wall of our building started to move and sway while I was leaning my hand on it. Later we discovered it was the beginning of the landmines. They came over very quietly and made the most enormous bang and created a terrific amount of damage. There was no warning with them. One day I was walking through Walpole Park to go to the dentist when one landed a couple of miles away. It was a devastating noise and I could see smoke rising from where it had landed. I couldn't help wondering how we could go on with our ordinary lives with death and destruction an everyday occurrence all around us. All I could think at the time was that some poor souls had met their Maker.

With all this going on, I began to feel guilty about keeping the children living such a way of life and finally agreed to evacuate with them to a very nice, friendly family in Porth, in the Rhondda Valley, in Wales. I had to go to Ealing Broadway to get the tickets and vouchers for the journey. While at that end of Ealing, and having collected my tickets, I went to catch a trolley bus to come home and, just as we were pulling in to the shopping area, we were completely deafened and struck immobile. The bus came to an immediate halt, as did everything else in the area. The conductor told us to duck, but, of course, it was already too late. We were all very shocked and shaken. When I realized just how close the bomb was, I knew I had to get home immediately as I had left my daughter in the Morrison shelter and the place could have collapsed around her. I couldn't even be sure at the time where the bomb had dropped. All I can remember is running and clambering over the destruction all the way home, until I arrived practically in hysterics. Every human being I passed was completely covered in a white dust, like flour, and there was a deathly silence everywhere. All the people on the bus in front of us were killed – and we were right behind them!

I was so relieved to find our house still standing when I got home, although the windows and doors had been blown out. My friend, who I had left in charge of my daughter, couldn't even get the front door open to let me in.

While we were suffering under the bombs ourselves, we became aware of another different noise at nights. It was our own bombers on their way to Germany to drop their loads. We would hear waves of them droning overhead and later coming back. I didn't realize until after the war what devastation we had created over there.

In July 1953 I married a German prisoner of war. We are still together and enjoying a happy retirement.

HILDEGARD GRATZ, was born in Januschkau, East Prussia, and now lives in East Berlin. Working for a time in her sister's post office, she saw the effect of the dreaded telegrams on the women of the community at first hand:

'Postmen came to dread their round'

In 1939 I was a happy young woman, married for just three years. For in 1936, after years of unemployment, my fiancé had finally found a regular job in Königsberg (nowadays Kaliningrad in the Soviet Union) and that meant we could at last get married.

The 27th of August 1939 was a Saturday, a lovely warm summer's evening. We were going for a walk through the town. We could sense a certain tension in the air. It got stronger the nearer we got to the stock exchange building. There we met other young couples. The men were going into the building in civilian clothes and coming out in soldiers' uniforms. That gave me an almighty shock. Unconsciously I gripped my husband's arm more tightly. He tried to reassure me by telling me that there was a big military parade planned for Sunday at the Hindenburg Memorial just outside our town to celebrate the First World War victory at Tannenberg. He didn't succeed in calming my fears. I had already seen the women's tears as they said goodbye to their menfolk.

The next anxious moment, in those last and strangely tense days of peace, came when a telegram arrived from my sister that same evening. She was postmistress in my native village and had sent an urgent message for me to come and help her with the telephone exchange. All phone calls had to be connected up by hand in those days. The village of Grossschmückwalde lay about seven kilometres from the Polish border, and four weeks earlier the German military staff had established a base in the neighbourhood. A lot of phone calls were being made in those last days before the outbreak of war. So I went there and plugged in phone calls from seven in the morning till seven in the evening.

On the 29th of August I got a phone call myself. It was from a neighbour in Königsberg who had rung to tell me that my husband had got his call-up papers the day before and had to leave immediately. I thought, 'So it wasn't just celebrations for Hindenburg after all.' Two days later – it was the 31st of August 1939 – I had the radio on while on night-duty when I heard the news: 'The Poles have attacked the radio station at Gleiwitz. Deaths have been reported.' I couldn't get to sleep that night. The phones just never stopped ringing. The little I managed to pick up from the conversations I was connecting up only increased my fears. The next morning the awful truth became known. We heard the Führer declare on the radio: 'Our soldiers have crossed the Polish border and have been returning fire for the past five hours.' And my husband Ewald was now a soldier!

All of a sudden I had plenty of time to think things over. An uncanny peace had returned to our post office. The hectic ringing of the telephones had stopped. The military staff had left the neighbourhood and gone off to war in Poland. There was a growing anxiety amongst the young women of the village. So many men had been called up in those last days. One heard rumours, but no one knew anything for certain. We were just like a lot of scared chickens.

On the 4th of September came the first news of my husband. He was with his company, the Railway Pioneer Corps, just four stations along the line in Deutsch-Eylau. Naturally I went there straight away. We were able to see each other, and what we arranged was that whenever he could, he would come and find me at my parents' house in the village or phone me at work at my sister's post office. We said our farewells without knowing what the future would bring. Gradually I settled down a bit, just as we all did. After all, we heard nothing but victory fanfares and all the special news bulletins were optimistic. None of us fully realized in those days that war also meant death. And there were never any reports of the dead. None of the women in our village had yet to get out their black mourning clothes. In 1939 none of those dreaded letters were arriving in my sister's postal district. When the announcement came 18 days later that the Polish campaign had ended in victory, all we young women in the village thought that our husbands would soon be home, that the war was only a short one. And the men did come home – but it was only on leave, and not a single one of them ever got out of his uniform. Not one. My husband Ewald didn't even get leave. Instead of seeing him, I got a letter on 14 November 1939 to say he had been transferred to Cologne. 'If you can, come and visit me here!' he wrote. Which is what I did. On 16 November I set out for the second time in this war to find my husband.

To get from East Prussia, where we lived, to Cologne you had to go through the Polish Corridor. There had been war in Poland – a blitzkrieg – which so far seemed to have left us unscathed. At Dirschau the train crossed the river Weichsel. It crawled along at a snail's pace because the bridge had been partially destroyed. I couldn't sleep for the whole of the rest of the 24-hour journey to Cologne. I had encountered the war – a war which might treat my husband the same way it had treated the bridge.

Once in Cologne I planned to ask at the army command post where I could find my husband. I knew only that he was one of the Railway Pioneer Corps in Cologne. The officer bellowed at me, 'You've got a nerve asking the whereabouts of military personnel!' I burst into tears and just stood there. Finally a note was pushed into my hand by a junior officer who whispered to me, 'Don't say who you got it from, or I'm for the high jump!' On the note was the name of the place my husband was stationed. I think it was Köln Ehrenfeld. So off I set across the big, unfamiliar city. And I was in luck. I found Ewald.

From Cologne he was sent to France. But at the end of May 1941 he was sent east again, to a place called Angerburg. I followed him there, too.

Then came the war against Russia and that brought the first 'black letter' for our family. The very first day of the campaign Ewald's eldest brother was killed. Suddenly everything changed. The radio carried on broadcasting news of victories. But the daily papers carried endless columns of death notices.

Being a postman suddenly became an unpleasant occupation: he became the bringer of bad news. There were these terrible letters, and the postmen told stories of pitiful scenes of grief. The postmen came to dread their round if ever there was one of those black-edged letters to be delivered. It wasn't just a question of witnessing grief and suffering. You could get drawn into conflicts. The official line was that women were bearing their news 'with proud grief', but many of the women in their despair screamed out curses on this 'damned war'. It was a risky business even hearing them, because you were supposed to report them to the police for 'undermining the spirit of defence'. For that reason I felt quite relieved that my sister didn't ask me to help with this harrowing work. But I knew very well the three young women who went around our village in black that autumn of 1941. I had danced at their weddings, and they at mine.

But it was impossible to forget about the war even by throwing yourself into your work. There were little reminders every day. Then my father, who was the village schoolmaster, asked for my help. I had already helped out in the school from time to time before I got married. But now it became a regular job. The young male teachers had been drafted, and now father was on his own with all eight classes in two classrooms. There sitting in front of me were children whose fathers would never come home. I was supposed to teach them something about 'a hero's death'. There were other official instructions for teachers, too. We had to get the schoolchildren to work for the 'Winter Relief', collecting or knitting warm clothing for our soldiers on the Eastern Front. That work made you think anxious, despairing, 'forbidden' thoughts. Especially after the defeat at Stalingrad. After that the Nazi government ordered six weeks national mourning. When our husbands had been in France we had all shown round the presents they had sent back. Now we swapped things amongst ourselves, hoping to get something to send off to help our soldier husbands survive the Russian winter. But at least my husband did survive.

ELAINE WYATT, of Saltdean, West Sussex, remembers life in London during the blitz, when part of her duties was to keep a watch on the animal population:

'The packet came to life'

Travelling to London from Bromley in Kent during the blitz was extraordinary. Whole areas disappeared overnight, such as Holborn between the Viaduct and Southampton Row. Animal ARP was what we were in. But, of course, the idea of small domestic animals, or zoo animals, running amok during a raid never seemed to happen. I also worked as a part-time ambulance driver, on duty on a Saturday night. I was called out only once, but the injured person had recovered by the time I got there and preferred to stay at home! So much for all that training.

Finding an animal in the devastation wasn't easy and we had to queue for horsemeat (tinted green to avoid it being eaten by humans) for them. One had to keep an 'iron ration' at the ready and mine was a packet of meat kept on top of the kitchen cabinet. One day during a heat-wave the packet came to life. Hundreds of maggots were crawling around inside it and outside the cupboard!

The worst year for shortages was 1943. There was a severe scarcity of even such essential things as a potty. My mother came back from Wales in triumph with a blue enamel job, which she carried home full of gooseberries. I still have it!

Preparing for the birth of a baby, and living in an upstairs flat, it was necessary to have somewhere at the end of the garden to keep the pram, so it would be under cover. To widen the narrow path, bricks seemed a good idea and there were some in a nearby lane from a bombed building. So each time we went by, we brought one home, feeling quite guilty as we didn't know to whom they belonged. Our Scottie dog was always with us on these excursions and for long after we had collected enough bricks, she refused to go past the site without stopping.

ELSIE LEE, from Walsall, the West Midlands, knew only too well the trials and terrors of bringing up small children alone beneath the bombs:

'Is that why you're crying, Mum?'

The first time we heard the air-raid sirens I was in bed with my three children. Talk about panic stations! There was I jumping out of bed and shaking my fist at the sky and calling Hitler all kinds of names, then turning to get my children downstairs. I'd got two of them down when my friend from across the road came running over shouting, 'Come on, Elsie, the sirens have gone! Where's the kids?' I unlocked the door and said, 'I've got two.' She rushed upstairs and got the other. I was putting some clothes on and happened to look around for my elder son and he was calmly putting on his shoes and socks and no amount of begging him to hurry did any good. And then someone at the back was shouting, 'Come on, Els, get them kids out!' And then the door was being thumped and a voice was yelling, 'Put that bloody light out!' There was a streak of light showing where the door hadn't closed properly. However, we did eventually get into a shelter. After a while I asked my son why he stopped to put his socks and shoes on instead of helping me. His reply was, 'I'm going to the swimming baths tomorrow and didn't want to dirty my feet.' What could I say?

Anyway, about a couple of hours later, the all-clear went. We hadn't heard any planes or anything but, believe me, did those husbands get to work later to cover in the shelters which they boasted we wouldn't need! I hadn't got one because I'd only moved in a week before war broke out, so I had to share. What nights we had after that, going to bed, getting up and going back again. It began to get nerve-racking.

My son came home from school one day and told me the head-master would take the twins into school. I'd already had their names down. They were four on the Friday, in school on the Monday.

My old boss asked if I'd go back to work and, as army pay was then only £2 2s, I went, so I was working all day and in between looking after the children. Their school was only five minutes from my work and only three of us worked there and the boss used to let them come and wait for me. I've got up at five o'clock in the morning, done my washing and pegged it out, came home dinner time, fetched it in and folded it, and got some dinner for us, then back to work, came home, got tea and ironed it all, got the children washed and in bed early in case of sirens going. I would then have a good wash (no bathrooms in those days), do a bit of mending and then go to bed dead licked. Would be in a lovely sleep when 'Moaning Minnie' started again. Up we'd all get and away to the shelter. Back again to bed for a couple of hours, then time to get up.

Things got gradually worse at night. My little girl developed a lung cough going out to the shelter, so I didn't go again. I made a shelter for us by the chimney breast and there we stayed, but we weren't getting any rest. I was sleeping on a chair pushed up against them. We could hear the ack-ack of gunfire and planes roaring overhead. It was terrifying, but still we wouldn't go to bed. I believe we slept like that for three years or more.

We had it very bad one night. It went on all night and seemed to be right over our heads. I couldn't get any closer to my children. They weren't too afraid. I used to keep talking to them, waiting for morning to come. I went to put the milk bottle out on the step and got the shock of my life. The whole street was roped off. I was told there was a 1,000 lb bomb at the bottom of the street. It had fallen into a brook and hadn't gone off. They had aimed at the gas-works at the back. I went back indoors and grabbed my kids and we ran for our lives. I took them to school and went off to my work. It was a heavy job, making thick chains and using a brazing torch, which was like working in a furnace, it was so hot. Anyway, we all went home together and what a relief to find the ropes had been taken away and the bomb defused.

We hadn't got a lot in to eat as I'd been too afraid to go to the shops and hadn't got my ration books. Anyway, the old lady next door used to give me half a pound of margarine and there was only one egg, so I sliced the bread and spread it with some marge and boiled the egg, and each of us had a spoonful of it between a couple of rounds of bread. I'd stopped having sugar so the children could have it. I'm afraid I went without a lot so they wouldn't go hungry.

By now, Birmingham and Coventry were really having a pasting. My sister lived in Birmingham and was marooned in her shelter with her children, surrounded by fire-bombs. The fire service came to their aid.

At about half past six one morning the sirens went and I could hear this plane right over my house and a bomb came whizzing down. What a screech it made! I put my hands over my ears, waiting for it to hit us and then there was a terrible bang and the kitchen floor shook, the fire-bricks came down the chimney, soot as well. I thought, well, we haven't been hit, but it's very close. Luckily, I found out later, it had landed on a golf course about one and a half miles away, just missing a new housing estate. But we all suffered. My kitchen was a real mess – another job to do before going to work! My children were really marvellous all through it all.

Then I had some good news. My husband was coming home on leave from Antwerp. I went to go across to tell my friend (her husband was in Tobruk) and I had just opened my front door when I heard a terrible explosion. No sirens had gone. Some of the neighbours came out and said, 'That was close!' It had hit a factory. A direct hit. The night firemen were there, just getting ready to end their shift and all were killed. One was a friend of mine. I thought, will it never end?

I went back indoors to get ready for work and just sat down and cried and cried and cried. The children were alarmed as they had never seen me cry before, but it was my husband's letter which had opened the flood gates. My children were growing up by now. I told them their daddy would soon be home. They said, 'Is that why you're crying, Mum?' I said, 'Yes', but they were tears of joy.

He did come home and, when he saw his kids, he looked at me and said, 'Els, you've done a wonderful job.'

Thankfully, he came home for good in 1946, after it was all over. Also my friend's husband was safe.

We had 51½ years together and then I lost him. I'm a great-grandma now, but many's the time, as I sit alone, I go through the war again and wonder how I really did cope all on my own through that terrible bombing. My children saved my sanity through all those years. My husband didn't come through it unscathed. He had been buried alive. He was dug out, but his two mates were blown to smithereens. But he had gone white-haired, whereas he used to have lovely chestnut hair.

DORA BÖHM, of Baden-Baden, Baden-Württemberg, lived with her children in the Südetenland. They were a long way from the bombs, had a large comfortable house and a big garden, which kept them well provided with fruit and vegetables for most of the war years. In October 1944 she had her fourth baby. In February 1945, with the advance of Soviet troops, the time came to leave Silesia. They boarded one of the last trains out without knowing where they were headed:

'What dumbfounded faces greeted us'

It was a long, long train journey. My sister and I were huddled together for days and nights on end with our seven children. Often the train stopped for ages. We were travelling into the unknown, with no real idea what our destination would be.

Somehow or other we discovered we were in Thuringia. During one of the endless waits, we saw a town being bombed and fires raging. We didn't know where it was. That was our first real contact with the war.

We two young mothers were able to breastfeed our youngest babies. At least there were no worries about where their food was coming from. It was a different matter with the other five children. They were starving. Our food supplies had run out long ago. Finally we recognized the name of one of the stations where we stopped. We had relatives not far away and so changed trains and arrived at the first of our destinations.

So there we stood with our many hungry children and our few bags and cases in the early hours of the morning on a little station platform in Thuringia. Our relatives had a small farm in the neighbourhood and we soon managed to find out the address. Hoping they would have room for us, we set off. A helpful old man loaded all our luggage and the two three-year-olds on to his handcart. I shall never forget the way those wheels rattled over the cobble-stones of the little town in those quiet hours of the morning. All along the way inquisitive people were peeping out of their windows at us all. We were the first refugees they had seen.

Finally we reached the farm and timidly knocked at the door. What dumbfounded faces greeted us! The family was sitting at a well-stocked breakfast-table. They couldn't believe it. There were we, the once proud owners of a splendid house in Silesia, now poor, tired and hungry, and asking for shelter. Almost overnight we had been reduced to the level of beggars. But however poor we might be, we had the children, and that was riches enough. The little ones' eyes were bulging at the sight of the food on the table. But they didn't say a word. We waited and waited, our hopes of being asked in dwindling.

That was our first experience of being impoverished refugees. Finally we did manage to get a place to live, in an ancient cottage belonging to an uncle. It was primitive, but it sufficed in an emergency. After what we had been through we felt safe there. We had a roof over our heads, an old kitchen stove to warm us, and three beds. The children had their prams to sleep in. It would do, and we all slept fine that first night despite the ghastly mattresses and lack of blankets. We could now think about getting back some sort of order into our lives.

MARGARET HOLLAND, from Farnborough, Hampshire. When war broke out, Margaret's husband was seconded by the Air Ministry and moved from Farnborough to de Havillands, in Edgeware, Middlesex, as the resident technical officer. Getting decent accommodation in wartime London could pose a problem:

'They are safe. These planes have men in them'

The winter of 1939 was very severe and the roads were lined with mounds of 'black' snow. Very depressing – but the state of the houses was even more so. People had fled out of London at the outbreak of war and had not even bothered to turn their water off or arrange for their telephones to be disconnected. In many houses the telephone was ringing when we arrived. The hard winter meant burst pipes and, in many cases, we were met at the gate by water flowing out of the front door, down the garden path and out into the gutter. Wallpaper, loosened by the damp, was festooned across the downstairs rooms. All this only emphasized the fact that we were moving into an area where the normal residents had decided it was unsafe to stay.

Eventually we found a suitable house in a pleasant part of Mill Hill. It was still furnished, although the owners had moved away. My father came down from Cheshire and went to Mill Hill on the day of the removal to receive the furniture, while we followed by car. He obtained the keys of the house and, to his horror, on his arrival, he was confronted by water pouring through the entrance-hall ceiling from the bathroom above. He was desperate. He didn't know the district, or where to find a plumber. When we finally arrived, I put Richard inside my coat, lowered my head, and ran through a cascade of water into the back of the house!

Eventually, however, we got settled in and all was quiet at first until the evacuation of British troops from Dunkirk. The boys of the nearby Mill Hill School were evacuated to St Bees, on the north-west coast, and their school was taken over by St Bartholomew's Hospital as their neurological unit. From the hill above our house we could look down on Hendon Aerodrome. During the evacuation from Dunkirk, ambulances were parked around the airfield awaiting the planes from France flying out the casualties. As the planes landed, the wounded were put into the ambulances and then a procession of them would set off for the hospital, only to return empty for the next lot of planes. This went on for days.

By this time my husband was working seven days a week, coming home late (about 8 p.m.), having a meal, sleeping for a few hours, and then working on paperwork until one or two o'clock in the morning, when he would finally retire to bed. When France fell, he decided to send Richard and me to my parents, as he would have to stay in the factory all the time if the Germans invaded, and he didn't want us to be alone. It was a hard decision to make but, as the blitz started almost immediately, it was probably wise. For nine months my husband would often not get home before the siren sounded, and many nights he had only half prepared his meal before he had to retire under the stairs, where he had fixed up a makeshift bed. In fact, he never slept upstairs for the whole period of the blitz.

Meanwhile Richard and I lived with my parents in Sale. I was anxious that my little boy shouldn't forget his father, so I put a photograph over his cot, but he was so distressed whenever he saw it that I had to remove it.

When the Battle of Britain was over we returned to Mill Hill. Despite the rationing, people seemed to keep fairly fit on the whole. We were afraid to stay in bed in case there was an air-raid! Many commodities which were not rationed were, nevertheless, often in short supply and shared out to regular customers by the shopkeepers themselves. One cold, snowy day when my daughter was about two, and in her push-chair, the grocer said to me, 'Bring the little girl into the shop. It's too cold to leave her outside.' When I said she would come to no harm, he insisted and said, 'I'll bring her push-chair in. I can't bear her to be left outside in this weather.' With that, he pushed her pram inside. The shop was full and, to my embarrassment, my little daughter stood up and in a clear piping voice said, 'What have you got under the counter today, Mr Dunster?'

In 1942 my parents moved to a Shropshire market town when my father retired. They had a garden and the small field behind their house belonged to three old ladies who lived next door. They told my father he could use it in any way he liked. He bought a hen-house and put a wire netting fence round it; he got a farmer friend to plough up a large area where he could grow vegetables, and he also had a pig-sty and run for a couple of pigs. He made two wooden boxes, each with 12 compartments, which he lined with felt. In these he placed 12 eggs, each wrapped in greaseproof paper so that if any cracked in transit the egg could be emptied into a basin without loss. These two boxes did a shuttle service in the post to keep us supplied with eggs. When he got the butcher to kill a pig and cure the meat, my father would also send us a piece of bacon through the post.

My daughter Elizabeth was born slightly earlier than expected, in May 1943. She arrived in great haste during an air-raid. We seemed to have very cold winters during the war. Coal was rationed and it was very difficult to keep the house adequately warm in winter. There were not the practical clothes for children that there are now and I remember Elizabeth's little legs being chapped all up the back.

Another problem was the lack of imported fruit and Richard suffered from mild scurvy. We have photographs of him with bandaged arms due to the rash. He was given tablets by the doctor to supply the Vitamin C that he lacked, but although they may have prevented it becoming more serious, it certainly didn't show any improvement. The introduction of rose-hip syrup was his salvation and later the introduction of concentrated orange juice – 'baby orange' – that was available at the clinics.

When the flying bombs started Richard had just developed whooping cough which he had very badly. The doctor said he must be kept away from Elizabeth, now a year old, as she was too young to risk her getting it. My husband slept in the dining room with Richard, and Elizabeth and I slept in the Morrison shelter in the kitchen. But one night the flying bombs were so near that my husband brought Richard into the shelter as he felt the risk of infection was less than the risk of being bombed. We lay between the children and hoped for the best. The two 'boys' had only just joined us when we heard a flying bomb very near and it cut out right over our house.

We waited for the bang, knowing that Mill Hill was doomed. Time passed and nothing happened. It was really eerie and we couldn't understand it. Several days afterwards we heard that a man, fire watching on the roof of the fire station, saw the bomb coming, heard it cut out, and realized the danger, but to his amazement a sudden gust of wind lifted the bomb and it was carried on to Watford, where it fell harmlessly in a field. A miracle!

When Richard was out of quarantine and could finally be taken out again, the two children and I were able to travel to Shropshire to stay with my parents. By this time Richard was five and old enough to be aware of the danger. At home he wouldn't go into the garden alone because of the danger of flying bombs, but when we got to my parents' home he ran out into the garden even though there were planes in the air. When I asked him why he had gone out alone into the garden, he replied, 'They are safe. These planes have men in them.'

The people in the countryside had little conception what the people in the cities were suffering. They knew nothing of the horror. Iron railings from gardens were confiscated for melting down to help the war effort and one woman my mother knew cried all day when the railings were taken from the front of her house. That was the only impact the war made on her – except that she received regular parcels of dried fruit and other luxuries from relatives in Canada!

FRIEDEL SCHLEMMER of Hagen, North Rhine-Westphalia, lived in Silesia and occupied Poland for most of the war, where her husband worked as a factory manager. She recalls that for her and her husband the hardest time was after they returned as refugees to West Germany:

'Hard work and effort'

I moved in with my parents who had been bombed out of their home in Cologne and were now living in Arolsen, near Kassel. My husband was still in the East. That was the beginning of very hard times for me. Hardly any clothes, almost nothing to eat. Refugees like myself, and those who had been bombed out, were in the worst possible situation, because we had nothing to barter for food. You would have starved on what you got on the ration-books. So you got to thinking up the most improbable schemes just to get something to eat or wear. I used to get remnants from a relative and made ties and other little things out of them. These would then be bartered for food.

In March 1945 my husband joined us, after escaping from the East. When the Americans took over he used to distil schnaps in a back-room. Highly illegal of course. But the Americans loved it and used to come regularly, giving us cigarettes which we then exchanged for other things. Soon after, we found work together on a farm. We had our meals there and were paid in butter, eggs, milk and flour. People were always coming out from the towns with things to barter, so that they could take food back to their families. They were often swindled. I know for a fact that the farmer's wife where I was always used to take the cream off the milk and then pretend it was full-cream milk.

My husband and I used to go into the woods and collect tree-bark, which we then tied up in bundles. What hard, dirty work that was. But it did earn us a little. The bark was sold to the tanneries. We did a lot of scavenging in the countryside in those days. There were lots of berries and fungi that we could pick. In the autumn and winter of 1946 and 1947 we worked for weeks gathering beechnuts. What painstaking work that was! We used to kneel down on sacks and grub around for hours on end. You had to watch out you didn't pick up those with a tiny hole in them. Those were always empty and were no use. By evenings our backs would be aching so much that we just used to go straight off to bed. I can't remember how many full sacks we had to collect to get a litre of cooking-oil. But I do know we got several litres of it, and that was invaluable to us.

Hard work and effort! That's how we managed to get through the years between 1945 and 1948. In 1948 my husband got work in Heidelberg. We had only a couple of pieces of furniture to take with us. But it was a new beginning, and that thought made us happy.

IRENE MARTIN, of Balham, London, remained in London for part of the blitz then, fearful for her children, she decided they could remain there no longer. Evacuation, however, proved to have its drawbacks and homesickness brought her back from the safety of rural Wales to brave the bombs in London, where she was soon to realize that her troubles were far from over:

'We covered them in goosegrease and brown paper'

We could see the City of London on fire; the blaze in the sky was horrific. It drew all the neighbours out. We knew we were in for another dreadful night. And it was. The enemy bombers dropped load after load on the flames. Uneasy days and sleepless nights followed, but food still had to be bought and washing done. My dear, brave mother still went to work, catching the tram into Westminster every morning. But we worried constantly about the children. They should have some kind of normal life. So, although unhappy about leaving my mother, I again became an evacuee.

We were sent to Wales, where my husband came from. The

family we were billeted with were very friendly, but it was very cramped for space, so I got us another billet. This one was not so isolated and near an English-speaking school. Most of the Welsh people had no idea how we had been living during the raids. Some were friendly, some suspicious, some resentful. They were delighted I had a Welsh husband and that he was on his way somewhere to fight in this bloody war. (He was with the Eighth Army and I knew he was on his way to Africa from the first airmail I received, in which was a censored poem.)

Most people in the village understood English, but seldom spoke it. I took the children to Aberdare to visit my husband's relatives for Christmas, but we were too many for one small house. The children became ill, so we covered them with goosegrease and brown paper, wrapped them in woollies, and took the coach back to the village of Saron, where we were billeted.

When we got back to Saron the children took measles, so I arranged with the landlady that my mother should come and visit us. We were so happy to see each other, and so excited. We all shed a few tears. We had such a lot to talk about. Were the raids still as heavy? Was she able to sleep at night? Had she news of my brothers? It proved to be a restful time for her and when it was time for her to go back, I knew I could not settle to rural life, and decided to go with her.

It was good to be home, even though there was a lot of rubble and a lot of houses down. People were using the Underground stations to sleep in at night, thinking it would be safe, but our local one here in Balham was hit and a lot of people lost their lives. The crater the bomb made was so deep that the big red double-decker bus in it was just visible. It was lifted out eventually by a crane.

Although I was apprehensive about bringing the children back to London, I didn't regret it because by now my mother badly needed me. She was taken into hospital with a lump in her breast which proved to be malignant. She suffered for six months and died in June 1942. None of her sons stood with bowed heads at her funeral. In fact, no men at all. They were all in different parts of the world fighting a war. She never saw the lorries full of fighting men that we cheered along the high road before D-Day, nor did she experience the misery of the buzz bombs, which brought our ceilings down and put out all our windows. Our poor old house was badly shaken about, but when the three houses next door fell down around us, I felt she was still here somehow, looking after us.

When my husband was finally demobbed at the end of 1945, we were so thrilled to have him back with us. It was wonderful when he arrived. He looked so different, so much older, so tired, and yet so very much the same. A lot had happened in those five years and I wondered how long it would take for us to knit together as a family again. Five years of separation is a long time for children to be without a father. They were very shy and treated him very much like a stranger for quite a while. Our eldest daughter accepted him, but the youngest found it much more difficult. But we all had to adjust. It seemed just like starting all over again. But, happily, we worked it all out, and we pray to God that we can continue to live in peace.

KÄTHE RICKEN, of Krefeld, North Rhine-Westphalia, was living with her one-year-old baby in a flat in Hamburg in July 1943. Her husband was an officer in the German army, had served in Poland and France, and had twice been wounded on the Russian Front. There was a heatwave in Hamburg that July. During the hot summer's night of 24 July, British bombers were heard over the city. It was the start of a massive four-day offensive against the civilian population of the city that unleashed a devastating fire-storm, reduced half the city to rubble, and left over 50,000 dead, mostly civilians. Through Käthe Ricken's wartime diary, we can experience some of those horrendous nights and the days that followed:

'I breathed on their little hands and feet'

25 July 1943

How terrified I was in our little cellar last night. I sat there, cowering, with my head tucked down between my shoulders. We all prayed out loud together with our landlord. The whole world was shaking like in an earthquake. You could actually feel our house moving up and down. Every bomb made a hissing and whistling noise as it fell. Then there would be a bang, followed by a rumbling sound. How often we thought: 'This one's for us!' Frau Stuhr wanted us to put the candle out. She thought that the light might escape outside. That feeble gleam! If only she knew! Some of the men who had gone outside to see how bad things were told us that the whole of Hamburg was blazing like a torch. I held little Wolfgang close and just prayed to get out of that hell-hole alive. Even if it meant being a poor suffering beggar for the rest of my days!

27 July 1943
Can't go on living here in the flat. No water, no gas, no electricity. There are no houses left and no shops. How am I going to look after Wolfgang? He's got a little brother or sister coming, too! Escape was the only way. The streets were full of dead bodies. There were mothers with children in their arms, shrivelled by the heat into mummies. They had obviously had to get out of their burning cellar, but death found them just as surely out in the streets. Before we went out, I wrapped a piece of clothing loosely around Wolfgang, leaving him just enough room to breathe.

Christmas 1943
We have been given a little room out in the suburbs, but will have to share it with others. All the upheaval has given Wolfgang diarrhoea. Have to fetch water from a long way off. I can't cook or wash, so the nappies can't be kept clean. I threw them in a nearby stream just to be rid of the smell. Now I'm having to cut up my own underwear for nappies. We have hardly had any bread again these last few days. Wolfgang keeps pleading and pleading for more. Will we ever see the day again when I can push a piece of chocolate into their little mouths? I asked Wolfgang what he would like Father Christmas to bring him. He said, 'Bread.'

January 1945
The children have stayed in bed for most of this month, just to keep

warm. It has been so cold that the milk on the kitchen table keeps freezing. The food hand-outs are getting smaller and smaller, and our hunger greater. I'm now expecting my third baby. Someone said that they were giving out special allocations of soup for small children. So today I got them dressed up warm – as warm as I can with the few clothes we have left – and we left the cold flat and went out to the even colder street. The children soon forgot the pain of the cold with all the excitement of getting some warm soup. We walked miles and when we arrived we were chilled to the bone. The soup was all finished. What could I say to the children to console them? They were so heart-broken. I hadn't got a thing in the cupboard here. 'I'll just have to make something out of nothing,' I said to myself, half determined, half despairing.

'Mummy, why don't you make yourself something to eat and then you can come to bed and keep warm?' little Wolfgang said to me. If only! Once home, I breathed on their little hands and feet, then rubbed them between my hands. Then I told them all the cheerful things I could think of, and especially about how lovely everything was going to be when all this was over.

NELLIE RICHARDS, of Liverpool, Merseyside, was the wife of a master on the tug boats belonging to the Rea Towing Company on the River Mersey. With her five-year-old son, she was evacuated to Denbigh, to live with a blind lady and her sister, but they returned after eight weeks, just in time for the first terrifying air-raid on Liverpool:

'I screamed as the fire got nearer'

My husband had made bunk beds in the small air-raid shelter in our backyard. My son and I slept in there when my husband was at work. The first night the incendiary bombs dropped, one fell directly on to our backyard wall, right opposite the door of the shelter where we were. I was so frightened. I screamed as the fire got nearer the wooden door. There was no escape. But, luckily for us, an air-raid warden ran to us and put the fire out. After that experience, I no longer wanted to stay on my own with my little boy, so my husband built more bunks in a friend's cellar, where about eight people gathered when the sirens sounded.

My husband worked 24-hour shifts in a very dangerous occupation. One day a mine was dropped into the Mersey and as a boat went over it, it drew the pin higher. My husband's tug then went over it, drawing the pin to the top, and the next tug that came after them was blown to pieces, with all hands lost. Another day his shift duty was altered to replace another man, and the tug he should have been on was blown up. Yet another time, his tug was at the dockside in Birkenhead when the sirens sounded, so the crew ran for safety into a nearby air-raid shelter. A landmine dropped close by and the blast blew in the door and the front of the shelter collapsed, trapping everyone inside. They had to be dug out.

My mother, who was a midwife, worked right through the period of the May blitz, delivering babies, often high up in blocks of flats.

Nellie Richards, who is now a widow, still lives in Liverpool, in a bungalow close by her son and daughter-in-law.

BARBARA PINNEY, of Brewood, Stafford, found that the joy of pregnancy, and the birth of her first baby, was marred by worry about others in her family:

'My brother never walked again'

I lived with my parents when I married in September 1943. My father said that this was what I should do, until my husband, who was in the RAF, could provide a home. My only brother was also in the RAF, flying Spitfires and Hurricanes, firstly in the Middle East and later in Burma as air support to Wingate's Chindits.

When one received a 'yellow telegram' it meant bad news. We received them when my brother met with accidents in the air. I remember the feeling of dread. We would look at each other, wondering who would have the courage to open the envelope. My father was in poor health, with what proved to be a terminal illness, and became very morose under the strain.

I was three months pregnant when we had one of the dreaded yellow telegrams to say that my brother had collapsed after returning from a flight in Burma. Many pilots did the same through too much flying. He had polio and was in an iron-lung. Six months later, on the very day my baby was due, my brother was due to arrive back in Britain by hospital ship. Although my father was by now very ill, my parents arranged to go to a hospital in Hereford to meet him. My brother never walked again, although he had many operations of nerve-grafting to give some mobility to his hands and arms.

Barbara Pinney now lives in happy retirement with her husband. Her brother married his nurse, and they had a daughter, but, sadly, his health deteriorated and he died when his little girl was only six years old.

HILDEGARD BALTZ, of Haan, North Rhine-Westphalia, lived in Wiesbaden during the first years of the war. Her husband was in the Signals Corps and stationed nearby. When he was promoted to major and transferred east, Hildegard Baltz decided to train as a Red Cross nurse. After completing her nursing training she was posted in 1942 to Military Hospital IV in Wiesbaden.

'Doctor, you'd better come'

On 15 January 1942 a hospital train arrived from Russia bringing wounded soldiers for treatment in our hospital. In the surgical section there were five of us Red Cross nurses under the direction of the section doctor, Dr Levandovsky. The stream of infantrymen brought in to us was endless. They had been travelling for days in cattle-trucks. All were exhausted and many were suffering from frostbite wounds. Outside it was cold, deathly cold, and deep snow. By the time we had treated them all, bandaged them and tucked them into clean beds it was well after midnight. My bandaging was too slow for the section doctor. He said to me, 'Nurse Hilde, you seem to think bandaging is some sort of religious act.' 'That's right, Doctor,' I replied. 'That's exactly what it is.'

One of the worst of the wounded was a young doctor, only 24 years old. He was a field doctor with the army and had seen action. In hand-to-hand fighting he had had an eye shot out and then lost both feet through frostbite. He also had seven badly infected wounds to his arms, back and legs. He was in very poor shape. He was depressed, spoke very little, but was always patient and helpful. Would he ever recover? One day a shaft of sunlight shone into the ward. My poor patient smiled and said, 'How beautiful. Sunshine! There's a poem by Mörike, only I have forgotten the words.' I knew the poem and recited the verse:

> Once more the springtime's banner blue
> Flutters through the balmy airs . . .

My patient, Dr Valentin Becker, positively beamed with delight. He said, 'Nurse Hilde, you have given me the most marvellous present. Many, many thanks!' It was a ray of sunshine for me, too, in those dark days. Dr Becker lived, despite his terrible injuries. He went back to medical life and became a consultant in a Mannheim hospital. Now he's in retirement.

In May 1942 I was on the night shift. I was left on my own to look after 100 beds in the surgical station and 40 beds on other wards. I even had to answer the phone myself. There was a doctor on call for emergencies. Most of the soldiers managed to sleep, but there were also those who were thirsty, and those who had to be given medicine or painkilling injections. Whenever I came on station at eight o'clock there were always a few empty beds, because the convalescent cases were allowed a five-hour pass for a trip into town and hadn't yet returned. One of them, a Sergeant Stipp, who had lost his right arm, once didn't get back till midnight. I caught him coming in looking very pleased with himself. 'How did you manage to get back in at this time?' I asked. 'We've bolted all the doors.' 'Same way you nurses do, when you've been out on the razzle,' was his reply. 'Has nobody ever told you? There's a hole in the hedge. All you do is swing yourself over the balcony downstairs and you're home and dry!' Then he said meekly, 'You wouldn't by any chance have a bite to eat for me?' I gave him my midnight meal: sauerkraut and mash. He wolfed it down, then slept like a baby.

One night a soldier had severe abdominal pains and was moaning so loudly he woke the whole ward. I telephoned the duty doctor and he said, 'Just give him painkillers.' My long-term patient, Dr Becker, didn't agree. 'Whatever you do don't give him painkillers. It's a blockage of the intestine. We had a case just like it in the field hospital, and the man died because he didn't get the right treatment.'

I telephoned the duty doctor again. 'Doctor, it's serious. The man has a blocked intestine.' He said, 'Just what qualifies you to make diagnoses?' I simply replied, 'Doctor, you'd better come.'

He came, saw the situation for himself and immediately got the surgeon to operate. Dr Becker had been right: ileus. All went well. As I was going off after my shift the duty doctor pressed my hand and said, 'We did a good job there, the pair of us.'

My husband had meanwhile been transferred with the Signals Corps to the Ukraine. He was on cable-laying and could put through phone calls to military centres. By getting through to Command HQ in Wiesbaden he managed to get connected up to the hospital where I was working. The phone rang on my desk at five o'clock one morning. I lifted the receiver: 'Hospital Unit IV, Wiesbaden. Nurse Hilde speaking.' 'Good morning, Nurse Hilde. Still cheerful after a busy night's work?' Hearing my husband's warm voice and feeling him so close for the few moments we spoke bridged the 2,000 kilometres that separated us and more than compensated for so many depressing hours.

WINNIE STEWART, of Dunkeld, Perthshire. After her husband was killed, Winnie left the bombs of Glasgow to marry a widower and move to the glens of Perthshire, so she experienced the war from both an urban and rural perspective:

'He was the only one on deck at the time'

At the start of the war my husband and I lived in a tenement in Glasgow, not far from Queen Street Station. My son was born on 1 August 1940, in the Maternity Hospital, Glasgow. He was only about half an hour old when the sirens went. By this time I'd been taken from the labour ward into the main ward and the nurses were running round snatching up the babies four at a time. The mothers had to walk down four flights of stairs. The lifts were only for those still in labour. We had to sit on mattresses on the floor in the gloom for over two hours, and then walk back up all those stairs again. I don't think it did me any harm. My only worry was, would I get the right baby back!

My husband was a member of the Peace Pledge Union, so when he was called up, just a month after our son was born, he registered as a conscientious objector. However, he had been in the merchant navy so, before he was due at Court, he went on an oil tanker. A more dangerous job he couldn't have taken on. The ship was torpedoed twice. They eventually limped into Haverford West on 2 April 1941. In the evening, before leaving the ship to come home, he went on deck and a lone German plane dropped a bomb on him. He was the only one on deck at the time. He was taken to hospital and I got a telegram at midnight to go down immediately. I would be given travel vouchers at Central Station.

I had to get a neighbour to look after my two children and my sister-in-law went with me. We had a nightmare journey lasting 24 hours. All the carriages were blacked out and full of airmen and soldiers. We were exhausted when we finally arrived. We went straight to the hospital. They had been waiting until we arrived before operating. My husband's face below the eyes had been blown away and there was a big piece of shrapnel in his windpipe. He was heavily drugged for the pain and was unable to speak, but he managed to write things down. We had cousins in New York and he had been to see them. They had given him coffee, sugar, toys for the children, and dresses for me. He wrote that they were all in his kitbag. After we'd been there about 20 minutes, they took him away to operate and we were asked to wait in a corridor. Then I saw a nurse running with a cylinder of oxygen and I knew immediately that he had died.

The doctor told me that if he had lived he would never have been able to speak again and his face was so badly mutilated that he would have been kept in some institution because at that time plastic surgery could have done very little. As my husband was a great talker, I think it would have been a living death for him.

After Alec died I got his kitbag. It was full of his working clothes and nothing else. I asked the captain about the other things and he said he was sorry there was nothing else. 'But, of course,' he added, 'the salvage people have been on the boat.'

The same type of thing happened to my mother. She lived in a flat in the West End of Glasgow. When the sirens went, she used to put on her fur coat, carry her personal belongings in a bag, and hide underneath the grand piano. Well, the house across the road got a direct hit and the blast hit the building she was in. She suffered some broken ribs and other minor injuries and was taken to the Western Infirmary. I went straight in to see her and she said, 'Go to my house – my glasses and my teeth are on a table beside the bed and I want them.' When I got there I met a policeman and when I told him what I wanted he laughed and pointed to the house. All that was left was a pile of rubble, with a bit of staircase sticking out of it. She had had a lot of jewellery and diamond brooches, etc. but she never got any of them back. All she got was £150 compensation.

While my husband was at sea, the first series of bombs were dropped on the centre of Glasgow. There were five all aimed at Queen Street Station. I didn't know about it till next morning when the postman knocked at the door. I went rushing to answer it, as he usually just put the mail through the letterbox, and he said, 'Did you know your letterbox has been blown off, missus?' There was just a hole where it had been. I had shutters drawn in my sitting-room and when I opened them, a shower of glass fell over me. The children and I had slept through it all.

After Alec was killed I went to stay with my sister in Bearsden, on the outskirts of Glasgow, as it was getting too dangerous in the city centre. She worked in the censorship department of the Post Office. She used to say that there wasn't much left in a letter after they had censored all the vital words.

What used to get me down was the attitude of the shopkeepers. Some of them turned into little Hitlers. They all had their favourites. You would go into a shop and ask for, say, elastic, and you would get this insolent stare and, 'Don't you know there's a war on?' This infuriated me. I only once retaliated when a particularly nasty shopkeeper said this, and I said, 'I'm quite aware of the fact. My husband was killed protecting people like you!' and I walked out. The shop was full of people and I felt dreadful afterwards. I never did it again, but there were a lot of little frustrations and sometimes you just had to let off steam.

We used to be able to buy stuff called Snoek which was absolutely ghastly. Even the cat wouldn't eat it. I think it was whale meat. There was also a brown loaf called a National Loaf. It was long and coarse and not very popular, but I liked it very much. I remember we used to cook mashed parsnips and put a little sugar and essence of bananas in it and tell the kids it was mashed bananas in their sandwiches.

The garden of our house had a little stone wall, about two-and-a-half feet high, with railings on top of it, but in 1942 the authorities came and took everyone's railings away. I had a terrible job keeping an eye on Peter, my two-year-old son, after that. He would simply climb over the wall and be away. People were always bringing him back. Fortunately there were very few cars as petrol was unobtainable unless you were a doctor or something like that.

I got married again on Hogmanay 1943 and went to live in a fairly isolated hamlet in the hills of Perthshire. My second husband had been a widower for 11 years and had four children. However, the three eldest were 17, 19 and 20, so they stayed on in their old house, and the youngest boy, aged 14, came with us.

The house was badly in need of repair and had no water, no sanitation, and no electricity. It was another 18 years before the house was modernized and I got a kitchenette and electricity. By that time the family were up and away.

When I first came up here there were a handful of refugees, mainly from Glasgow, in various houses. There were some pathetic sights. Some had to be taught simple sanitation and some of them had to be deloused. The people who took them in were very good to them, but they got homesick and soon returned home. As one wee boy said, 'There's naething to dae here – nae chippie, nae pictures, naething but grass and trees and sheep.'

There was a prisoner-of-war camp nearby, at Blair Atholl, and some of the German soldiers were sent to help out on the big estates, such as this one, where my husband was head forester. We had two and we all got on fine. They were excellent workers. When they left they brought presents for us that they had made themselves. There was a painted butterfly on wheels for my little girl and a wooden painted train for my son. My husband got a tobacco pouch and I got a purse – all beautifully made.

The big house near us was turned into a depot for soldiers. After the British soldiers left, the Poles arrived. The officers were based at Taymouth Castle, the rank and file near us. Some of the officers would come and visit the locals and one day one of them walked into the gardener's house while his wife was washing herself at the kitchen sink. (We had no bathrooms in those days.) She protested to the factor and when he investigated, he was told, 'A Polish officer does not knock on a peasant's door!'

When the war was finally over and everyone safely home, we staged a huge Welcome Home Party, with money we had been collecting from raffles, sales of work, etc. Everyone in the district packed into our village hall for dinner, which was supplied and served by the Dunkeld Hotel. Every returning serviceman was given a wallet and a small gift of money.

INGEBORG PFITZINGER, of Bad Oeynhausen, North Rhine-West-phalia, was right in the middle of Berlin during the Russian encirclement and siege of April 1945. She was 21 years old and spent the last few days before the capitulation working as an auxiliary nurse in temporary first-aid stations set up in cellars, as the artillery bombardment intensified. From the diaries she kept at the time, Ingeborg Pfitzinger has sent us this graphic description of those last chaotic days in the German capital, when the Berliners went to ground and Berlin became a city of cellar-dwellers. The Sunday that starts her narration was 30 April 1945 – the day on which at half past three in the afternoon Adolf Hitler committed suicide:

'A trap from which there is no escape'

Sunday 30 April 1945
Saturday and Sunday are quiet enough, except for the continuous artillery fire. It is now getting closer to the university buildings where we are. Food supplies are down to iron rations, which are issued in small amounts, as we have no idea how long they are going

to have to last. An army command post has been set up in the cellar next to us. Through them we at long last get official news from the German High Command. The people of Berlin are asked to hold out for just another one or two days. Armies are racing to relieve the capital. Paratroopers are going to be landed in the Tiergarten on the east-west axis.

Alas, there is never any sign of either the relief army or the paratroopers. The story is just a sop to keep the people calm.

No new first-aid station can be set up, so we nurses now have nothing left to do. It's dark down in the cellars. There has been no electricity for days, and candles are now getting scarce. No one says much. We're all too busy listening to the noises as they get closer.

The university has been under artillery bombardment for several hours. The upper storeys come crashing down over us, making the cellars unsafe. The ceilings are already sagging and threatening to collapse under the crushing weight of the falling masonry. We move out to another wing of the university to avoid being buried alive.

Monday 1 May 1945

How much longer can we hold out here? The Russian shellfire is getting worse. We huddle together. At around ten o'clock at night we get the order to leave the university and head for Kleine Mauer Strasse, from where we will be escorted to the cellars of the Reich Chancellery, where we shall be safer.

We set off, clambering over mountains of rubble and fallen masonry. We pass burning houses and keep close in to the walls to gain cover from the shells and sharpshooters. There is no direct way through. Huge craters in the pavement and piles of débris block our path. We keep having to turn back to look for an alternative way. After one and a half hours we have hardly covered any distance at all. When we finally reach Kleine Mauer Strasse we see nothing but a sea of flames. Not a house is left standing. The street has been levelled to the ground.

There is no way through to the Reich Chancellery. We set off instead for Friedrich Strasse which is the rallying point for all the units left in the city centre.

Tuesday 2 May 1945

It is midnight. All the troops left in Berlin are gathered here in Friedrich Strasse. It is jammed with soldiers, cars, trucks of every sort, tanks and ammunition. The Waidendamm Bridge by Friedrich Strasse Station is to be the battleground. Here all remaining resources are going to be deployed in one big effort to break out to the north, to provide an escape route for all those now sheltering and trapped in Friedrich Strasse. Russian troops are positioned in Karl Strasse, just behind the Waidendamm Bridge and firing down Friedrich Strasse. And here am I in the thick of it!

Men pass me carrying bazookas. Everyone is dashing about. But the superior strength of the Russians is apparent enough. There is no leadership among our soldiers. Everyone is running and shouting, and in the confusion no one knows what to do next. I press myself to a wall and watch a German tank trundling towards the bridge. Seconds later it stands helpless, crippled by a Russian anti-tank rocket.

Things are getting too dangerous on the streets. I manage to find a hidey-hole in the cellar of the Admiral's Palace. I can now breathe more easily. We are obviously caught in a trap from which there is no escape. Rumours are circulating that the city is about to surrender. Another says that Hitler is already dead. Then the news becomes more definite: Berlin is going to surrender at twelve o'clock tomorrow.

Next morning people start to come out on the streets again. I can see soldiers ripping the badges off their uniforms and throwing away their weapons. Others start lending a hand where they can. Just after twelve o'clock Russian tanks and armoured cars rumble by. For the first time I see Russian soldiers. How frightening they look! The first Russians to enter Berlin are Mongols. The tears run down my cheeks as I witness the fall of Berlin and the end of a terrible war.

LILIAN BORTHWICK, of Liverpool, Merseyside, was a young war-bride who, in a few short months, was to know both the heaven and the hell experienced by so many young women in her position:

'Memories live longer than dreams'

I was 19 years old when the war started in 1939. I was working as a football-pools clerk in Littlewoods, in Bootle, Liverpool. As we lived and worked near the docks we were being bombed every night. One morning, in October 1939, I went as usual to work, only to find the place had been bombed to the ground. I was told to report, with others of the staff, to the other department of Littlewoods Pools in Crosby, Liverpool.

When we arrived there it had been changed from a Pools office into a factory making barrage-balloons and oxygen bags. I also received a letter telling me to report to the Labour Exchange for war work. I was sent to the Aircraft Factory at Speke, just outside Liverpool. There were about six of us girls – the first females to work there. We were working on Spitfire planes – putting rivets in the doors and windows.

When I was working at the Aircraft Factory (I still laugh to myself when I think of this), we started work at 7.30 a.m. and caught the bus to work at 6.30 a.m. It was an hour's bus-ride to work. The mornings were very dark, with often no moon and, of course, it was the blackout. I used to come out of the house and feel my way down the street (we lived in the old-fashioned terraced houses). I would feel round the doors and window-sills until I came to a wall at the end of the street and every time I came to that wall I walked into it. I had permanent bumps on my forehead.

Another night we came out of the factory at 5.30 p.m. to be met by dense fog. There were no buses to take us home so we walked home in groups. We ended up on an island and didn't know which way to go, so we had to stay there until the fog lifted. I think we arrived home about 10.30 that night. Another morning we had no difficulty seeing our way because there was a large timber yard on fire and we had to pass it in a very narrow road, dodging the flames.

We didn't really understand what it meant to be at war until the bombs started dropping, and even then we didn't really understand why it was happening to us. Our world was suddenly turned upside down, but we quickly began to take it all in our stride. We didn't just sit in our air-raid shelters afraid to go out. We went to work to do our best for the war effort, despite the bombing and loss of sleep. We spent most of our lunch-hours in the air-raid shelters though, as the bombers came over at that time each day. They also arrived when we finished work at night and a few times they machine-gunned the buses we were travelling home in. Most nights I had to eat my tea in the air-raid shelter in our backyard.

Our next door neighbours were in their shelter one night and they were all killed. We had to move to another house. I was living with a brother and his wife and children. I used to go to my sister's house every evening to help her with her three children. Her husband was abroad in the Royal Marines. I remember one awful night in particular when I had gone round to help with the children. A bomb dropped near our shelter. A nurse was delivering a baby in a house nearby and the house received a direct hit. The screams of the people could be heard in our shelter. The air-raid wardens came in and asked if we had anything to use as bandages. We gave them our handkerchiefs and tore our petticoats off. We even tore up our blouses. It was so tragic.

I was out one night with my younger sister when we bumped into two soldiers in the blackout. They were stationed at the docks and had lost their way. We invited them home. I courted one. His name was Bob and he was 19 years old. It was November 1939 when we met. We were the ideal loving couple.

In early 1940 he was transferred to Donnington in Shropshire. In the meantime I was staying half the time with my sister and the other half of the time at my brother's house. Then my sister had to evacuate because of the children. One night I went back to my brother's house to find it had been bombed to the ground. Luckily, my brother and his wife and family had already been evacuated. So I had to stay on my own at my sister's house.

Bob, my young man, came to see me on his weekend leave and asked me to go to Shropshire with him and take a chance of finding digs for me, or I could stay with his mother who was a widow and lived at Burton-on-Trent. I went to the evacuation office and received a free travel warrant to Burton. I was made very welcome at his home. His mother was like a real mother to me. (My own mother died when I was two and a half years old. She left nine of us children. My youngest sister was only six months old when she died. I was taken from my family and placed in a foster home where I suffered terrible experiences. I would have been better off in an orphanage.) I think that was why I loved my husband so much – because of his kindness to me. I stayed with his mother for about two months.

Bob and I were married in August, 1941. We were both 21 years old and very happy. We used to go home to his mother's when I wasn't working and he was not on duty. One night when we were coming back after the weekend, we missed our train connection at ten o'clock. I was worried because I knew if he was not back in camp by 7 a.m. on Monday morning he would be confined to barracks for seven days. I couldn't bear that so we decided to walk back to Donnington. We walked all the way from Stafford, which was 16 miles. I wore out two pairs of shoes and ended up walking in stockinged feet for the last two miles. We arrived back at 6.30 a.m. next morning. My husband had to go on duty straight away, but I couldn't go to work, my legs wouldn't let me.

I loved my husband so much. He was not a fighting man; he was so gentle and kind, and we were so happy together. He only joined the regular army in the first place because he wanted to play in the drum and fife band. He used to sound the bugle at camp.

We lived in digs for two and a half years, then we were given a council house. That was in January, 1944. We had a nice little home; not much because we were only allowed so many units for furniture. But to us it was heaven.

On August Bank Holiday Monday, 1944, Bob had to move. I was terribly upset when he had to go away and was unable to tell me where he was going. Neither of us knew where he would be sent to. It was as if I already knew I would never see him again. I saw him off on the train on the Holiday Monday and wrote to him every day. I always ended my letters the same as he did with 'Close to you', which was one of the popular songs of the war.

I was three-months pregnant when the awful news came. I lost the baby the same week I received the dreaded telegram to tell me that Bob had been killed on 23 September 1944 in northern France. I couldn't believe it. We worshipped each other. I wanted to die – and have often wished I had then.

I went to his mother's home for Christmas. I received his parcel of belongings on Christmas morning and a statement of his credits. They didn't get much money, but out of his few pounds there was a deduction of eleven shillings for the army blanket for his burial. I was disgusted.

I received £1 a week widow's pension. I only wish I could have had his child. It would have been part of him for me to love.

I went to France last year to see his grave. He is buried in the war cemetery at Tilly-sur-Seulle, near Caen. There was an inscription on the bottom of his gravestone which said, 'Close to you always, darling'. I was very touched. I didn't know about it as the only photo I had received was of the temporary grave, when he was first killed. It was a very sad experience, but I always think if there is a heaven we will meet again. I expect a lot of war widows felt like I did, and still do. It is a true saying that memories live longer than dreams.

HELGA BAUMHÄCKEL, was born in Berlin, but now lives in Mannheim. She married in March, 1940, but her husband did not enlist on medical grounds. Here she recalls the very different circumstances encountered when evacuating from the bombs of Berlin to the peace of the countryside:

'I said thanks and could have kissed him'

Berlin, 1 September 1939. I was working as a typist and went off as usual to the office on the Frankfurter Allee. Suddenly the loudspeaker system gave out an announcement which came as a shock to me and to everyone around: we were at war with Poland. Hitler had sent his troops over the border. I was just 20 years old, about to get engaged and full of the joys of life. And now came this dreadful news that would completely change all our lives. There had been all sorts of rumours that war was in the offing, but right up to the last we all hoped that nothing would come of it.

The first bombs fell in 1941. 'Aircraft approaching over Hanover and Brunswick', it said on the radio. Soon after that the sirens started howling. That meant dashing down to the cellar clutching just a few bare necessities. All the other occupants of the building would be down there, packed like sardines. When bombs fell nearby you could feel the whole cellar floor lift. It was a terrible feeling. Sometimes the lights would go out. Finally the all-clear would sound, and we would all dash upstairs to see what had happened. Once a whole block of flats in our neighbourhood got a direct hit with a blast bomb. It was completely flattened. We rushed to see if we could help, but there was just nothing left to help. In those days we used to say to each other, 'May God strengthen your air-raid shelter.'

More and more of my colleagues at work were being bombed out. It was especially bad in the city centre. That was where my in-laws were living. Many a time my husband would set off on his bike to go and see whether they were all right and whether their house was still standing. Broken windows were nothing in those days. There were far worse things to get worked up about. It was especially difficult for the old folks, having to cart themselves and their belongings continually down into the cellar and spend the night there.

It got to the point where there would be several raids the same night. Then we would go to bed with our coats on, so as to be able to dash down the stairs. They used to give out little allocations as comforters: a miniature bottle of brandy, 25 grams of real coffee, a few cigarettes. These were so foul to smoke that we nick-named them the 'Stambul' brand. (The letters were said to stand for 'Adolf's Passion Killers'.) I don't know how we were meant to survive on these 'bombing handouts'. But Berlin people don't easily get downhearted. We used to say, with typical wartime humour, 'Make

292

the most of the war, folks. Peace is going to be awful!'

In 1943 I was expecting a baby, so I was evacuated out to Lötzen in East Prussia. It was still peaceful there, and there was more to eat, too, so I was able to help out the rest of the family by sending them my ration cards. One day the 'Higher Authorities' told me that I would have to go to a place on the Baltic to have my baby. I wouldn't hear of it. All that way and so far from everyone I knew! My landlady, who had been so good to me, was horrified that I wanted to go back to all the bombs and destruction in Berlin. My parents almost fainted with astonishment when I turned up on their doorstep right out of the blue.

On 28 October 1943, in the maternity hospital at Buch, in Berlin, our little son first saw the light of a chaotic world. He took it all calmly enough. The second day after his birth there was an air-raid, so I tucked him under my arm and went down to the hospital cellar. This was his very first outing. Fortunately nothing happened. But a plane had crashed on one of the hospital buildings just a day or two before, so you can imagine how anxious I felt.

Back home the raids made feeding, changing and washing for the baby very difficult. In November 1943 I was evacuated again, this time to a God-forsaken little place called Staffelde, out east. And right in the middle of winter. I can remember standing there with the baby's pram in the slush, with the rain teeming down, and just crying my eyes out. We were taken in by a nice lady, but she didn't really want us. We were just billeted on her.

Then I remembered having an aunt in Landsberg on the Warthe. I hadn't heard from her in years, but I still had her address. I travelled by train and then left the baby at the Station Mission to warm up, while I set off to find my aunt. I just hoped she was still living there. She was. What a surprise she got, having me arrive like that. How different things were there. I just couldn't believe my eyes. We weren't far from Berlin, but it was just as if there was no war on. An Advent wreath stood on the table and all around it was warmth and comfort. I had come from a war-torn city, but here peace reigned once more. My cousin and I went back to the station to fetch the baby. They really took good care of me while I was there and I feel grateful to them to this day.

The bitter end came in 1945. We used to hide under the bedcovers and listen-in to BBC London, so we could hear the truth about what was happening. We had to be secretive about it, because listening to foreign radio stations was an offence that carried the death penalty. My husband, who was visiting us, had to return to Berlin. He was with the Volks Sturm [German equivalent of Home Guard] and was detailed to erecting tank-barriers. The Front was getting closer all the time. By now we could hear the gunfire. We would have to leave.

I packed my things and went down with some of the other Berlin women to see if we could get a lift with the army trucks. It was blowing a real blizzard and freezing cold. One of the drivers gave us a lift. What an odd crowd we were. Mothers with small children next to deserting soldiers still carrying bazookas. All along the road there were Russian prisoners of war marching. It took us 18 hours to reach Berlin. There were air-raids all the time, when we would have to jump down and rush for cover in nearby cellars. By the time we got to Berlin my baby boy had messed himself so often he was up to his eyebrows in it! But it kept him warm and protected him. All we had to do was scrape him down afterwards. But the cold had given him terrible bronchitis.

In Berlin the war was reaching its final stages. There were air-raids night and day. I shall never forget seeing my first Russian in May 1945. He was standing there with his machine-pistol under his arm. Just like the eternal Russian soldier on the shores of the Volga. It gave me the shock of my life to see him. But at the same time I felt a great sense of relief. I thought, whatever else may happen, at least the war is over! What might the Russian's thoughts have been? He'd probably much rather have been back home than here in Berlin.

I left my baby in the bunker and ran back to our flat. The doors were wide open; it was completely empty, and there was blood in the kitchen. Who's been shot, I thought? It was a German soldier. He had set up his gun in our kitchen window and a Russian had shot him from across the road.

I went back to the bunker and fetched the baby. Our bedroom was just like a fortress. My husband had propped mattresses up against the windows to protect us from splinters of flying glass. Soon my parents came back from their shelter at the school. My husband was gone. With the general panic, and thinking we must be dead since the Russians were already here, he had taken off. He was caught by the Russians outside Berlin and taken prisoner. He came back again. But that's another story.

I never thought I would be able to just walk over dead bodies without feeling anything. But I did. They were lying all over the street, together with the carcases of horses. People were already cutting up the animals for meat. That's how hungry we all were. I could never bring myself to do that. The shops were all being ransacked. The only thing left was ersatz coffee. All we had was our hunger – and my wrist-watch.

The first Russian troops in were the élite. They did us no harm. Then the backup-troops arrived with their cries of 'Uri, Uri,' and 'Frau komm!' ['Watches, watches,' and 'Women come!']. There were some of them wearing watches right up their arms. But I kept mine – for the time being at least. And none of the Russians did me any harm. Then I said to myself, 'Hunger hurts, and what do I need a watch for, anyway?'

Against my parents' advice I went out and round the corner to where there were some Russians standing beside their Studebaker cars. I showed one of them my watch. He opened it with his pocket-knife just like an expert. Then he checked the seven jewels and found them to be in good order. Fat and meat were just not to be had anywhere, but the Russian offered me a big sack of potatoes, two kilos of cube sugar, and some chocolate for our son. Some deal in those days! Then he motioned me to get into his car. I was trembling with fear, but had to do as I was told. He drove me right round to our front-door! You should have seen the neighbours all craning their necks out of the windows. Here was a Russian helping me carry in the potatoes! What a meal we were going to have!

I said thanks and could have kissed him. He was just a young man. I do hope he got back home safely, and that my watch kept on ticking for him. It was my Confirmation present.

I am now nearly seventy years old and I have lived through the war all over again in writing about it. I do hope that the coming generations will not have to share our fate and I hope that this book will help to let people understand all the suffering and sacrifice that was caused by a senseless war.

A little more peace, a little less strife,
A little more goodness, and not so much hate,
A little more we, and not so much I.
Give us the beauty of flowers while we live;
How pointless to strew them too late on our graves.

Epilogue

This book belongs not only to the women whose stories we have shared in the preceding pages, but to all the women of that generation who lived through those six years now known as the Second World War. Out of the many hundreds who took the time and trouble to get in touch with us and relive those fateful years, Hilda Shaw, of Llangefni, Anglesey, sums up the feelings of all, when she writes:

Looking back, which I have not done for a long time, I can't believe we came through it all. We have much to thank God for, and let us all hope that no one will ever have to live through those things again. Many lives were lost and sad things happened. War is awful. Women hate war, and want peace at all times to bring up their children with love towards their fellow men. May women all over the world pray for it.